Intercultural Reciprocal Learning in Chinese and Western Education

Series Editors
Michael Connelly
University of Toronto
Toronto, Ontario, Canada

Shijing Xu
Faculty of Education
University of Windsor
Windsor, Ontario, Canada

This book series grows out of the current global interest and turmoil over comparative education and its role in international competition. The specific series grows out of two ongoing educational programs which are integrated in the partnership, the University of Windsor-Southwest University Teacher Education Reciprocal Learning Program and the Shanghai-Toronto-Beijing Sister School Network. These programs provide a comprehensive educational approach ranging from preschool to teacher education programs. This framework provides a structure for a set of ongoing Canada-China research teams in school curriculum and teacher education areas. The overall aim of the Partnership program, and therefore of the proposed book series, is to draw on school and university educational programs to create a comprehensive cross-cultural knowledge base and understanding of school education, teacher education and the cultural contexts for education in China and the West.

More information about this series at
http://www.springer.com/series/15114

Shijing Xu

Cross-Cultural Schooling Experiences of Chinese Immigrant Families

In Search of Home in Times of Transition

Shijing Xu
Faculty of Education
University of Windsor
Windsor, Ontario, Canada

Intercultural Reciprocal Learning in Chinese and Western Education
ISBN 978-3-319-83441-2   ISBN 978-3-319-46103-8 (eBook)
DOI 10.1007/978-3-319-46103-8

© The Editor(s) (if applicable) and The Author(s) 2017
Softcover reprint of the hardcover 1st edition 2017
This book was advertised with a copyright holder in the name of the publisher in error, whereas the author holds the copyright.
This work is subject to copyright. All rights are solely and exclusively licensed by the Publisher, whether the whole or part of the material is concerned, specifically the rights of translation, reprinting, reuse of illustrations, recitation, broadcasting, reproduction on microfilms or in any other physical way, and transmission or information storage and retrieval, electronic adaptation, computer software, or by similar or dissimilar methodology now known or hereafter developed.
The use of general descriptive names, registered names, trademarks, service marks, etc. in this publication does not imply, even in the absence of a specific statement, that such names are exempt from the relevant protective laws and regulations and therefore free for general use.
The publisher, the authors and the editors are safe to assume that the advice and information in this book are believed to be true and accurate at the date of publication. Neither the publisher nor the authors or the editors give a warranty, express or implied, with respect to the material contained herein or for any errors or omissions that may have been made. The publisher remains neutral with regard to jurisdictional claims in published maps and institutional affiliations.

Cover image © Dennis Cox / Alamy Stock Photo

Printed on acid-free paper

This Palgrave Macmillan imprint is published by Springer Nature
The registered company is Springer International Publishing AG
The registered company address is: Gewerbestrasse 11, 6330 Cham, Switzerland

Series Editor Introduction

The Series and East–West Contrasting Educational Narratives

This book series focuses on Chinese and Western education for the purpose of mutual understanding and reciprocal learning between the East and the West. The East has been a puzzle for the West, romanticized or demonized depending on the times. East–West relations have a long history of inquiry, and action has often been framed in competitive, ideological, and colonialist terms. In 1926 Dewey complained that "As far as we have gone at all, we have gone in loco parentis, with advice, with instruction, with example and precept. Like a good parent we would have brought up China in the way in which she should go" (p. 188). This "paternal" attitude, as Dewey called it, has not always been so benign. Economic, cultural, and intellectual matters have often been in the forefront since the Opium Wars of the nineteenth century. Intellectually the East–West dynamic is equally dramatic as found in works by authors such as Said (1978), Tu Wei-ming (1993), Hall and Ames (1999), Hayhoe and Pan (2001) and many others. These writers are part of a rich conceptual knowledge across cultures literature on the historical, philosophical, cultural, and educational differences of the East and West.

Education is a vital topic of international discussion and essential component part of our global consciousness. Global discussions of economics, national and regional competition, and national and regional futures often turn to education. Meanwhile local educational discussions take place in social environments discourse of international awareness. 'How are our international neighbours doing?' 'How do they teach values?' 'We have to catch up.' These matters are vitally important. But they are not new. Higher education in universities and other forms of postsecondary education has occupied most of the attention. What is new, and what, in our view, is likely to have far-reaching impact, is the focus on school education and early childhood education as well as pre-service teacher education. For several reasons, not the least of which is national competition, the focus on school education has been driven by comparative achievement studies. When Shanghai school students topped the chart in the Program for International Student Assessment (PISA) studies, the information was broadcast worldwide and generated ferocious discussion. One of the positive outcomes of this discussion is comparative research interest, the process of comparing educational similarities and differences in school practices, official policies, and social cultural influences. This comparative interest is all too the good and should help frame potential positive comparative futures. But comparative research on similarity and difference is not enough. We believe we need to reach beyond the study of similarities and differences and to explore life-filled school practices of people in different cultures coming together and learning from one another. In this postmodern world of instant worldwide communication we need to go beyond comparative premises. Ideas, thoughts, images, research, knowledge, plans, and policies are in constant interaction. This book series hopes to move our international educational research onto this collaborative and interactive educational landscape of schools, parents, communities, policy, and international trends and forces.

THE SERIES AND EAST–WEST CONTRASTING EDUCATIONAL NARRATIVES

The book series grew out of our seven-year Canada–China partnership study on reciprocal educational learning between Canada and China (Xu & Connelly, 2013–2020). The partnership developed from the current global interest and turmoil over comparative education and its role in international competition. The specific series grows out of two ongoing educational programs that are integrated in the partnership, the *University of Windsor-Southwest University Teacher Education Reciprocal Learning Program* and the *Shanghai-Toronto-Beijing Sister School Network*. These programs provide a comprehensive educational approach ranging from preschool to teacher education programs. This framework provides a structure for a set of ongoing Canada–China research teams in school curriculum and teacher education areas. The overall aim of the *Partnership* program, and therefore of the proposed book series, is to draw on school and university educational programs to create a comprehensive cross-cultural knowledge base and understanding of school education, teacher education, and the cultural contexts for education in China and the West.

The first few books in the series will be direct outgrowths of our partnership study. But because of current global conditions, there is a great deal of important related work underway throughout the world. We encourage submissions to the series and expect the series to become a home for collaborative reciprocal learning educational work between the East and the West. The starting point in our Canada–China Reciprocal Learning Partnership's is the idea of a global community in which ideas, things, and people flow between countries and cultures (Xu & Connelly, 2013). There is intense public discussion in Canada over international relations with China. The publication of international student achievement scores that rank China at the top has resulted in growing scholarly and public discussion on the differences in our educational systems. The discussion tends to focus on economic and trade relations while educational reciprocity and reciprocal learning are often absent from educational discourse. Given that the Chinese are Canada's and Ontario's largest immigrant group and that Chinese students have statistically shown academic excellence, it is critical to explore what we can learn from Chinese philosophies of education and its educational system, and what Canada can offer to China in return.

The Partnership's overall goal is to compare and contrast Canadian and Chinese education in such a way that the cultural narratives of each provide frameworks for understanding and appreciating educational similarities and differences. We expect other work generated outside our partnership grant to have different starting points and socially relevant arguments. But we do expect all series works to share the twin goals of mutual understanding and reciprocal learning.

Built on these twin goals the purpose of the book series is to create and assemble the definitive collection of educational writings on the similarities, differences, and reciprocal learnings between education in the East and the West. Drawing on the work of partnership oriented researchers throughout the world, the series is designed to:

- build educational knowledge and understanding from a cross-cultural perspective;

- support new approaches to research on curriculum, teaching, and learning in schools and teacher education programs in response to change brought on by heightened global awareness;
- provide a compelling theoretical frame for conceptualizing the philosophical and narrative historical trajectories of these two compelling worldviews on education, society and culture;
- Provide state-of-the-art reviews of the comparative Chinese and English language literature on school curriculum and teacher education;
- Model, sustainable, school to school structures and methods of communication and educational sharing between Canada, other English-speaking countries, and China;
- Model, sustainable, structures, and methods of initial teacher training in cross-cultural understanding;
- Contribute to a documented knowledge base of similarities, differences, comparisons and reciprocal learnings in elementary and secondary school teaching and learning curricula.

Michael Connelly and Shijing Xu

REFERENCES

Dewey, J. (1926). America and the Far East. *Survey*, 1 May, *1926*, 188. Later published in: John Dewey, The Later works, 1925–1953, (1984). Volume 2: 1925-1927, pp. 1173–1175.

Hall, D. L., & Ames, R. T. (1999). *The democracy of the dead: Dewey, Confucius, and the hope of democracy in China*. USA: Carus Publishing Company.

Hayhoe, R., & Pan, J. (Eds.). (2001). *Knowledge across cultures: A contribution to dialogue among civilizations*. Hong Kong: Comparative Education Research Centre, The University of Hong Kong.

Said, E. W. (1978). *Orientalism*. New York: Vintage Books.

Tu, W. (1993). *Way, learning, and politics: Essays on the Confucian intellectual*. Albany: State University of New York Press.

Xu, S., & Connelly F. M. (Project Directors) (2013). *Reciprocal learning in teacher education and school education between Canada and China*. Social Sciences and Humanities Research Council of Canada (SSHRC) 2013–2020 *[Grant 895-2012-1011]*.

Foreword

In *Cross-Cultural Schooling Experiences of Chinese Immigrant Families: In Search of Home in Times of Transition*, Shijing Xu reveals her intellectual and cultural passions and frames the purposes and content of this book series. Chinese education has gained worldwide attention. The Chinese have spread far and wide, and many communities and school systems throughout the world have large numbers of Chinese immigrant and international students. Often, as is commonly the case in Canada, Chinese students have become the school population majority. Second language learning Mandarin programs and Mandarin immersion programs are springing up in North America, England, Australia, and elsewhere. Highly publicized student achievement results on standardized tests, and comparative school system analyses, are widely reported in the popular press often accompanied by tensions and associated policy initiatives. Educational discussions are contextually spiced by the rise of China as an economic and political global force. Studies on best practices and competitive educational programs to level the playing field proliferate. Xu's passions to build multidimensional reciprocal learning bridges and cross-cultural communication links are particularly welcome at this moment of tension-infused global awareness.

Xu's work is not only scholarly, it is practical and compassionate. She put it well in her statement as Canada Research Chair (CRC) prepared for the Canadian government when she wrote, "Since I started my academic journey in Canada, my work has been programmatically-oriented with my hope of building a multidimensional cultural bridge between the East and West. I began my research with Chinese immigrant families' cross-cultural schooling experiences in Canada". The book cites a wonderful, not well-known, Chinese literature, to support this idea. Classic Confucian works are brought forward. There is Tao Chi's brilliant insight on time in his statement that mountains flow like rivers and are like ocean waves frozen in time; Jiayi Zhuang and Chongzhang Nie's descriptions of Chinese river painting scrolls as unfolding narratives of Chinese life; and many other ancient and current Chinese writers like Wayming Tu and Ruth Hayhoe. In this book Xu hopes to reach beyond the unidirectional liberal help-the-newcomers Euro-centric thinking in teaching and learning as she calls for mutual appreciation and reciprocal learning between cultures and educational systems. For readers, the simplicity of a bridge where people cross a divide, meet with one another, learn *about* the other, and learn *from* the other, is the simplest and most direct way to understand what this book offers. Throughout the book newcomer family educational stories are presented in detail. The stories are analyzed and interpreted in ways that reach beyond the social justice goal of providing the best possible education for newcomers as she explores what the other children, the teachers and the community at large can learn from the Chinese newcomers in their midst. Helping newcomers is only a start. Respecting and valuing newcomers, and learning from their differing cultural norms and practices is the important added educational dimension. Again, as she wrote in her CRC statement, "My study with newcomer immigrant Chinese families and intergenerational narratives of their cross-cultural schooling experience in Canada and China reveals the importance of reciprocal learning between newcomer families and mainstream schools".

Xu's drive to build bridges led to institutional developments, which formed the core of the Social Sciences and Research Council of Canada (SSHRC) Partnership Project, which gave rise to this book series. She was instrumental in setting up a Toronto–Beijing and Shanghai Sister Schools Network in which schools in Canada were paired with schools in China and specific Canadian and Chinese classes were paired. The second institutional initiative was the translation of her passion and ideas into a collaborative Preservice Teacher Education Reciprocal Learning Program involving the University of Windsor, the Windsor Public School Board, and Southwest University. The Preservice Teacher Education Reciprocal Learning Program was not a look-and-see program but, rather, a participatory program. Teams of students with supervising faculty visited back and forth and the process of crossing teacher education and school education cultural bridges was pursued as student teachers studied in their host university and undertook teaching and learning practicums in host schools. This initiative expanded the original sister school network to include Windsor and Chongqing and added the important dimension of preservice teacher education to the mix. The two programs, the Sister School Project and the Teacher Education Reciprocal Learning Program, were joined in the SSHRC Partnership Project and are integral to the purposes and intentions of the book series.

By way of summary, Xu's book is important reading for anyone searching for the passion, the concept, and the components of reciprocal learning between the East and the West. The book lays out, on a global scale, the socio-cultural need for cross-cultural understanding and reciprocal learning. It frames the SSHRC partnership project that serves as the nucleus for this book series. The book reveals the theory and practice of reciprocal learning as it was embedded in the study of newcomer education in Canada grew, into a SSHRC Canada-China Partnership Grant, and frames the book series.

January 31, 2017   F. Michael Connelly

Acknowledgements

A Chinese proverb says, "Give me a fish and I eat for a day. Teach me to fish and I eat for a lifetime." I wish to thank Professor Michael Connelly who has taught me how to fish. I forever see Dr. Connelly as my 导师 *Dao Shi* no matter how far I am walking along my academic and professional path. I prefer the Chinese term for *an academic mentor* as it carries deeper connotations. 导 *Dao* means leading you, guiding you, supporting you and advising you; 师 *Shi* means the master of knowledge, who knows much more than you and hence who is a great teacher for you. I greatly appreciate Dr. Connelly as my academic mentor who has taught me how to fish and appreciate his essential guidance and support in completing this book project and in co-directing our collaborative partnership project between Canada and China.

My special thanks go to Professor Ruth Hayhoe and Jim Cummins whose work has been my inspiration and whose participation in my East–West reciprocal learning bridge-making endeavor is encouraging and supportive. Thanks to Dr. Antoinette Gagne and Dr. William Ayers for their academic support and encouragement. Special appreciation to Dr. Cheryl Craig, Dr. Ian Westbury and Dr. Zongyi Deng for their academic and professional support and help.

I wish to state my special appreciation to the Chinese families, school principals, teachers, supporting staff members, and community workers at the research school, who participated or got involved in my research work. Because of research ethics restrictions, I can only thank all participants anonymously although they each have played a crucial role for me to get my work done as it is.

Thanks to the Narrative Inquiry Community and the Chinese academic community at OISE/UT. My special appreciation goes to *Do-As-a-Team* and *Dames-Who-Dine*, who have played an important supportive part of my journey in completing the work illustrated in this book. **DO-AS-a-Team** is an acronym made up of the initials of our given names: **D**ianne Stevens, **O**dilia Ng, **A**lison Neilson, **S**hijing Xu, and **T**ed Howe and the Dames included Dianne Stevens, Alison Neilson, Anne Fraser, Susan London McNab, Dilshad Ashraf, Hong Zhu, and myself.

Great appreciation is for Mr. and Mrs. Wong, Walther's, Xie's, Dong's, Lane-Smith's families and Lingqin, along with the *Dames Who Dine*, who are like a family to me! Special thanks are for Lao Chen and my family in China. It is our shared understanding of the Confucian notion of learning that has sustained our sense of home and sense of family in between China and Canada across the mountains and oceans throughout the many years of my cross-cultural inquiry journey.

Last, but not least, I would like to thank Palgrave Macmillan for making this work accessible to academic, professional, and public readers.

Contents

1 **Being "Chinese" on Landscapes in Transition**   1
   龙的传人 Descendants of the Dragon   1
   Canada Is My Home   2
   In Search of Home on Landscapes in Transition   3
   An Inquiry into Chinese Newcomer Families' Educational Narratives   5
   A Fluid and Open Inquiry   7
      The Fieldwork   9
      Parent Centre, My Research "Home"   10
      Framing the Book in Episodes and Scenes   10
   Core Family Stories   11
   Why Boys Only?   12
   Note   14

2 **In the Midst of Stories: Is Seeing Believing?**   15
   Walking into the Midst of Stories   15
      Who Tells Whose Stories?   15
      "To See Is to Believe" or "To Believe Is to See"?   17
      Multiple Stories the Toy Boxes May Tell   19
      Intersecting Diverse Cultural Histories in Learning   20
   Living in the Midst of Stories   21
      Thinking Narratively   21
      Untold Stories in the Story about "The Granny with a Doggie Bag"   23

xvi CONTENTS

    Intersecting Narratives of Diverse Experiences in Living   24
    Double Agendas in My Inquiry   25

3 Grandparents' Sense of Home: "Money Cannot Buy the Heart"   27
    Prelude   27
    Episode One: Making Sense of Life in-between China and Canada   28
        Scene I: Julian's Grandma, a Retired Teacher from China   28
        Scene II: Dissonance on the New Land   29
        Scene III: Disillusion about the New Life   30
    Episode Two: Making Meaning of Schooling   31
        Scene I: Different Views on How to Educate Children   31
        Scene II: Dissatisfaction with Canadian Elementary Education   33
        Scene III: Buddy Reading Program   34
    Episode Three: Julian's Grandma Making Efforts to Learn English   34
        Scene I: "Difficult to Live in Toronto Without English"   34
        Scene II: Helping the Grandma with Her ESL Homework   35
    Episode Four: Grandparents' Sacrifices and Contributions   37
        Scene I: Julian's Grandma's Sense of Family   37
        Scene II: Grandpa Jiang's Joy: Another Perspective   38
    Episode Five: Sense of Family and Education: Interview with Grandpa Jiang   38
        Scene I: Grandpa Jiang's Life Story   39
        Scene II: How to Be a Person in Confucian Values   40
    Episode Six: Grandparents' Role in Children's Education   43
        Scene I: Julian's Grandma's Teaching Chinese   43
        Scene II: A Multilingual and Multicultural Family   45
    Episode Seven: Tensions at Home   47
        Scene I: Conflicts on Changing Landscapes   47
        Scene II: Issues Beyond Language Learning   48
        Scene III: Moving out of Downtown: Another Sacrifice   49
    Interlude   50
        The Ongoing Story   50
        点评: *Shi Jing's Reflection*   51
    Note   52

4 A Mother's Hope: Hui Lan's Family Stories   53
    Prelude   53

  Episode One: Two Little Brothers and the Buddy Reading Program 55
   Scene I: Yong Sheng and Yong Ming, Hui Lan's Younger Sons 55
   Scene II: Buddy Reading Program 56
   Scene III: A Child Who Loves Learning 58
  Episode Two: Hui Lan, Mother of Sons 59
   Scene I: An Indispensable Parent Centre Helper 59
   Scene II: Hui Lan's Large Backpack 60
   Scene III: Hui Lan's Family Values and Educational
   Approaches 60
  Episode Three: The Family's Priority 62
   Scene I: One Home, Many Languages 62
   Scene II: Hui Lan's Dilemmas 64
   Scene III: Values in Life that Hui Lan and Her
   Husband Hold On To 65
  Episode Four: Hui Lan's Family with the Police
  and the Children's Aid 66
   Scene I: Yong Sheng, the Little Caring Soul of the Family 66
   Scene II: Yong Sheng and 911 67
   Scene III: Unexpected Drama in Hui Lan's Life 68
  Episode Five: Beyond Languages 71
   Scene I: English Is Difficult to Learn 71
   Scene II: The Boys' Language Preferences 72
   Scene III: Hui Lan's Efforts to Learn English 73
  Episode Six: Learning from Life and "Schooling" at Home 73
   Scene I: Learning from Life: Yong Chang's Options
   for His Future 73
   Scene II: "Schooling" at Home 77
  Episode Seven: Communication between School and Home 79
   Scene I: Communication Barriers and Expectation Discrepancy 80
   Scene II: Communication Breakdown between School and Home 82
  Interlude 83
   Life Moves On 83
  Shi Jing's Reflection 85

5 **Life in Transition: Newcomer Boy Zhi Gao** 87
  Prelude 87
  Episode One: Newcomer Boys on Landscapes of Schools in
  Transition 89

Scene I: "Do you like milk?"—Language and Culture
Dissonance   90
Scene II: "Democracy wouldn't work here"   91
Episode Two: Diverged Path from Parent Centre to Room 48   92
Scene I: What Language Do You Speak?—Meeting
the New Boy Zhi Gao   92
Scene II: Marching along Toronto Streets   93
Scene III: Zhi Gao, the Angry New Boy   95
Episode Three: Locating Zhi Gao and Newcomer Students on
Diverging Paths   96
Scene I: Zhi Gao Taking the Leadership Role   96
Scene II: Math Tutorial for Newcomer Grade 8 Students   97
Scene III: Parent–Teacher Interview   99
Episode Four: "Why was Zhi Gao frustrated?"   100
Scene I: Getting Ready for High School   100
Scene II: "Why is Zhi Gao upset?"   102
Scene III: Learning How to Play   104
Episode Five: Zhi Gao Tells His Stories   104
Scene I: "Life is so unpleasant"   105
Scene II: "太白了… At school a minute is like
an hour to me"   106
Scene III: "太白了. 我太白了. 我是个白痴.
(I am an idiot.)"   107
Scene IV: Zhi Gao's Narrativization of His Childhood
in China   109
Episode Six: Finding Zhi Gao in-between Landscapes of Schools
in Transition   111
Scene I: The Parents' Worries   111
Scene II: Zhi Gao at High School   116
Scene III: "No shame from the family should be made
public 家丑不可外扬"   118
Scene IV: Why Was Zhi Gao Unwilling to Go to School?   120
Scene V: "Children's Aid did not come"   122
Interlude   123
At the Verge of the Cliff   123
点评: 125
Shi Jing's Reflection   125
Note   126

6	**Life in Transition: Newcomer Boy Yang Yang**	127
	Prologue	127
	Episode One: Yang Yang's Father's Concerns	128
	Scene I: Yang Yang's Father Came to the School Council Meeting	128
	Scene II: Yang Yang's Father's Expectations and Worries	129
	Episode Two: Yang Yang at School	130
	Scene I: Yang Yang at the Math Tutorial	131
	Scene II: Making a Bridge out of Straws	131
	Episode Three: Yang Yang Back to China?	133
	Scene I: Parent–Teacher Interview	133
	Scene II: Is Yang Yang returning to China?	134
	Scene III: Newcomer Students' Farewell Party for Yang Yang	135
	Episode Four: Yang Yang Working in His Family Store?	137
	Scene I: Yang Yang at His Family Store	137
	Scene II: Talking With Yang Yang's Mom	138
	Episode Five: Yang Yang's Mom's Concerns and Hopes	140
	Scene I: Yang Yang's Ups and Downs	140
	Scene II: Yang Yang's Family Store	141
	Scene III: Yang Yang Back Home in Toronto	142
	Scene IV: Trip to St. George Campus of the University of Toronto	143
	Episode Six: Yang Yang back to Bay Street Community School	145
	Scene I: Yang Yang Re-registered at Bay Street Community School	145
	Scene II: Yang Yang's Special Needs	146
	Scene III: Second Visit To Yang Yang's Home	147
	Scene IV: Yang Yang's Unseen Lives in School and out of School	147
	Interlude	148
	Yang Yang's Graduation	148
	点评:	149
	Shi Jing's Reflection	149
	Note	149
7	**Life in Transition: Newcomer Boy Jia Ming**	151
	Prelude	151
	Episode One: Jia Ming's Life in Shanghai and Toronto	152
	Scene I: Life in Shanghai	153

Scene II: Schooling in Shanghai	153
Scene III: The Journey to Canada	154
Scene III: Life in Transition	155
Scene IV: Changes in Life after Immigration	158
Episode Two: Phoning Jia Ming's Home – Mom's Worries	159
Scene I: Mom's Worries about Jia Ming's Education	159
Scene II: Mom's Worries about Peer Influence	160
Scene III: Meeting Jia Ming's Mom	160
Episode Three: Mom's Expectations and Efforts in Jia Ming's Education	161
Scene I: Learning and Playing	162
Scene II: Parental Involvement and Expectation in Children's Education	163
Scene III: Computers and Learning	164
Scene IV: Language Issues	165
Scene V: Mom's Involvement in Son's Education	166
Scene VI: Mom's View of the Teacher's Role on Jia Ming's Learning	166
Scene VII: Learning and Testing – Efficiency and Accuracy	167
Scene VIII: Differences in Educational Expectations and Approaches between Chinese Parents and Canadian Teachers	168
Episode Four: A Dragon in Shanghai but a Fish Out of Water in Toronto	170
Scene I: Jia Ming's Mom's Education and Career in Shanghai	170
Scene II: From a Shanghai Career Woman to a Toronto Stay-at-home Mom	171
Scene III: Self-value and Sense of Belonging	172
Scene IV: Values and Traditions to Let Go or Hold On To	173
Scene V: Respect the Elderly and Care for the Young	174
Episode Five: Efforts, Sacrifices, Dissonance, and Hopes	174
Scene I: Different Accounts of Discrimination at School	175
Scene II: A Father's Sacrifices and Hopes	176
Scene III: Jia Ming's Reflections on His First Year in Canada	178
Scene IV: Dissonance and Hope in the New Homeland	180
Interlude	183
A Positive Light on the Way	183
点评:	184
Shi Jing's Reflection	184

8 Intersecting Newcomer Families' Narratives on Landscapes in Transition   187
Landscapes in Transition   187
No Longer Others' Stories: Why We Should Care?   189
   Changing Face and Changing Landscape   190
   Emerging Issues in New Situations   191
   Family Narratives versus Public Discourse   193
   Reciprocal Learning Needs   194
Through the Lens of Generational Narratives   195
   Notion of Home and Notion of Learning   195
   Essential Roles of Grandparents   196
   Role modeling in Chinese Parenting   199
   Homework in Chinese Learning   202
   To Be Human in Confucian Values   204
   To Help Others   205
   Return to Others in Abundance   205
   Share With Others and Care for Others   206
   Think of Others   207
Bridging the East and West Dichotomy: Confucian Continuity of Being and Deweyian Continuity of Knowing   209
   Confucian Notion of Being   209
   The Self in Chinese Society versus the Self in Western Society   210
   The Need for Reciprocal Learning between the East and the West   212
   Finding a Way for Reciprocal Learning   214
   Curriculum, Commonplaces, and Harmonizing Newcomers' Educational Practices   216
   I, We, and Reciprocal Learning   217
Notes   218

9 Sketching Unseen Lives of Immigrant Children between Home and School   219
Exploring Curricular Issues from Personal and Social Narrative Perspectives   219
   Learning with Reflection   219
   Narratives of Newcomer Student Experience   220
   Curriculum as Experience in Situations   220
   Commonplaces in Joseph Schwab's (1971) Concept of Curriculum   221

Sketching Immigrant Children's Unseen Lives in Curricular
Terms   222
  The Subject Matter   222
  The Learner   232
  The Teacher   236
  The Milieu   243
Multidimensional Bridge across Cultures on Landscapes
in Transition   249
  Culture and Experience   249
  Bridges across Cultural Boundaries   250
Notes   252

Epilogue   253

References   255

Index   269

CHAPTER 1

Being "Chinese" on Landscapes in Transition

龙的传人 Descendants of the Dragon

Since the ancient times, the Chinese people have referred to themselves as "the Descendants of the Dragon". On the morning of May 17, 2004, I was awakened by CBC Radio in Toronto when it was broadcasting *Descendants of the Dragon*, the Chinese song, written by a Taiwanese singer named Dejian Hou (侯德健) in 1978. "遥远的东方有一条江, 它的名字就叫长江…古老的东方有一群人, 他们全都是龙的传人…There is a river in the Far East; it is called Long River…There is a group of people in the Ancient East; they are all descendants of the dragon…" This song became popular in Mainland China in 1985 when an American Chinese singer first sang the song in Beijing at the Chinese New Year's Eve Gala televised live by CCTV (China Central TV). At that time, China had just begun its open-door policy to modernize the country.

I was not too surprised when I heard *Descendants of the Dragon* broadcast by CBC Radio in Canada, for its special program, *Descendants of the Dragon*, the same name as the song, which was to honor Asian Heritage Month in May 2004. This was a time when, in Canada, China was ranked by Citizenship and Immigration Canada (2004) as the first of the top 10 source countries of immigrants in the past five years. In 1996, Chinese overtook Italian as Canada's third most common mother tongue and it retained that position in the Canadian census publicized in December 2002 (Carey 2002; CIC 2004). According to the Canadian Census

2001, 41 percent of all Canadian residents whose mother tongue is Chinese live in the Greater Toronto area. That is, Chinese, Toronto's second most populous language after English, is the first language of 355,270 residents in the Great Toronto area (Carey 2002). The total number of Chinese immigrants to Canada in 2001 alone was 40,296, with 21,487 of them choosing Toronto as their landing destination (CIC Canada 2001). According to the most recent immigration overview reported by Canada Immigration and Citizenship (CIC 2015), between 2005 and 2014, there appears to be a decline in the total number of Chinese newcomer permanent residents year on year. However, the People's Republic of China has remained as one of the top three source countries for immigration, with a total of 314,090 newcomer Chinese having landed in Canada as permanent residents in the recent 10 years (CIC 2015). The influx of newly arrived Chinese immigrants in the recent decade has made Chinese students a visible majority among the student population at some schools in Canadian metropolitan cities, such as Toronto.

Canada Is My Home

Why have so many Chinese people chosen to immigrate to Canada? The study on parenting issues of newcomer families in Ontario, completed by the Centre for Research and Education in Human Services (CREHS) and the Joint Centre of Excellence for Research on Immigration and Settlement (CERIS) in 2001, shows that, diverse as their ethnic backgrounds are, most newcomer families came to Canada for the sake of their children. They "sacrifice everything to come here" in order to give their children a better life (Anisef et al. 2001, p. 27). The Chinese community in Toronto has a tradition of celebrating Canada Day in a "Canada IS My Home" parade. Thousands of Chinese immigrants and their families participate in the parade each year. "Home" and "family" are represented by one word in Chinese, " 家 " [jia]. "Canada", in Chinese, is 加拿大 [Jia-Na-Da]. The first syllable of "Canada" in Chinese 加 [jia] is pronounced exactly the same as " 家 " [jia], "home" or "family". Many consulting companies for immigration to Canada have used Chinese advertisements such as "夫妻双双把'加'还!"—"Having your family immigrate to Canada is like going home", a pun played on the word of "Jia" in a popular local Chinese opera song. Sentiments like this, which are associated with the idea of home, are attempts to encourage potential immigrants to come to Canada. What I heard on CBC coincides with these recruitment efforts to make Chinese immigrants feel at home in Toronto.

So, Canada is the home for Chinese immigrant families. "Is it?" I wondered, as I watched the parade in Chinatown in downtown Toronto. In a study on newcomer families, a father of a non-Chinese newcomer family said, "What we do not know is that we will be asked to make an even bigger sacrifice: we will be asked to give up our children, as they become not children we know and understand, but Canadian children, and so we lose them" (Anisef et al. 2001, p. 27). Does this happen among Chinese newcomer families? If so, how does this affect their experience of Canada as home? Do they remain "forever the descendants of the dragon"? Will they be able to do so, situated as they are, on cross-cultural landscapes in transition? How does all of this impact how Chinese immigrant families and their children experience the Canadian school system?

IN SEARCH OF HOME ON LANDSCAPES IN TRANSITION

In Search of Home on Landscapes in Transition through the Narratives of Chinese Newcomer Families' Cross-Cultural Schooling Experience was the starting point of my narrative inquiry, which has now resulted in a longitudinal research program focused on reciprocal learning in teacher education and school education between Canada and China (Xu and Connelly 2013). My initial research fieldwork was located in Bay Street Community School (pseudonym), one of the Toronto District School Board (TDSB)'s inner-city schools and one of the research sites in Professors Connelly and Clandinin's longitudinal research program. The TDSB is so linguistically and culturally diverse that 52 percent of secondary students and 47 percent of elementary students do not speak English as their first language (Carey 2002). According to a more recent report based on the 2011–12 Student and Parent Census among Grades 7–12 students (TDSB, 2013), the proportion of both White and East Asian students in TDSB schools has dropped by two percentage points while there has been a slight increase in South Asian students by one percentage point and also in students who identified themselves as "Mixed" by two percentage points (TDSB, 2013). Chinese still remains the top language among the top five non-English languages spoken at home. English is the sole first language for less than half (44 percent) of TDSB students. This diversity is reflected in Bay Street Community School where 64 percent of students do not speak English as their first language (Connelly et al. 2004).

In many urban schools across Canada and the United States (Coelho 1998; Cummins 1996, 2000; Cummins et al. 1994; Gagne et al. 2003; Goldstein 1999; Hing 2001; G. Li 2002; S. Lee 1996; Nieto 1995, 2000; C. Park et al. 2001, 2003; Schecter and Cummins, 2003; Soto 1997, 2002; Zhou 2003) and other countries such as Australia and Hong Kong (Chong 2005; Leung 2002; Macphee 2003; Parry,, 1998; Piper and Garratt 2004; Rao and Yuen 2001), culturally and linguistically diverse students constitute the mainstream school population. The Bay Street Community School reveals Canada's changing immigration patterns (Connelly et al. 2004), with a sharp increase of students of Chinese origin in its school community in the recent decade. I began my research contextualized within Connelly and Clandinin's longitudinal research program on the diverse cultural histories that individuals bring to school settings, with my focus on the role of Chinese newcomer families in school landscapes in transition. It is my belief that it is not only student diversity, but also changing patterns of diversity that create educational needs and difficulties. For instance, programs for Central European immigrants may not work well for Caribbean Black immigrants and these, again, may not work well for Asian immigrants.

There are many studies on Chinese family's cultural values and the relationship between these values and those at work in Canadian and American schools (Lee and Hawkins 2015; Chao 2013; Chen and Tse 2010; Costigan et al., 2010; Guo 2012, 2007; Chen et al., 2005; Chin 2005; Dyson 2001; Wong Fillmore 2000; Lai and Ishiyama 2004; G. Li 2002; J.2001; Louie 2001; J. Xu 1999). These studies have drawn attention to conflicts and tensions between home and school for Chinese immigrants. Many studies (e.g., S. Lee 1996; C. Park et al. 2003; Zhou 2003) point out one of the downsides for a multicultural society: differences and separations tend to be highlighted in a less than positive light. Furthermore, as Park et al. (2003) point out, the diverse Asian Pacific American groups are often labeled as "Asian model minorities" in a monolithic racial category in the United States. The label, "model minorities", tends to doubly marginalize groups with Asian origins. Academic achievements are often attributed to the cultural group (e.g., Cheng and Starks 2002; H. Park and Bauer 2002; R. Lee and Liu 2001) while individual variations and differences within one cultural group are overlooked. Hence, difficulties, as well as resulting tensions experienced by

Chinese and other Asian groups, tend to be ignored. Kim et al. (2015), for example, in their study of 444 Chinese American families, highlight the importance of distinguishing among different types of parent–child acculturation dissonance on academic trajectories.

An Inquiry into Chinese Newcomer Families' Educational Narratives

In my inquiry into Chinese newcomer families' educational narratives, I perceive differences differently. The family as the unit of analysis is the focus of my inquiry. The Chinese song broadcast by CBC and the celebration of *Descendants of the Dragon* symbolizes the importance of family and community context for understanding immigrant children/students' education. The assumption in my inquiry is that to properly understand Chinese students' education, it is necessary to understand something of their families' culture, hopes, and ambitions. However, rather than distinguishing newcomer families from the larger Canadian society in the East and West dichotomy, I study each family in the context of family and community in their own terms. I focus on their lived experience to study and understand each family's detailed educational narratives. I "see the family as fluid and constantly being negotiated and reconstituted both spatially and temporally" (Creese et al. 1999, p. 3) on cross-cultural landscapes in transition, not only for newcomer families, but also for the larger Canadian society. My research is not designed to focus on immigrant issues such as the settlement of new immigrants, struggles for survival, or conflicts between parents and schools; neither is it designed to improve parent–school relationships in terms of parent involvement or empowerment, or parent–school partnerships that often tend to carry the connotation "very much within the mainstream of educational thinking" (Valdés 1996, p. 191). This work is developed to explore and understand newcomer families' beliefs and values in what is important in their children's education from their lived experience on their journey in search of home in Canada.

My three-year intensive fieldwork with follow-ups at Bay Street Community School, an inner-city school in Toronto has helped me develop a narrative understanding of linguistically and culturally diverse school life. The stories told from the perspectives of newcomer Chinese families about their lived experience in the Canadian educational system point to a Canadian multicultural discourse that has categorized the Chinese as one of the visible minorities who have been perceived as ethnically "othered" Canadians with static cultural values and practices in their cultural heritage that are homogenized. Moreover, the newcomers are perceived more as the ones who need to adapt to their new life rather than as people who contribute valuable social, cultural, economic and educational resources to the increasingly diverse society.

With a special interest in cross-cultural issues between the East and the West, I am particularly interested in finding ways to bridge cultural and educational values. Narrative methodology enables me to simultaneously study the cultural tensions and communications in the processes of cultural adaptation while appreciating the knowledge and values brought to Canada by new immigrants. As Hayhoe (1997) points out, Confucian, Taoist, and Buddhist views of society, knowledge, and the human person are useful to identify core values that have persisted in modern education in East Asia, but they have been neglected as a resource useful for the West. The increasing number of Chinese immigrants in the Canadian population may open up various channels whereby they can introduce their values to Canadian and American societies (Hayhoe 1997; Hayhoe and Li 2017). By examining family narratives, I hope to gain insights into one of the ways this communication of values occurs through schooling. It is my assumption that the larger Canadian society, with its increasing diversity, is embraced with great opportunities as well as reciprocal educational needs for both newcomers of ethnically diverse groups and the mainstream people in mutual sharing of ideas, knowledge, and values. Hence, the broad purposes proposed in this research transform into the following specific objectives:

1. To make meaning of Chinese newcomer families' experience on landscapes in transition by focusing on understanding their notion of home, and to understand the relationship between their notion of home and their notion of learning and schooling for children's education;
2. To explore and understand inter-generational education issues and school–family–community connections for the purpose of contributing to cross-cultural curriculum studies and teacher education;
3. To provide a narrative understanding of multicultural school life in Canada in the hope of providing insights for bridging culturally diverse families, communities, and schools in the complexity of

multiculturalism, and stimulating the reciprocal learning and adaptation of newcomers and the larger Canadian society in order to foster mutual communication and appreciation of values in education.

A Fluid and Open Inquiry

> Children of Julian's age in China have learned a lot, both in literacy and math, but here in Canada, Julian is playing all day long. There is no homework... Children of Julian's age need spoon-feeding, as they do not know the importance of study, yet.... Canadian schools are good for children like Julian who are not willing to study hard but play all day long (Conversation with Julian's grandma at the Parent Centre of Bay Street Community School).

This is not the first time I heard such comments among Chinese immigrant parents. Though most immigrant families came to Canada for the sake of their children, Canadian education often does not meet their expectations (An 2001; Anisef et al. 2001; Greenfield 1999; Mapp 1997). Views, however, are mixed.

In contrast to Julian's grandma's view, a Chinese professor, one of the participants in my research with Chinese visiting scholars in Toronto (Xu 2000), said:

> Whenever I pass by the primary schools here, I always see happy children's faces. I rarely see a child unhappily carrying a big schoolbag because of school pressure. They are sunny boys and girls. Their life is full of sunshine and happiness. They don't take study as a burden. However, in China, we think we have to study very hard. Student life is always very hard. Yes, one has to study hard, but it has become a conception that one cannot learn well if one doesn't go through a very hard time.

> I am a father of a 10-year-old boy. I always think it is important to find the best way to teach young children. I really appreciate the western teaching methodology. We should adopt it in the primary school or even kindergarten.

The contrasting views about Chinese and Canadian schools held by a Chinese grandmother and a Chinese visiting professor puzzled me. I wondered what might explain their different views on education. Connelly and Clandinin (1988) point out that people make sense of learning in relation to their own experiences, both past and present, their beliefs about education, their present needs within a particular situation, and their hopes for the future. Thinking in terms of defined categories and cultural groups, one might be led to think that the Chinese grandmother was "more Chinese" than the visiting professor who, it might be said, was more modern and westernized because of age and access to Western values. But the Chinese grandmother had been in Canada much longer than the visiting professor and was, perhaps, more knowledgeable and involved in the educational system. Thinking narratively, the question of why these two participants' assessments of the school system differed so greatly is best explained in terms of their particular experiences, both past and present, and their particular beliefs and needs, within the particular situation in which they find themselves. This is the kind of thinking that governs my research with the Chinese families and their children in Bay Street Community School. Accordingly, I wonder how Chinese families' cultural and cross-cultural experiences are making and reconstituting their sense of home in their transition from China to Canada. In turn, how does this shape and reshape their notions of schooling and learning over time and space on school landscapes in transition?

The study of experience in narrative inquiry, while methodologically fluid and open, has an analytic inquiry structure for the construction of narrative histories and profiles. Drawing on Dewey's theory of experience (Dewey 1938), in which he analyzed the structure of "a situation", Clandinin and Connelly (2000) developed the idea of a three-dimensional narrative inquiry space: temporal dimension, social dimension, and place. For my study, this means that I explore family narratives temporally, in terms of their past, present, and future; socially, in terms of other family members, interacting school and community members and so on; and through place, primarily the Chinese settings before immigration, places involved throughout immigration, and places where key elements of life are lived out in Toronto. I write narrative family profiles that, in varying degrees depending on the family, reflect aspects of this three-dimensional structure. Therefore, my narrative accounts and explanations of education are contextualized accounts. They have a conditional quality and tend to lack the precision and certainty of methods more focused on cultural groups and/or statistical/demographic analysis.

By studying families this way, I believe I can give a nuanced account of Chinese families' journey searching for "home" in Canada. Narrative inquiry builds on Dewey's metaphor, "life is education" and "education is life" and I hope to bring forward some of life's complexities as Chinese immigrants meet up with the Canadian school system. As Connelly and Clandinin (Clandinin and Connelly 2000) say, life is filled with narrative fragments, enacted in storied moments of time and space, and reflected upon and understood in terms of narrative unities and discontinuities. Hence, educational studies, such as mine, as a form of experience, are designed to explore and understand experience by thinking narratively of the continuity and wholeness of people's life experience. This narrative perspective guides my inquiry into Chinese families' lived experience on cross-cultural landscapes in transition, through which I hope to bridge culturally diverse families, communities, and schools in the complexity of multiculturalism. Furthermore, I turn to work on international studies (Hall and Ames 1999; Harrison and Huntington 2000; Hayhoe 1997; Hayhoe and PAn 2001; Tu 1994, 2002), cross-cultural studies (He 2003; Lee 1996; Li 2002; Valdés 1996), bilingualism and multiculturalism (Cummins 1989, 1996, 2000; Phillion 2002; Phillion et al. 2005; Schecter and Cummins 2003), and curriculum and teacher development (Ayers 2004, 2003, 1998, 1993; Clandinin ans Connelly 1992; Connelly and Clandinin 1992, 1988; Schwab 1971a, 1971b, 1971c, 1973, 1983; Schubert and Ayers 1992) for the theoretical underpinning and social significance of my study.

The Fieldwork

With the narrative approach taken, narrative thinking and understanding of fieldwork is key to my inquiry. My fieldwork consisted of—three to five days a week of school visits for three years and two-year follow-up visits and continuous participation in school events and projects. These visits involved observing and volunteering in the School's Parent Centre, English as a Second Language (ESL) programs, International Languages program (such as Mandarin classes), and extra-curricular programs. Fieldwork also included participant observation of teacher–parent interviews, field trips, and School Council meetings. In addition, I interviewed parents, grandparents, children, the school principal, teachers, and community workers. When turning the fieldnotes into research text in family narratives, as part of the ethical considerations, I used "the 1st year", "the 2nd year", "the 3rd year," and "the 4th year" to indicate the year of my fieldwork in the school when the events were taking place in those narratives.

Parent Centre, My Research "Home"

When I began my work in the Parent Centre located at Bay Street Community School, I first made the following friends: Carmen, the staff member at the Parent Centre; Freeman, a Chinese grandpa who had been a volunteer at the school for a dozen years and a School Council member; Julian's grandma with Julian and his baby brother Allen; and 惠兰 Hui Lan, whose two little sons were the first two children I talked with at the Parent Centre. I met Hui Lan's eldest son later in the Literacy Enrichment Academic Program (LEAP) when I followed up with my other student participants at the beginning of another school year. I also interacted with many other families, both Chinese and non-Chinese, at the Parent Centre and at various settings in the school. The Parent Centre is a room set aside in a Canadian school where parents, grandparents, and other caregivers can drop in, socialize, interact with children, and familiarize themselves with schooling. It was the Parent Centre at Bay Street Community School that connected me with the linguistically and culturally diverse school life where I observed the interactions among Chinese families and between themselves and non-Chinese families. 亲子中心, the Chinese translation of Parent Center on its door, was done by Freeman, the Chinese grandpa, who had been an essential bridge between the Chinese community and the school. It was at the Parent Centre where I first met Mr. Anderson and his Chinese newcomer students such as 智辉 Zhi Hui, 琳琳 Lin Lin, 志高 Zhi Gao, 嘉明 Jia Ming, and 亮亮 Liang Liang. With the Parent Centre as my "home base" at the school, I followed the Chinese newcomer students to their classrooms and on fieldtrips. My inquiry path diverged from the Parent Centre into several classrooms, extra-curricular programs, school events, School Council meetings, parent–teacher interviews, newcomer students' homes, and the local community centers.

Framing the Book in Episodes and Scenes

At a "settling" school, like Bay Street Community School, with people moving in and out and with so many people interacting with one another on the school landscape, I was sometimes perplexed by the fluidity of the inquiry and unsure of how to proceed. I wondered how all the threads could be woven together to capture the diversity and dynamics of the interactions among the families, the school, and the communities. It occurred to me that I might use the form of an opera program to narrate many different characters in my book when I watched a series of operas presented by the Canadian National Opera Company with Catherine, my landlady and friend in Toronto. I was further reassured of the feasibility of this form when I saw how Anne Fraser beautifully presented her research structured in the image of theatre with a stage as the major metaphor (Fraser 2005). I decided to borrow the form of an opera program to introduce the many characters in my stories and structure the core of my book. I found the idea of an opera program helpful because it is a form for displaying aspects of life as they unfold. I found that it helped structure and present the fluidity in my inquiry, and believe that it helps convey the holistic, lifelike, qualities of the family stories in my study. The purpose is not to present the work in the form of a play, but to help me, and you, the reader of the book, to follow and identify more vividly with the characters whose life paths are interwoven with one another on the changing school landscapes in my journey, and whose narratives have their own individual family shape in the three-dimensional narrative inquiry space.

CORE FAMILY STORIES

The core book chapters each start with a *Prelude* that serves as a chapter overview as well as a connection between chapters. At the end of each chapter I offer a brief summary of the themes that emerge from the chapter from the eye of the inquirer in *Shi Jing's Reflection*. My reflection is more of a transitional section bridging the family story being told and the one to come. As the life paths of the major characters in different family stories are often interwoven with one another on the landscapes of schools in transition,[1] I intend to keep the narrative flow of the family stories and let you, the reader, to read and understand these family stories in their own terms as well as in yours. Therefore, I do not offer a full-length discussion of the themes emerging from each family story until the last interpretive chapters. The time in each episode refers to the time of my fieldwork in the school as the first year, the second year, or the third year, which not only shows the number of years of my fieldwork, but also prevents the teacher participants and student participants from being identified by using their pseudonyms and not listing the actual school year.

The first family story, Chapter 3, tells a grandmother's sense of home with Julian's grandma as the major character. The story features Julian's grandma, Julian, and Julian's little brother, Allen, at the Parent Centre. The intersecting narratives of the grandmother, her family members and other Chinese grandparents and parents reveal the family values as well as tensions that have impact on children's learning and schooling, mainly from the grandparents' perspective. Chapter 4 is a story about 惠兰 Hui Lan's family. It is a story about a typical Chinese mother and wife who holds on to traditional Chinese family values in her education of her three children, both at school and at home. It is a story about a shared family dream that is hoped to come true in the success of their children's education. Chapters 5 through 7 tell stories about newcomer boys: 志高 Zhi Gao, 洋洋 Yang Yang, and 嘉明 Jia Ming respectively. What is common for these three chapters is that the stories are all about life in transition: life in transition between China and Canada, between middle school and high school, and between childhood and adolescence. However, each of the three chapters also features different characters. The first story is about Zhi Gao, a 13/14-year-old boy from 广东 Guangdong (Canton), who, because of his fragmented school life and fragmented home life, eventually "fell in between" and dropped out of high school before he finished Grade 9. Yang Yang, a boy from 福建 Fujian, returned to Bay Street Community School for Grade 8 and graduated from the school as a double-award winner. Earlier he had been seen working in his family store, and his family sent him to a school far away from the downtown neighborhood for the purpose of reducing the negative peer influence on him in his addiction to video games. Jia Ming, a boy from 上海 Shanghai, who was once in the same Newcomer Support Class with Zhi Gao and Yang Yang, was one of the few newcomer students at Bay Street Community School whose families came to Canada in the category of *professional immigrants/skilled workers* 技术移民, people with higher education, professional skills, and an established life in their home country. Hence, each chapter tells a different core family story with a different focus varying from grandparents, parents, to children/students in the flow of life as it has evolved. Different as they first appear, these five family stories all tell the same or similar dreams and hopes of the Chinese immigrant families for their children's education and future on landscapes in transition.

Why Boys Only?

Following the flow of life on the changing landscape in the fluid inquiry, I featured five core families who turned out to be families of boys. It was not my intention to study only families of boys. I did have girls like 琳琳 Lin Lin, 秀华 Xiu Hua, and 红红 Hong Hong and their families as my potential participants. Intellectually, it had been my intention to present a picture of the diversity and the dynamics of the linguistically and culturally diverse school life in which Chinese families were not homogeneous but diverse from family to family. However, during my intensive fieldwork at the school with the children, the families, and the teachers, my attention was drawn more to the boys who were more difficult than the girls. They got into the minds of the grandparents and parents, of the teachers, the principal, social worker, and the community workers because the boys tended to turn everything upside down at the Parent Centre, in the classroom and on the street during the field trips. My attention and energy went particularly to Zhi Gao, Yang Yang, and other newcomer boys when they seemed to be at risk of failing the school system in their transition from China to Canada, between childhood to adolescence. From an observing researcher, I became a participant in the lives of those under study. I helped the principal to contact the Chinese families, and served as an interpreter and culture broker between home and school at parent–teacher interviews, Parent School Council meetings and other school events and activities; as well, I was a teacher and friend to the families and the children. The newcomer boys and girls from two classes would often fight for me to join their class every time I visited the school. The boys' mothers sometimes called me at home late in the evening after their work to discuss issues about their boys. They often asked me to talk with their boys, as several mothers told me, "My boy listens to you. One word said by you is worth 10 words said by me to my son". Some mothers, whose boys were not in the classes I worked with and who heard about me from other Chinese parents and students, asked Freeman if he could ask me to talk with their boys. It was during the intensive work of helping the Chinese newcomer families of boys, as well as my work at different settings in the school, that I realized how the issues of boys' education stood out. In contrast to the boys who tended to draw most of the attention and energy from those who worked with them, the newcomer Chinese girls in my observation were mostly well-behaved, hard-working, friendly, and respectful. They also tended to be targeted by the misbehaving boys. From my conversations with them and their parents, the girls were expected to share family responsibilities in housework chores and caregiving for younger siblings more than the boys. I could, therefore, have featured gender issues in an effort to understand how immigrant boys and girls experienced schooling and learning differently both at school and at home. However, I have focused my study on the family unit, and the family unfolding narratives. My data on the girls and their families are informative and supplementary to my principal understanding and interpretation of the educational issues reflected in those core family stories. These data also open up new areas for future work.

It is my hope that this book will provide a narrative thinking and understanding of multicultural school life and develop a conceptual bridge for communication of values in education that will serve our linguistically and culturally diverse children and youth.

Note

1. On landscapes in transition: The preposition of "on" is used intentionally to illustrate the challenges of newcomer families in their adaption to the host society. They stay "on" the landscapes in transition, rather than immersing in the landscape.

CHAPTER 2

In the Midst of Stories: Is Seeing Believing?

In this chapter, I make a methodological inquiry into some issues and challenges in my narrative inquiry into Chinese families' lived experience on landscapes of schools in transition from China to Canada. When I first walked into the midst of the research field, the issue of truth in narrative became a methodological challenge to me as I was bouncing in between the boundaries of educational research. By understanding story as the phenomenon, and narrative as the inquiry (Clandinin and Connelly 2000), two questions arose in my mind while I was located in a place of stories: "Who tells whose stories and why?" and "Which is true, 'To see is to believe', or 'To believe is to see'?"

The issue of truth in narrative research has received attention with diverse views (Carter 1993; Elbaz-Luwisch 1997; Phillips 1994, 1997). Living in the midst of stories with these two questions in mind, I explore and understand the complexities of the issue of credibility that counts most for educational research.

WALKING INTO THE MIDST OF STORIES

Who Tells Whose Stories?

It was already 9:00 a.m. by the time we reached the entrance to the school building. The loudspeaker was playing "Oh, Canada". Two boys and one girl, Asian-looking from behind, were standing right in front of us by the door.

Teachers were standing in the hallway by their classrooms. I was impressed by the children who learned to show their respect to the national anthem by standing still when they heard "Oh, Canada". My eyes were drawn to the colourful little hands on the wall to my left. It must be the shapes of real hands of children, for there were also names signed in those little hands. When the music stopped, there were announcements on the loudspeaker. People started moving around. We went inside the building. I saw four Chinese characters, 亲子中心 Qin Zi Zhong Xin, on the door to my right. It was the Parent Centre. A Chinese grandpa was standing by the door. He told me that in the past there were only Cantonese-speaking children at the school but now there were more and more Mandarin speakers.

This was the first day of my entry into the research school. It was a time when Citizenship and Immigration Canada showed that Mainland China had ranked the first of the top ten source countries for three years, with an ever-increasing number of people immigrating to Canada every year.

At the beginning of my inquiry, I looked for Chinese parents in the category of "Independent Immigrants or Skilled Workers", people with higher education and good professional skills. I was disappointed when most parents and grandparents I met at the Parent Centre were from the villages of Guangdong (Canton) and Fujian, two coastal provinces in China that have had a long history of people seeking better life opportunities overseas. Most parents or grandparents spoke Cantonese and came to Canada in the category of "Family Reunion" (CIC 2001, 2004). A few Mandarin-speaking parents were from Fujian, which was known to the public from the media for having "boat people" (Li 2001) coming to Canada or the United States illegally. They spoke Fujian dialects among themselves. Both Fujian dialects and Cantonese sounded like another language to me, so I felt foreign among the Chinese families who spoke Cantonese or Fujian dialects among themselves at the Parent Centre. Therefore, during my early visits, most of my conversations were with Carmen, the school staff member who worked with the families and children at the Parent Centre, and Freeman, a Chinese grandfather who had volunteered at the school, mostly at the Parent Centre, for more than 10 years.

My conversations with Carmen and Freeman were the major entries of my initial field notes at the Parent Centre. I heard stories about someone taking snacks home in a doggie bag, about parents not helping when it was Snack Time or Circle Time, about some grandparent spanking a child or another grandparent totally ignoring a child's misbehavior.

I was bothered by the stories I heard about these newcomer families at the school.

I was seeking a bridge that would link the West and the East, with newcomers bringing good values from the East and contributing to the multiculturalism in Canada. Therefore, I was looking for Chinese families who were well educated and well established in China in their life and career before they immigrated to Canada, and ideally who had children more than 10 years old. I believed that families belonging to this category would have developed a sophisticated understanding of the Chinese educational philosophy and values as well as the Chinese educational system. They would, I thought, be able to elaborate their views when comparing Eastern and Western educational systems. For months, I came back from the school telling Professor Connelly that I could not find the participants I wanted for my studies in the Parent Centre. I told him about Carmen's frustration and Freeman's concerns. I said I could not see these grandparents and parents as potential participants for my studies. Also, most of them did not have any higher education, and some had had little or no schooling experience in China.

Listening to my briefings of what I "observed" in the Parent Centre, Professor Connelly said to me, "When a husband or a wife came to complain about the other person, he or she doesn't tell me much about the other person. He or she is telling me about him or herself. Don't judge: Carmen is frustrated … parents are not helping. Is Carmen frustrated? Are parents not helping? You don't know. Is Freeman frustrated? Why does Freeman feel bad? You are not telling me much about the parents in the Parent Centre. You are telling me about you yourself, your own values". Professor Connelly advised me that I take an inquiry attitude into the research field, instead of my strong beliefs as to what I was trying to do for my research. I thought I understood. I did not realize, at the time, that this incident was the beginning of my inquiry into the issue of truth in narrative.

"To See Is to Believe" or "To Believe Is to See"?

Tuesday, November 12
    Mr. Anderson, the Newcomer Support Class teacher, suggested to Carmen that he bring his Grade7/8 students to have a Buddy Reading program with the little ones in the Parent Centre on Monday afternoons. Mr. Anderson was busy

yesterday afternoon so they changed the time to this afternoon. Around 1:30 p.m., Carmen called out, "Tidy up! Tidy up time!" Several grandparents were talking on the couch. Michael's mother was putting puzzle pieces together with Michael on the carpet. Two boys were running across the room one after another. It was very noisy in the room. Nobody seemed to pay attention. Carmen looked around; then she asked Freeman to tell the parents to help tidy up. Freeman got up and went over to tell people in Cantonese and Mandarin that it was time to tidy up. The carpet was full of toys and puzzle pieces. I went to help and heard Michael asking his mom in Chinese, "Why should we tidy up now? It is not time, yet." Michael's mom told me that usually it was not the time yet to tidy up. They usually tidied up around 2 p.m. Children were used to the routine. They didn't know that today they had to tidy up earlier because the Buddy Reading Program was switched from yesterday to today.

At Circle Time, I noticed the grandparents and parents tried to follow Carmen when she was counting in English. They were trying to learn English from Carmen as she taught the little ones. Julian's grandma said she found Chinese actually more difficult to learn than English, as there were more complicated characters in Chinese. She said Julian didn't like to write Chinese words at home. He was a little bit naughty. I looked at Julian. He was playing with Danny. Danny hit Julian with his elbow. Julian hit back. "No, Julian!" Julian's grandma said. Danny's grandma was sitting on the sofa watching without saying anything. Danny did not sit quietly like the other children who listened to Carmen when she started reading to them. Danny made a lot of noise. Carmen had to stop to discipline him. Yong Sheng and Yong Ming's mother got up to take Danny away from the circle and took him in her arms, trying to calm him down and keep him quiet....

"OK, let's do our last song. 'Twinkle, twinkle little star....'"

Yong Sheng and Yong Ming were singing loudly along with Carmen and following every movement Carmen made along with the song....

Wednesday, November 13

In the afternoon, Carmen spent most of her time tidying the room and sorting out the toys because they were all mixed up. She had different buckets to contain different toys, such as wild animals, farm animals, dinosaurs, fish, cars, little people, etc. She also sorted different colorful pieces according to their shapes or purposes. I didn't grow up with these toys, so I had to check with Carmen which pieces should go into which buckets or containers. It took us a long while to sort out all of the toys and put them into the right buckets or containers. Carmen said she would wash these toys once in a while to make sure they were clean for children to play with. Yong Sheng and Yong Ming, the two little brothers, were helping as well. Yong Sheng, the five-year-old boy, with tiny little glasses on his nose, looked very cute. He was a better helper to Carmen than me as he knew mostly where the right place was. For example, he knew where to put the baby stuff, and where to put the kitchen utensils. I didn't know, at first, that at the Parent Centre there was a baby's corner with toys particularly for babies and a tiny kitchen place for children to play with toy kitchen stuff. Yong Sheng was there helping Carmen all the time. Like myself, some parents tried to help but seemed to get lost and did not know how to help. Jeff's Grandpa helped a little while. But he looked confused. He didn't know which toy should go to which bucket, so he stopped.

Carmen said it was really a lot of work for her at the Centre every day and she asked Freeman to tell the parents to help. I noticed someone was vacuuming the carpet and Yong Sheng and Yong Ming's mother was sweeping the room. Someone was doing the dishes....

Multiple Stories the Toy Boxes May Tell

Almost every Wednesday afternoon, Carmen would pour out all the toys mixed in different containers onto the carpet and sort them out before she returned them to the right containers according to type or category. I helped her whenever I was there. As I had difficulties figuring out which piece should go to which container, I came to understand why many parents did not seem to help with toy sorting. I had been told to bite my tongue and not to give suggestions in the research field. So I did for many weeks, but eventually I suggested to Carmen that it might be a good idea to ask children to draw a picture of the toys and put them outside of each bucket so that parents would know which piece should go into which container. Carmen thought it was a good idea, so she glued some pieces outside each bucket. It helped, but not much. Parents and children still mixed them altogether without checking. One day before the Circle Time, when I was trying to figure out which bucket was for the toys in my hands, one mother said to me, "Don't bother. The children will make a mess again in just one minute. We just put them away and make the room tidy for the Circle Time." Her hands were moving up and down very fast and putting away the toys from the carpet. In a minute she cleared the carpet for Circle Time. Still, Carmen repeated sorting out the toys every Wednesday afternoon. After many weeks, I could not help asking Carmen why she bothered to repeat this tedious work every week since the children would mess the toys all up in a minute. She said she thought it was important for children to be able to sort out things according to colors, shapes, purposes, or categories. The children would learn to make distinctions between colors, shapes, or categories and learn how to say the word for each toy. She thought it was also a way of learning skills that would be important in their lives; for example, to be well organized and tidy. Carmen said she did not grow up with some of the toys, but she used to work in a toyshop, so it was very easy for her. She understood it was difficult for parents to know exactly what was the right way to do it. "There is no right way. It is just my way." Carmen laughed. "Because I bought every single piece, so I have the idea where each one of them should go." I laughed and then remembered that the other day I had no idea that a red square shape with some white stripes on it should go to the bucket with farm animals until Carmen explained to me that the piece was a barn door and that was why she put it together with farm animals.

Intersecting Diverse Cultural Histories in Learning

Simple as these everyday routines seem to be, I found I was in the midst of stories of people with different cultural histories and lived experiences. Carmen's "taken-for-granted, habitual ways" (Connelly and Clandinin 1988, p. 81) of doing her routine work at the Parent Centre actually reveal her concept of learning and her notion of curriculum. She is consciously and unconsciously constructing and enacting a hidden curriculum that can be related to Dewey's (1938) notion of learning through direct experience. However, it is also because of that the Chinese grandparents/parents in the Parent Centre, who do not share the same lived experience as Carmen, did not seem to be able to make meaning of the weekly toy sorting as a learning process for their children intended by Carmen in her "hidden curriculum" (King 1986; Jackson 1992).

Hence, in the single room of the Parent Centre at Bay Street Community School in downtown Toronto, Carmen and the Chinese families, with their diverse cultural histories and lived experiences, meet and interact in their intersecting narratives, bouncing in-between cultural borders or boundaries, while constituting a shared cross-cultural lived experience.

These people are both characters in, and narrators of, their diverse stories. I, as a researcher, am also "both a character in, and the narrator of, the story" (Connelly and Clandinin 1990; Conle 1999) of the multicultural life and interactions in the Parent Centre between Carmen and

Chinese families, as well as families of other ethnic backgrounds, and between all families with diverse narrative histories. I came to understand that story as a mode of thought (Hardy 1968), a mode of thinking (Bruner 1996), and a mode of knowing (Carter 1993) is in such multiple and complex forms that it constitutes and reveals multiple layers and dimensions of life. In other words, life is a story. While I am telling stories about events happening among people of diverse cultural histories at the school, what I am doing is not merely storytelling. It is life, an experience I live together with the people that I bring under study.

Living in the Midst of Stories

Thinking Narratively

In the previous sections of the chapter, "Being in the Midst of Stories and Walking in the Midst of Stories", I intended to say that, in educational narrative studies, it is important to make meaning of the intersecting narratives of people with diverse cultural histories and lived experiences in seemingly everyday routines. To do so, someone who wishes to become a narrative researcher needs to learn that an inquiry sense is key in his or her mode of inquiry into people's life, and it is important to think narratively and be part of the living rather than simply telling about people's life in defined terms or categories.

With a sense of inquiry aimed at understanding the multiplicity and complexity of stories, I began to think of the question "Who is telling whose stories by whom, and why". I reflect on my early ideas about having "well-educated" potential participants in my research. How shall we define "well-educated"? Who has the right to define whom? Who is well educated and who is not? Are those who do not have regular schooling or do not have higher education not "well-educated"? The presumptions I had about what education should be like were associated with my educational beliefs and values in the definition of "truth" about knowledge and education as 'the quest for grand theories, themes, or systems in the academic disciplines that will provide us with "final understandings" of how the world works, how human beings behave, and, "finally", how these "final understanding" will guide us to "social harmony" (Jones 2002, p. 111). I was looking for people who would fit into my defined categories and whom I would be able to study in my defined terms. My presumptions of "being well-educated" were only related to formal schooling, but ignored what was educational in people's lives, "life stories people have lived about their childhood, their relationship to their parents, siblings and other people, their immigration to a new country... endless life stories that may peripherally be connected to the school system but not intimately connected" (Connelly & Beattie, 1992, p. 130).

With a sense of inquiry developed by living in and thinking narratively of Chinese families' immigrant experience from the past to the present and their hopes for the future, I am able to "see the family as fluid and constantly being negotiated and reconstituted both spatially and temporally" (Creese et al. 1999, p. 3) on cross-cultural landscapes in transition. By living in their stories, I am able to see people with a narrative perspective and in their own terms, not as what I thought they were in my mind, or what I was told they were in others' stories. Rather than complaining that I could not find the right people as participants for my studies, I found that every person I met and every conversation we had constitutes a fascinating narrative with significant educational values. With the sense of inquiry I acquired in my lived experience with my participants moving in and out of the school landscapes in transition, I see *what I see* and hear *what I hear* with a narrative perspective instead of seeing *what I think or believe what I see* or hearing *what I think or believe what I hear*. That is, by living in the midst of stories, I start to see an event as an expression of something happening over time, instead of thinking of it as a thing happening at that moment.

This narrative perspective guides me consciously and unconsciously to the narrativized telling of the day-to-day and moment-to-moment life fragments captured in my inquiry.

The story of toy sorting turned out to be more complex than mere daily routines in the Parent Centre, or a story about "parents not helping" in the process of narrativization. As well, untold stories of "the granny with a doggie bag", which would otherwise have remained frozen as a negative fragment about the granny, became much more complex than it was in the narrativized telling. Narrativization helps to avoid telling a single story by itself and helps to prevent interpreting or retelling a story in defined terms and categories. The following stories about "the granny with a doggie bag", interwoven one after another, reveal the complex multigenerational relationships in which the granny lived: she had been an indispensable caregiver to Danny's father, her grandson, and she was then a caregiver both to Danny, her great grandson, and to her granddaughter Daphne, her daughter's daughter at the Parent Centre. These otherwise untold stories about the granny reveal the complexity and multiplicity of stories embedded in the multiple dimensions of people's life.

Untold Stories in the Story about "The Granny with a Doggie Bag"

One and a half years since I first walked into the Parent Centre, a place of stories, many children had reached school age. Yong Sheng and Danny became Grade-1 students in September. I still saw Yong Ming and Julian in the Parent Centre as they would go to kindergarten for a half day in the morning and come to the Parent Centre in the afternoon. Danny's great grandmother, one of the grandmothers who were seen putting snacks into a doggie bag, now came to the Parent Centre with her granddaughter Daphne, her daughter's daughter. Several times, while at the Parent Centre, I saw the granny teaching her granddaughter Daphne to read and write Chinese. I was amazed at her beautiful Chinese handwriting. Julian's grandma said that the granny was born into a rich family. I wondered if she had attended a private school as daughters of some rich families in China did in the old days before girls were allowed to attend schools. "No, she didn't go to school", Julian's grandma said. "How did she learn to read and write then?" Julian's grandma shook her head. The granny seldom talked. She was either attending to Daphne or sitting there lost in her own thoughts. She often dozed off in the tiny chair beside Daphne. During the Circle Time, she moved to the couch with Daphne, sitting in front of her. She fell asleep when Carmen started singing with the children. The granny spoke only a sub-dialect of Cantonese which only a few other grandmothers could understand. Her life remained as fragmented stories to us. A mother told me that Danny was actually the granny's great grandson. She brought up her grandson, Danny's father, and now, in her 80 s, she is taking care of Danny, the great grandson, while also looking after the housework for the family. Daphne, the granny's daughter's daughter, often fell asleep during the Circle Time. The granny carried her in her arms. Looking at the 80-year-old granny with her 3-year-old granddaughter in her arms, I wondered what miraculous energy burst out of her tiny aged body that was often bent at a 90-degree angle.

One afternoon, I walked into the Parent Centre, and saw quite a few grandmothers and mothers sitting around the big table talking. They said hello to me but all looked solemn. I noticed that the granny was sitting among them. Half of her right cheek was black and blue. The granny looked sad and confused. The grandmothers and mothers listened and sighed. One grandmother who could speak Mandarin told me the story. The granny was hit by Danny, her great grandson. No one knew what exactly had happened. One fragment of the granny's story, somewhat related to the granny's black-and-blue cheek, was that Danny's mother, the granny's granddaughter in-law, often blamed the granny for eating too much. She often complained to the granny that she did not understand why the granny at her age still ate so much. The granny came to the dinner table often to see only leftovers from the family after she finished the housework. All the grandmothers and mothers sighed with the granny. Yong Sheng's mother said angrily that she knew that woman. Over one year ago, Danny had a serious skin allergy. Carmen asked him to stay at home in her concern about other children in the room. Danny's mother came to the Parent Centre shouting at Carmen. Freeman tried to explain on behalf of Carmen. Danny's mother turned around, shouting at Freeman. I remembered Freeman had told me the same story a while ago.

"Why wouldn't the granny go to live with her daughter?" I looked at the deep wrinkles in the granny's saddened face, wondering what stories each of those wrinkles would tell about the granny's life. Yong Sheng's mother said that the granny's eldest son, Danny's grandfather, had a good business at home in China. He asked the granny to go back home to Guangdong, but the granny would not listen. She brought up Danny's father and she is now taking care of Danny, her great grandson. It looked as if she felt Danny's family could not do without her.

The week before Christmas, the granny came into the Parent Centre with two grandchildren who came to visit her from Paris where another daughter of hers lived. All the wrinkles on her face expanded comfortably like a fully blooming chrysanthemum.

No one knew exactly why the granny chose to stay with Danny's family even though she seemed to be so mistreated while she had many better choices.

Intersecting Narratives of Diverse Experiences in Living

The granny's life is most likely to remain a puzzle. My "narrativization" of the fragmented stories about her helps to give a narrative understanding of the story about "the granny with a doggie bag" and pulls out more narrative threads that put together stories that would otherwise remain fragmented, frozen or untold.

Obviously, many more stories embedded in the story about "the granny with a doggie bag" are personally and socially complicated. However, coming back to the point of telling the story about the granny with a doggie bag, I recall what Rosanna's grandma murmured to me, "What a waste!" when looking at the leftover cookies dumped in the garbage bin after the Snack Time while I was standing by the sink washing the dishes.

I understand the untold stories, unstated in her comments, thinking of grandparents of her age who had experienced starvation during the Japanese invasion, the Chinese Civil War, and the Great Leap Movement consecutively in China in the early half of the twentieth century. In the meantime, by "living" in the Parent Centre for over two years, I also understand why Carmen has been so careful as to make sure nothing the children eat, drink, or play with is unclean or unhealthy, after we have been faced with the crises of severe acute respiratory syndrome (SARS), bird flu, mad cow disease, and West Nile virus.

Just as narratives of diverse cultural histories intersect in making meaning of toy sorting, narratives of diverse lived experiences intersect and interact in the story about "the granny with a doggie bag". These intersecting narratives of people's diverse lived experiences are no longer simply storytelling of an event. They tell people's diverse lives from the past to the present across cultural and spatial borders on landscapes in transition. They tell both personal and social dimensions of people's lived experiences from the past to the present, the transition and interactions of people's lives across social and cultural boundaries, their adaptation and frustration in their life on landscapes in transition, and their values, traditions, and habits that they hold on to or let go. Above all, the intersecting narratives of people from diverse cultural narratives on landscapes in transition reveal the multiplicity and complexity of narrative and storytelling. Accordingly, in narrative educational studies, it is important to develop a sense of inquiry into people's storied life by living in the midst of stories temporally, personally, socially, and spatially. Living in the midst of stories with a sense of inquiry enables a narrative inquirer to consciously and unconsciously narrativize fragmented stories of people's life and to understand narratively the continuity and wholeness of an individual's life experience in narrative unities and discontinuities.

Double Agendas in My Inquiry

Conle (2000) distinguishes "narrative inquiry" from more traditional didactic and strategic uses of narrative in education by pointing out that its open-ended, experiential, and quest-like qualities are useful in the two areas of research and professional development. According to Connelly and Clandinin (1990, 2000), narrative is both the phenomenon and the method in the social sciences because experience is what narrative inquirers study and narrative thinking is a key form of experience and a key way of writing and thinking about it. Narrative inquiry as a methodology derives its strength from narrative inquiry as phenomenon in which *story* is the phenomenon and *narrative* is the inquiry (Connelly 2001; Connelly and Clandinin 1990). Using this narrative approach, I have double agendas in my inquiry. On one hand, I present Chinese families' lived experience on cross-cultural landscapes of schools in transition, the phenomenon under study: Chapters 3 through 7, in narrative form, are structured in episodes and scenes. On the other hand, I try to bridge cultures not only between the East and the West, but also between the culture of the reader and the narrative culture of the text in a narrative inquiry sense. Hence, in the following chapters I present the core family stories in the way life they evolved during my inquiry journey. I would like to invite you to read the episodes of these Chinese families' lived experience in their own terms. The family stories are, to a certain extent, interrelated and embedded in one another. I hope to accomplish my double agenda in the inquiry journey: the inquiry into the stories of /about my participants; and, the inquiry into the narrative process of my thinking and understanding of the phenomenon under study.

CHAPTER 3

Grandparents' Sense of Home: "Money Cannot Buy the Heart"

爷爷奶奶的心事: 钱财难买真情

PRELUDE

Julian's grandma,[1] Mrs. Fang 房老师, a retired elementary school teacher from Guangdong (Canton), China, is the major character in this chapter. Her family story represents the stories of many other grandparents I met during my visits to the Parent Centre for a period of three years. Important characters in the family stories are Julian, Julian's little brother Allen, Julian's parents, and two grandfathers. Although I called the grandma *Teacher Fang* in Chinese 房老师 (Mrs. Fang), the grandma was referred to as *Julian's grandma* in Carmen's and other grandparents' and parents' daily conversations and interactions. Similarly, at the Parent Centre, other parents or grandparents are identified as *Tommy's mom, Tommy's grandma, Sally's grandma,* or *Steve's grandpa*. However, Freeman, Stephen's grandpa, who had been in Canada for over 30 years, preferred to be called by his English name at the school. In the past dozen years,

---

A couple of quotes from my interviews with the grandparents in Chapter 3 were cited in the following book chapter when I discussed the roles of grandparents in immigrant children's education: Xu, S. J. (2011). Bridging the East and West dichotomy: Harmonizing Eastern learning with Western knowledge. In Janette, Ryan (Ed.). *Understanding China's education reform: Creating cross cultural knowledge, pedagogies and dialogue* (Ch 11, pp. 224–242). London, UK: Routledge.

Freeman was a volunteer at the school and provided indispensable support to the Chinese families and the school staff members, not only at the center, but at school and community activities as well. Most Chinese families insisted on calling him 黄先生 Mr. Wong, as it is not customary in the Chinese culture to call seniors by their given name.

Following leads that often surprised me, I discovered evolving stories about my participants as life paths interwove. Every weekday evening, Julian's grandma went to the Language Instruction for Newcomers to Canada (LINC) program to learn ESL with Yong Sheng and Yong Ming's mother. She also taught Chinese to Freeman's grandsons every Sunday afternoon. In addition, Grandpa Jiang, from another family, is included as a supplementary character to enrich the grandparents' perspective in the chapter. Grandpa Jiang's grandsons, and the little boys' mother, Jane, also appear in this chapter. They were regular visitors to the Parent Centre.

Carmen, the Parent Centre staff member, is a crucial figure in this chapter. The Parent Centre was, to a great extent, a home for the parents and grandparents with their children and grandchildren. This was one of the main places they made meaning of schooling and their transitional life on the cross-cultural school landscape. It was also a home for me as I moved from place to place on the school landscape: Parent Centre, classrooms, library, gym, School Council meetings, Main Office, school events, and field trips. Because the Parent Centre is so central to my inquiry, both Carmen and Freeman are important characters in this, and other chapters of my book.

Episode One: Making Sense of Life in-between China and Canada

Scene I: Julian's Grandma, a Retired Teacher from China

November of the 1st year, Parent Centre
Julian's grandma was a literacy teacher who taught the Chinese language for over 30 years in a central elementary school in downtown Guangzhou, the capital city of Guangdong (Canton) in south China. She retired in her early fifties and came to Toronto to help her daughter take care of Julian. When I first met her at Bay Street Community School's Parent Centre in September during the first year of my fieldwork at the school, she told me that she came to Toronto two years earlier when Julian was one and half years old. Carmen told me that Julian's grandma looked unhappy and seldom talked or smiled

when she first came to the Parent Centre with Julian. Carmen noticed that the grandma started talking and smiling as she gradually found friends among the Chinese parents and grandparents at the Parent Centre. Carmen wondered what the grandma gave up to come to a new country where she could not speak the language and knew little about its culture.

I met Julian's grandma when I started intensive observation in the Parent Centre in September. From the very beginning, Julian's grandma and I connected as she was the only Mandarin-speaking grandmother. She usually came with Julian and his 13-month-old brother, Allen, in the afternoon because Julian, at age four, attended kindergarten in the morning. She told me that her son-in-law, Julian's father, came to Toronto 12 years ago. He works in a restaurant. Her daughter, Julian's mother, came to Toronto a few years later. She works in a clothes factory. Mrs. Fang and her husband, Julian's grandfather, joined their daughter's family in Toronto two years ago. The grandfather works in a factory.

In one of our conversations she said:

> When in China, everyone in the family came home from work around the same time and we would have dinner together at home or go out together and spend the evening in a restaurant or cinema. Now, one person might come home around 7:00 p.m., another around 8:00 p.m., and another might be still not yet home. There has never been a time for the whole family to be together for dinner since coming to Canada.... Money is important but money cannot buy everything; and money cannot buy the heart.

Julian's grandma raised her voice when she uttered the word "heart". The look in her eyes made me wonder about the untold stories of her home in China and her new home in Canada. What does "home" mean to a newly arrived Chinese family? What motivated these families to move their "home" from China to Canada? The episodes and themes that follow help explore these questions.

Scene II: Dissonance on the New Land

After the Chinese New Year of the 2nd year, Parent Centre
Julian's grandma had not come to the Parent Centre as regularly as other Chinese grandparents for a while. In January after the Chinese New Year, I saw her again in the school. She asked me about the application procedure for a visitor's visa to Canada. Her son wanted to come. Later she said: "My

husband is reluctant to sponsor our son. He said our daughter has become westernized. It would not make sense to have a son come here to become westernized as well."

Still later she explained her husband's reluctance:

> Here, people are very individual. They do not seem to care about one another. When one person eats something, s/he just eats it by her/himself. In China, we always share with others whenever we eat something, or at least we ask if others would like to have some before we eat alone. It would be rude if a person started eating without asking others.

Julian's grandma said that her husband did not like living in Canada. They wanted to return to China when Julian and Allen grew older. But, for now, they had to stay to take care of the little boys.

The grandma was worried about Julian. She said: "Julian is naughty. He never wants to lose at anything. If he loses, he becomes unhappy. At home, he often wants to do something to beat his father and grandpa." The grandma said she thought spanking was necessary to discipline boys like Julian. He needed to learn that he could be punished for doing something wrong.

Scene III: Disillusion about the New Life

April of the 2nd year, Parent Centre
While I was talking with Julian's grandma, I noticed Allen playing with a little girl at the children's kitchen corner. He pretended to drink from a toy cup and seemed to be enjoying himself. I recalled that my friend's son, Da Wei 大伟, who was cared for by his grandmother before he went to daycare, liked to play with cooking utensils and pretended he was cooking. Allen, who also spent a great deal of his time with his grandmother, was doing the things he saw his grandmother do at home; cooking and washing dishes.

Julian's grandma said she had the flu but felt better today. I said, "I noticed that you often have a cold. You must be too tired or overworked. Maybe you need to rest." I asked her if she was able to take a nap as Chinese people often did when in China. She replied that it was impossible. Jane, a Chinese mother, joined our conversation and said that it was also impossible for her to take a nap as she now had three children, Steve, Henry, and the new baby Andrew. Julian's grandma added that she often stayed up until 2:00 a.m. because Allen wanted her attention and banged on her door. She said she had to ignore him and he was learning to go to bed around 10:00 p.m. When I asked if her daughter took care of the children on holidays or the weekend, she replied:

> My daughter hardly has any holidays. She has to work hard at the clothes factory, sometimes, 12 hours a day and her work requires her to stand all day. Her work is counted according to the items she makes, not according to the hours or days she works. So, like many Chinese workers, she has to work overtime. When she gets home she is exhausted. She looks so skinny. When she has a day off, she is too tired to help with the housework. I'd rather she rest when she is home.

I asked, "Why not just work regular hours so as not to ruin your health?" Jane pointed out, "If you don't work overtime, you can be fired. You have to work overtime to keep the job. There are so many people without a job. If you don't work overtime, somebody else will." I asked the grandma if Julian's mother would have a pension and other benefits, and if there was a union to protect the factory workers' rights. She did not know.

This story reminded me of a report in the Chinese morning newspaper in Toronto. Three Chinese women were fired from a Toronto company even though they had worked hard and often worked overtime. They sought help but were told to accept reality. When I asked Julian's grandma if her husband still wanted to go back to China, she said:

> Yes. We want to go back to China when the boys grow older. I told my daughter that I did not like her laboring like a farm animal. She is not living as a human. She has no time to enjoy life.... People came to Canada with their dreams for a better life, but it turns out they cannot enjoy life.

Episode Two: Making Meaning of Schooling

Scene I: Different Views on How to Educate Children

Fall to Spring, Parent Centre
The following conversations took place during my visits at the Parent Centre for a period of over two years. Many of my conversations with Julian's grandma touched on education. As a retired elementary school

teacher, she preferred Chinese schools to Canadian ones. Her views were tied to her concerns for Julian. She once told me:

> Children of Julian's age in China have learned a lot in language and math, but Julian plays all day long. There is no homework. ... Children of Julian's age need spoon-feeding. They do not know the importance of study ... Canadian schools make it easy for children like Julian.

On another occasion, she said:

> Here they do not teach students how to write properly. In China, if a child does not hold the pencil properly, they are corrected and shown good handwriting. But here children do whatever they like. Their handwriting is messy and not in good order.

Tommy's mother, also from Guangdong, came to the Parent Centre in the afternoon with Tommy after she sent her elder son Jimmy to kindergarten. Like Julian's grandma, the young mother could speak both Cantonese and Mandarin. She talked about schools and children in Canada and in China, but with a different perspective.

> Children like Canada better, for they have less pressure at school. In China children love holidays and do not want to go to school. On the contrary, children in Canada do not like holidays and want to go to school. Here, Jimmy and Tommy became bored even when the winter holidays were only two weeks long. They asked me when they could return to school. Children in Canada are encouraged and can do anything they like. In China, children have to study hard. If they do not study hard, they are blamed by their teachers and parents.

> I am sympathetic with my brother's daughter in China. She is still in kindergarten, but she has to read a whole book and recite a long article. If she cannot, her parents criticize her for not studying hard and sometimes even spank her.

Julian's grandma was not sympathetic to this view. On another occasion, she said: "Allen is much better at language than Julian, taking their age in consideration." She said she had taken care of Allen since he was born whereas Julian was one-and-half years old when she started caring for him. "Allen loves pens and papers," she said proudly, smiling. She went on to say:

Julian just loves watching TV. He doesn't like reading. He spends most of his time at home watching TV. That's why I always bring Julian and Allen to the Parent Centre no matter how bad the weather, so that Julian can play with other children and interact with people.

Scene II: Dissatisfaction with Canadian Elementary Education

January of the 2nd year, Parent Centre

Julian's grandma's views on the weakness of education in Canada were connected to her views on children and how best to teach them. Her previous teaching experience was in downtown Guangzhou, in what was regarded as one of the best city schools.

She compared elementary education in China and Canada by relating her teaching experience in urban south China to what she had seen and heard at Bay Street Community School, also an urban elementary school. She felt that "elementary education here is not good enough for children" who, she said, "do not know well how to learn, and have to be pushed." She commented:

> The teachers should stuff children with as much knowledge as possible. Because children in China have been trained since they were little, they can do things children here can't do. Chinese kids even in Grade 2 can do multiplication and mental computation, so they do not have to use the computer or calculator; nor do they use their fingers to count. Even in Grade 7 or Grade 8, kids here still cannot do mental computation. This is just wrong. Children in China have to write a lot and read a lot. They learn a lot in elementary school and even at preschool time. But children here just play and play.

She said this meant that Chinese teachers have more pressure than Canadian teachers.

> It seems that teachers here can do whatever they like. They do not seem to prepare for classes. In China, teachers have specific tasks and have to prepare the lessons very well. And they are inspected frequently: the principal or other administrators often sit at the back of your classroom and observe how you teach. There are regular evaluations of teachers. Those who do not do a good job can be fired. You have to work hard there.

I replied, "Teachers here have to prepare for their classes and have a heavy load as they have to teach everything including language, math, art, etc.; and report cards also add to their work."

Julian's grandma continued, "Teachers here have only about 18 kids in one class. We have 35 students and sometimes even over 50 in China."

Scene III: Buddy Reading Program

March of the 2nd year, Parent Centre
Mr. Anderson, the Newcomer Support Class teacher, had started to take the Grades 7 and 8 newcomer students to the Parent Centre for the Buddy Reading Program with the little ones on Tuesday afternoons since the beginning of the new school year in September. His idea was to help build newcomer students' self-esteem by making them feel useful when reading to the little ones. However, most of these students came from Fujian and Guangdong and had little English. Mostly they talked among themselves in Chinese and engaged in roughhouse play, fighting with one another using toy dinosaurs or crocodiles.

Watching this, Julian's grandma said, "The boys are killing time here. They are not studying at all ... you've got to listen to your teacher. How can you learn if you do not listen?"

The disruption brought on by the Newcomer Support Class affected parent/grandparent attendance, with many appearing to skip Tuesday afternoons. But Julian's grandma was always there, watching and listening when Carmen and Mr. Anderson read to the children during Circle Time. She would sit nearby and watch me work with a group of the naughtiest Newcomer Support Class boys.

EPISODE THREE: JULIAN'S GRANDMA MAKING EFFORTS TO LEARN ENGLISH

Scene I: "Difficult to Live in Toronto Without English"

Spring of the 2nd year, Parent Centre
When I first met Julian's grandma in September, she said that English was too difficult to learn. I encouraged her to learn English from Carmen, as did other parents who followed along when Carmen worked with children during Circle Time. As I worked with the newcomer boys on Tuesday afternoons, Julian's grandma often held Allen in her arms

EPISODE THREE: JULIAN'S GRANDMA MAKING EFFORTS TO LEARN ENGLISH

and listened to me reading to the boys. Sometimes she tried to read a word or two in English with us; sometimes she printed words such as *street* and *parking*, which she saw on her way to school. She would ask me what they meant.

After the Chinese New Year, Julian's grandma told me that she started an ESL class on Saturday mornings with some neighborhood friends. She said she found it difficult to live in Toronto without English. I was so happy for the grandma and suggested she could read children's books in the Parent Centre. With the help of pictures, the books can be easier to read. Carmen and I could help. She wondered where to begin learning English. "It is different in China," she said, "where Chinese is learned by starting with phonetic Pin Yin."

One day when she saw me, she remarked: "Oh, I didn't know you were coming today; otherwise, I would have brought you something to read for me." She had received a letter in English from the government.

Scene II: Helping the Grandma with Her ESL Homework

After the SARS Crisis, Parent Centre

In 2003 Toronto was plagued with SARS, a dreadful infectious disease which brought the city to a halt. Many families stopped bringing their children to the Parent Centre. Carmen was happy to see families returning to the Parent Centre in the middle of April when the SARS crisis abated. I did not see Julian's grandma during the crisis. She came to the center today because Julian's father finally said "yes" to the children's request to return to school. She settled the boys and joined us at the table.

She said she had missed two of her English classes. She showed me her homework – a TTC (Toronto Transit Commission, the city's public transportation system) map. She wanted to know what TTC stood for and how to pronounce the subway station names so that she could understand the subway announcements. We read aloud the names most important to her: Kennedy, Yonge, St. George, Spadina, Finch, Bloor, College, Dundas, and Union. She asked about the different subway lines. When I responded by asking her about her usual route, she said that she often went with other people and did not remember the directions. I said I used to be like that, too. When I first came to the university's downtown campus, the Spadina stop with intersecting lines confused me. Why, I wondered, did people go downstairs after getting off at St. George? It took me a long while to figure it out. I explained how the subway, bus, and streetcar lines connected, and how these tied in to GO (Government of Ontario) trains and GO buses for connecting travel outside Toronto.

As we talked, Freeman joined us and explained the Chinese–English digital dictionary. The digital dictionary pronounced words and sentences in Cantonese, Mandarin, and English. I noted that taped books could help in the same way. This was one of the ways I learned spoken English. Too often Chinese people learn silent English. Many may be able to read English, but are unable to speak it or to understand it when listening.

As a Chinese language teacher, Julian's grandma paid attention to pronunciation and tried to figure out English pronunciation rules. She printed the word *gate* and asked what it meant. I explained in Chinese, pointing out the difference between *door* and *gate* as she told me that she learned the word *door* at her Saturday ESL class. She said she saw Gate 12 at Stadium Skydome, but did not know what it meant.

Hui Lan, Yong Sheng, and Yong Ming's mom joined us and sighed that English was too difficult to read. I tried to encourage them by saying there were pronunciation rules that helped. For example, in the words *gate, skate, late*, which end with a silent *e*, the letter *a* is pronounced the same as the letter *a* itself while *a* is pronounced as [æ] in words like *cat, sat, sad*.

But Hui Lan said, this only works because "you know English well … we don't understand English and we find it too difficult to learn". Julian's grandma was interested, however. She wrote the word, *like*, and asked why sometimes the letter *i* is pronounced as [i] and sometimes as [ai].

I said, "It follows the same rule as the letter *a*. The letter *i* in words ending with a silent *e* is pronounced the same as the sound of the letter itself, such as *like, bike, bite*, or *side*, while it is pronounced as [i] when in words like *sit, did, kid*, or *lid*."

"Tidy up time, tidy up!" Carmen called out from somewhere near the sink. Hui Lan stood and asked Yong Ming and Yong Sheng to help tidy the room.

Julian's grandma continued to ask about English words. As we talked, Carmen suggested she ask Julian to help. Julian's grandma looked embarrassed and began to tidy up. Carmen said that she did not mean for her to do the work. I explained to the grandmother what Carmen meant. She smiled and spoke to Julian in Cantonese, but Julian did not listen.

Episode Four: Grandparents' Sacrifices and Contributions

Scene I: Julian's Grandma's Sense of Family

After the New Year of the 3rd year, Parent Centre
Time went by like flowing water. Soon the Year of the Goat left quietly. There came the Year of the Monkey, which Chinese people believe would be a better and healthier year than the Year of the Goat for people. It was the first day after the winter holidays. Julian's grandma arrived with Allen. Julian was already playing in the children's kitchen corner. I asked Julian's grandma how she spent her holiday. She said she stayed at home and rested while Julian's parents took Julian and Allen to different places. However, I knew that she worked on weekends caring for an elderly woman. I suggested she take a tour with her husband or friends on the weekends. Chinese travel agencies cater to groups. She said she would wait until the boys grew up.

We sat at the big center table. Tommy's grandma talked in Cantonese and Julian's grandma helped me follow the conversation by translating for me. Julian's grandma was saying that she was a fool because she and her husband had two fine homes in China, a house, and an apartment in Guangdong, but now lived poorly in Canada, working even on weekends. Her husband did not approve of her weekend work and asked "What is the point of making money only to leave it to the children?"

We talked about how elderly Chinese people sacrificed themselves for their children and grandchildren. Another mother joined our conversations saying that some grandparents bring food to their grandchildren. She said, "People ask them, 'Why don't you keep the food for yourself? Will your grandson remember and share his food with you in the future?'"

Julian's grandparents' situation was complicated in Chinese terms. They came to Toronto to support their daughter. The grandma looked after the children and the grandpa worked in a factory. They lived in one room of the daughter's house. They sent money to their son and his wife in China even though the son said he was not in need. It is traditional for a Chinese mother to live with a married son and help with housework and childcare. Julian's grandma appeared to feel the pressure of this obligation, while she supported her daughter instead.

I understand traditional Chinese customs and said, "It seems to go one way nowadays – parents sacrifice for their children, but not the other way round. I wonder if young parents who do things for their children remember to do the same for their own elderly parents." Julian's grandma said in an understanding way, "It is hard for them, a kind of burden, if they help both ways. It is enough to take care of their own children."

I knew about the weekend work from Freeman who told me the surprising news before Christmas. During the weekend, Julian's grandma took care of a 90-year-old deaf and blind woman. She stayed in the granny's home from Saturday evening until noontime Sunday taking care of her, cleaning the house, and doing her shopping. Then, on Sunday afternoon, she gave Chinese Mandarin lessons to Freeman's grandsons. Therefore, Julian's grandma had three jobs with no time to herself. Her time was so full that she had to sneak out to grocery shop while the boys were at the Parent Centre where Hui Lan or Tommy's grandma would keep an eye on the children for her.

Scene II: Grandpa Jiang's Joy: Another Perspective

Grandpa Jiang, Jane's father in-law, joined our conversation later, and spoke philosophically:

> It is a pleasure to take care of my grandsons. It is my happiness to watch them grow up. I do not feel lonely as I have so much to do every day. I do not feel sad about getting old, as I know my grandsons carry on my life. My family grows and moves on even though I will eventually die. The utmost happiness for a grandparent is to watch grandchildren growing up in front of you. My grandsons are my greatest joy. I am old now and cannot work for society. But I can help my son and daughter in-law care for their children, so they can work. My wife is in Scarborough helping our daughter with her children. It is fair for us to help both our son's and the daughter's families although we have to live separately. We've been old husband and wife for many years. Nothing can change our relationship. But they are young. It is hard for them to bring up the little ones while overloaded with worries of life and pressure from work. Although we two live separately, we are happy to help. Our sacrifices contribute to the harmony of their small families and hence of the big family, so it is worth it."

EPISODE FIVE: SENSE OF FAMILY AND EDUCATION: INTERVIEW WITH GRANDPA JIANG

> Parents need to be considerate of their sons and daughters. My life is very simple. I don't smoke nor drink. My sons and daughters give me money, but I

live with my eldest son and do not need money. So whenever one of my children is in difficulty, I help with my China pension – just give a hand to the one(s) in difficulty.

Grandpa Jiang had been in Canada for nine years when I interviewed him. I include his stories in this chapter to provide an enriched understanding of Chinese immigrants' values from a grandparent perspective. Grandpa Jiang was thoughtful and philosophical. Unlike Julian's grandma, he made few comparisons between Chinese and Canadian schools. He talked more substantially about the importance of how to be a person in the Confucian tradition. His stories and reflections help provide narrative context for understanding the educational experiences brought forward in this study.

Scene I: Grandpa Jiang's Life Story

June, the 3rd year, Interview with Grandpa Jiang, Parent Centre
As I did not see Grandpa Jiang as frequently as I saw Julian's grandma, I made an appointment through his daughter-in-law, Jane. He took my invitation seriously. Jane later told me with a laugh that he spent a long time in the morning getting properly dressed and checked with Jane to make sure he looked clean and nice before leaving for the interview. Grandpa Jiang reminded me of my parents who taught us to dress in clean tidy clothes to show respect to those we visited.

The interview was in the form of a casual conversation during which I followed the grandpa's train of thoughts. I did, however, pursue the question of tensions between grandparents, their children, and their grandchildren for immigrant families. Grandpa Jiang was born into a family of six sons and three daughters in the countryside of Jiangxi Province, China. Before he was born, his parents selected a girl to be his eldest brother's future wife. The girl, who later became the grandpa's "big sister in-law," was responsible for his care when he was a baby. Before 1949, when the People's Republic of China was established, it was customary for a family to adopt a girl from a poor family to be their future daughter-in-law. The girl was usually much older than the boy who would be her future husband and she often worked as a maidservant in her future husband's family.

Grandpa Jiang studied accounting at a private hometown school run by a retired professor. By 1949, he was working as an accountant. He was selected to study accounting at a university in Shanghai and eventually became a provincial official before the outbreak of the 1966 Cultural Revolution. After he left his hometown, Grandpa Jiang brought his younger sister and brother out of the poor area. He wanted to prevent his elder brothers from finding his 15-year-old sister a husband for the purpose of reducing family costs. With Grandpa Jiang's support, his sister became a midwife in Hong Kong and his younger brother became a technician. When Grandpa Jiang married, he and his wife supported his wife's younger sister to attend university. The sister-in-law became a professor in a university in south China.

When the Cultural Revolution began in 1966, Grandpa Jiang was labeled a "contemporary anti-revolutionary" and was sent to the mountainous countryside of Jiangxi Province for "re-education" for 10 years. He took two elder children with him while his wife, who was sent to a different place in the countryside, took two younger ones. The family met once or twice a year. Grandpa Jiang said that it was reading that had kept him calm and happy through this difficult time.

> While other people were denouncing people, I read world history, European history, Chinese history, and history of other countries. I read a lot and thought a lot. During the Cultural Revolution, I could keep calm. I was happy. Our family came back to the city with six children in good health and spirit. People asked, "Others couldn't live. How come you still have had so many children, Lao Jiang?"

This question was the grandpa's way of initiating one of his main themes – the importance of being a person in a Confucian value system.

> Now, in China, many people do not know how to be a person. What to do when so many people do not know how to be a person? Many Chinese traditional ways were good. They should be maintained. Not all tradition was good, though.

Scene II: How to Be a Person in Confucian Values

June, the 3rd year, Interview with Grandpa Jiang, a Chinese Restaurant
Grandpa Jiang reflected not only on the Cultural Revolution, but also on changes following the end of the revolution in 1976 and the opening up of China:

> In China, we have taken all the traditional ways as something bad and have denounced them all. It is wrong. The old ways were reasonable. For example, 3 years ago I asked a daughter of mine in China to send 1000 yuan from my

pension to her maternal uncle. But it was not sent until last month. I lost my temper. But she said, "We didn't stay in touch with this uncle. Why should we send him money?" I said, "You don't understand, but Papa (I) understands it. When Papa had a hard life and could barely survive, Papa and Mama would stay at your maternal grandparents and uncle's home. ... Now the uncle is over 70. He is a peasant and has no pension. One Dan 担 (50 kilo) of processed rice 米 cost 50 yuan. So 1000 yuan 3 years ago would buy 20 Dan of rice. Now the price is up. I said (to my daughter), "For my generation, we took our brothers-in-law as brothers. We are close." But, my daughter does not understand. We shouldn't have denounced all the old ways.

There was more to this story for Grandpa Jiang. He felt an obligation to his big sister-in-law, the woman who had come into his home as a bride-to-be and maidservant.

I often send money to my big sister in-law, who is my children's eldest aunt. My children cannot understand this, either. I asked them to send her 500 yuan. They were unwilling. They said, "She has her own sons and grandsons. Why should we send her money?" I said, "When I was little, your big aunt washed my diapers. Even when my brothers and I became big boys, she washed our clothes. I explained how an adopted would-be wife was a family maidservant. But, the young people, my children, do not understand.

Grandpa Jiang told me other stories that helped explain his view of being human and the value of the old, rejected, ways.

In 1986 when I visited my hometown, I made tombs for my parents and for my eldest brother and his wife. They were very pleased. My big sister in-law even sat in the tomb to feel it. A local person commented, "Sons nowadays are not willing to build a tomb for their parents. But a younger brother does?" I said, "I do not drink, nor smoke. I save the money from alcohol and cigarettes to do something good for others. It is better, isn't it?"

Grandpa Jiang continued his reflections:

It is good to do something for others. Nowadays in China many people do not want to help others. They say, "Ah, the relative is useless." Who is useful? It is not that the relative is useless. Maybe he is poor. Sometimes with help, a person might change his life. I supported my younger brother and sister and also my sister in-law. When they graduated from university, I had 6 children. Then they supported me to help raise my children. This is how it works.

Grandpa Jiang told several other stories to illustrate his idea of knowing how to be a person when we left the Parent Centre and continued our conversation during lunch at a Chinese restaurant. The stories also revealed views on education.

He told a story of an uncle, who passed the classical exams at age 17 and considered himself a scholar. When asked by his mother, Grandpa Jiang's maternal grandmother, to carry manure pails to the fields, the uncle was ashamed and committed suicide. In a more recent story, a top university physics student killed four roommates when ridiculed by them during a card-playing game. Grandpa Jiang saw these stories as illustrating the idea that "formal education does not necessarily teach a person how to live and be a person."

> In old China, we followed the Confucian principles of how to be a person and how to live life with others. In the old days, in Confucian thought, there were specific ways to deal with human relationships such as between husband and wife, between older generation and younger generation, among classmates, and between parents and children. In the old days, people were poor but lived in harmony. Now the old humanity is destroyed but the new one has not yet been established.

He told a story of poor people to show what he meant by living in harmony.

> How to be a person? For example, if a man and a woman in a family live together and get along well, they can have a happy life. They do not need high social status or much money. They will be happy if they are in love and in harmony. In Yunnan Province, the people in the mountains were really poor. They were so poor that a husband and a wife had only one set of clothes in the old days. Yunnan is hot and they could survive. When they needed to go to town, one would wear the clothes and go. The other would stay at home without clothes. Still they had a happy family life. They had children. Some might call them savage, but they were just poor. The whole village was like that.

He returned to his theme that too much had been lost when the old ways were rejected. "The Confucian way kept society peaceful and stable. Now there is no Confucian way. Confucius was denounced. But the current way is neither the western way, nor the ancient Chinese way."

I was immersed in his train of thought and asked the Grandpa how he would educate his grandsons in Canada. He seemed at a loss, saying:

It is very hard to say... the western way or the traditional Chinese way? They won't accept it if you educate them in the traditional Chinese way. In the western way? You may ruin their life. You may ruin their life...

What the grandpa was sure of was that he and his wife made the right decision to live separately at their son and daughter's homes to help the two young families care for the grandchildren. They saw sacrificing themselves as the best way to reduce stress for the younger ones. They saw it as their contribution, not only to family harmony but also to society. "So, it is worth it," said the grandpa.

EPISODE SIX: GRANDPARENTS' ROLE IN CHILDREN'S EDUCATION

Scene I: Julian's Grandma's Teaching Chinese

Summer, the 3rd Year, at Freeman's Home
I had been to Freeman's home several times for lunch and always enjoyed listening to Freeman and his wife's fascinating personal and family stories across oceans and generations: From Mainland China, to Hong Kong; from South Asia to Canada. For this summer visit, I chose a Sunday, so I would also talk with Julian's grandma and see her teaching Freeman's grandchildren.

As I walked downstairs, I heard chanting of a Chinese classic poem by 王之焕 Wang Zhihuan, a poet of Tang Dynasty.

登鹳鹊楼
Deng Guan Que Lou
白日依山尽, 黄河入海流.
Bai Ri Yi Shan Jing, Huang He Ru Hai Liu.
欲穷千里目, 更上一层楼.
Yu Qiong Qian Li Mu, Geng Shang Yi Ceng Lou.
Ascending the Stork Tower
The bright sun is setting behind the mountains,
The Yellow River speeding into the sea;
Climb a storey higher
And you'll get a view of a thousand *li*.

Julian's grandma sat at one end of the desk against the east wall. Stephen, son of Freeman's eldest son, and Donald, son of Freeman's eldest daughter, sat across the table facing the wall. "Go on. Go on. Please don't let me interrupt you," I said.

Bai Ri – Yi Shang Jing... 白日依山尽...
Huang He – Ru Hai Liu! 黄河入海流!

She taught the boys to read the poem in an impassioned tone. Some words were emphasized; others pronounced longer. The boys read after her again and again. When they pronounced words incorrectly, she repeated the words.

Freeman's family and I respectfully referred to Julian's grandma as Fang Lao Shi 房老师 (Teacher Fang). She appeared transformed from the grandma in the Parent Centre. She wore a pair of golden-framed glasses, which she never wore at the Parent Centre. Her tone, look, and gesture were those of a dedicated Chinese teacher. She showed me the Chinese language textbook, Book 2, for students in Grade 1, second semester. Unlike the textbook I had when I was in Grade 1 in China, this textbook had colorful pictures. She said they had already finished Book 1, Pin Yin, the phonetic Chinese alphabet.

The boys each had a copy of the book. After they memorized the four-line, five-word, poem, they wrote the words in the exercise space on the left page of the text. She made sure the handwriting was neat and tidy. The two boys spoke four languages, like Freeman and his wife, Mrs. Wong: Cantonese, English, Burmese, and Mandarin. Freeman and his wife, the boys' grandparents, have been cultural bridges for the boys who were born in Canada.

The class was for one hour. The boys stood up to stretch. I asked them if they found it difficult to learn Chinese. "I know a boy who said his cheek muscles hurt when he read and spoke Chinese. Is that true for you?" I asked the two boys. Julian's grandma repeated the question in Cantonese. They said it was.

It was interesting to observe how Julian's grandma taught the boys. She taught Mandarin like many English language teachers in China teach English, with Chinese as the medium of instruction. She spoke Cantonese and Mandarin bilingually. As Cantonese is their home language, Julian's grandma would read the text aloud in Mandarin, but would explain the text in Cantonese, more accurately, in the Tai-shan dialect. Freeman's grandparents' family had lived in that region in Guangdong (Canton). So Freeman spoke the same sub-dialect of Cantonese as Julian's grandma.

The boys went upstairs. I asked Julian's grandma if she was still working for the 90-year-old granny. She said the granny's son was back from Hong Kong for the summer. She would work for them again in the fall.

"You do not have any break: From Monday to Friday you take care of your grandsons and do housework at home, with Saturday for the granny and Sunday for the Mandarin Class," I said.

She said it was actually a rest for her to work for the granny and to sleep over at her quiet home for the weekend. It was not much work. All she needed to do was to cook the meal, clean the house, and pick up some groceries.

I understood what she meant. At home, she took care of two grandsons, bought groceries, cooked three meals a day for the whole family, cleaned the house, did laundry, and tutored Julian in math and Chinese.

She said she was very happy that Freeman's grandsons were so enthusiastic learning Chinese and both of them had made remarkable progress. She got a sense of satisfaction and pleasure, and was happy and willing to teach the boys. "But not my own grandson," she sighed. "Julian doesn't like studying."

Scene II: A Multilingual and Multicultural Family

Summer, the 3rd Year, Freeman's Home
While Julian's grandma and I were talking, Freeman asked us to come upstairs for a drink. He gave me a note from his wife, Mrs. Wong, who I respectfully called "Auntie 伯母" by following the Chinese custom. I called Freeman by his English name at school as this is how he was known in the school community. However, it would be inappropriate for me, someone of his daughter's age, to call him by his given name in front of his family members; so, following Julian's grandma's lead, I called him "黄先生 Mr. Wong" at his home. I read the note. Mrs. Wong wrote in Chinese: "Shi Jing: I am sorry that I cannot stay at home to welcome you, for I have to go to see my old Ma. Please feel at home." I knew that almost every Sunday morning Mr. and Mrs. Wong would go to see the granny, Freeman's mother in-law, and have dim sum with her.

We went upstairs with Freeman. He pointed at a Burmese picture on the wall of a young woman in Burmese traditional costume. I commented, "How beautiful the traditional dress is!" Freeman said, "Yes, the traditional Burmese dress is very beautiful. Now people still keep the style with some modification. It looks somewhat like Chinese Qi-Pao" (a traditional Chinese dress with a slit skirt).

Christie, Freeman's eldest daughter, had home-made cookies ready on a plate. She served watermelon with a bowl of litchi. She made tea as we sat around the kitchen table, apologizing that her tea might not taste as good as her mother's. I remembered the tasty special Burmese tea Mrs. Wong made every time I visited them. We thanked Christie for making the tea. It tasted good. Her husband, Donald's father, joined us. Freeman said that he and his wife could speak Mandarin, Cantonese, and Burmese, but the younger generation could not speak Mandarin, for when it was time for Christie to go to school, Mandarin was abandoned by the then Burmese government. Christie, nevertheless, is trilingual: She spoke their home language Tai-shan dialect, a sub-dialect of Cantonese; she learned Burmese at school in Burma and learned English at school in Canada. She is now a successful career woman, working in a big Canadian corporation. Her husband, from Hong Kong, speaks both Mandarin and Cantonese and is fluent in English.

Because Christie could not speak Mandarin and I could not speak Cantonese, we spoke English to one another. Since this excluded Julian's grandma, I switched back and forth between English and Mandarin. Among themselves, they spoke Cantonese. When this happened, either Freeman or Julian's grandma switched to Mandarin to translate for me. It was an interesting conversation as we tried to include everyone.

Christie and her husband live in the east end of Toronto, but said they did not mind driving downtown to her parents' home each Sunday so that their son, Donald, could take Julian's grandma's Mandarin lessons with Stephen. Freeman said Stephen and Donald both enjoyed the Mandarin lessons.

Earlier Freeman and his wife told me that their two grandsons both loved staying at the grandparents' home, for it had been their "daycare center" since they were born. Mrs. Wong said she used to take the two boys to the Parent Centre every day before they attended Grade 1 at Bay Street Community School. The grandmother said the two cousins were as close as brothers and never fought or argued with each other. They were together every day at the grandparents' home until two years ago when Donald moved to the east end of the city. As the two boys spent most of their pre-school years and after-school time with their grandparents, they could manage several languages like their grandparents: English, Hong Kong Cantonese, Tai-shan Cantonese, Mandarin, and Burmese. They preferred the grandma's home-made Chinese meals and Burmese special food. Freeman and his wife celebrated Canadian, Chinese, and Burmese cultural holidays at home with their big family. So, not long after the two boys enjoyed Christmas at the grandparents' home, they celebrated Chinese New Year together. The boys learned many Chinese and Burmese customs and Buddhist values when various Chinese and/or Burmese traditional holidays were celebrated at the grandparents' home throughout the year.

Freeman said, "Next Sunday is my 91-year-old mother-in-law's birthday. The whole big family will go to celebrate the granny's birthday. The great grandma loves the two great grandsons very much. She would like them to be there for the whole day. Stephen asked his grandma if they would have a day off next Sunday. She said, 'You have to ask Grandpa if you can skip Chinese class.' So Stephen asked me. I teased him that they would go to the great grandma's birthday celebration, but would have to come back in time for the Chinese lesson. Of course, they will have a whole day off next Sunday for great granny's celebration."

Freeman's eldest son, Stephen's father, came to pick up Stephen. Julian's grandma said she had to go. I got up along with her. I gave Freeman $40 and explained that his wife lent it to me two weeks ago. Mrs. Wong took me to a ginseng store to help me select ginseng. The store would not take credit cards, so she lent me money. The store owner was impressed and kept saying, "Oh, how nice she is! How nice she is!"

Episode Seven: Tensions at Home

Scene I: Conflicts on Changing Landscapes

Summer, the 3rd year, on the Way from Freeman's Home to Julian's Home
I walked with Julian's grandma when she returned to her daughter's home following the lesson with Freeman's grandsons. We walked slowly and talked. She told me how her son-in-law complained about her even though she took care of his boys and did the housework. Finally, one day she spoke back saying:

> My husband may not be good-looking, but he has a good heart. For 8 years, he helped me take care of my old mother. He gave money to my poor siblings. What have you done for us? We do not want a penny from you. We two old people make our own living here. We stay in your house because we love and care for our daughter and want to help her. I cannot stand seeing her so overworked. We are not dependent on you!

Now she said, "He doesn't complain as much."

"Why was he complaining?" I asked.

The main thing was the fact she sent money to China. She laughed, saying, "What can I do? I have to support my mother, the great grandmother, and the siblings. It is money we two old people earned ourselves. I said to my daughter. 'What a fuss you make! When I am gone, the money we made in Canada will be yours.'"

She went on to say the son-in-law was unhappy because his brother in China had a motorcar and new house and seemed to be better off in China than he was in Canada. She thought this might be the reason he was moving to a new house in Scarborough even though he lacked the money. She said he would not listen to reasons against the move.

We reached their home. The son-in-law, Julian's father, was on the front porch. He said nothing when he saw us and went inside. The grandma pointed at the sign saying, "The house is for sale."

She asked, "Would you like to come in?" Given the son-in-law's reaction, I sensed this invitation was extended mainly out of courtesy and said, "No, thanks, next time."

Scene II: Issues Beyond Language Learning

Summer, Parent Centre
I sensed the tensions in the grandma's life, which could be traced back to one of our early conversations. Julian's grandma had worked hard trying to learn English. She started English lessons at a community center on Saturdays in January the year before and, since September regularly attended a LINK program: ESL adult class, four evenings a week, in the basement of Bay Street Community School. She told me she asked her daughter to come with her, but the daughter dropped out after one week because the son-in-law did not let her attend the classes.

"Why not?" I asked.

> You know the reason. He doesn't want his wife to learn English or do anything to be better than he. He wants a traditional wife who obeys her husband. He does not like change. My daughter has been here for over six years and still cannot speak good English.

She said both her daughter and son-in-law laughed at her, saying that it was useless at her age to learn English. Her son-in-law said to her, "No

Cantonese people learn English because they don't need to. Only people from the north parts of China learn English because they cannot speak Cantonese. They learn English to find a job."

But the grandma did not agree, saying, "They are short-sighted. They think money is more important than anything else." The grandma took Allen to a painting class which he enjoyed, but the father objected because of the cost.

This troubled the grandma but she did not interfere. She sighed, "My daughter is married, so I cannot say anything. She follows her husband. What can we do? We can take care of the boys and do the housework. Cantonese people can be silly. They care more about money than life." The grandma seemed to have more to say, but it was time for her to go home to make dinner for the family. She collected the boys and left.

Scene III: *Moving out of Downtown: Another Sacrifice*

Fall, Parent Centre
Although two years earlier Julian's grandma said that her husband did not want to sponsor their son to come to Canada, she asked me how to apply for a visitor's visa. She said she compared her life here with that in China and felt life was better in Canada. Their daughter's family had just bought a new house and would soon move out of the neighborhood.

The move to Scarborough was an important event in the grandma's life and she talked about it again in the fall. She said her daughter and son-in-law found the downtown house too small and thought the neighborhood was unsafe. Their house was broken into one afternoon, when Julian and Allen were at the Parent Centre with the grandma. Then, later of the year a young Chinese woman was robbed on her way home from work, and the father of a boy in the Parent Centre was robbed one evening as he and his friend walked in the neighborhood. Even so, Julian's grandma and grandpa liked the Chinatown neighborhood and did not want to move. "But," she sighed, "we have no choice; we came to Canada to look after our daughter and her children." The grandma seemed to have made the downtown neighborhood her home; more so, it would seem, than the daughter's home where she lived. Carmen said she remembered how unhappy the grandma looked when she first came to the Parent Centre. But she met other grandmas, made friends, and "Now," said Carmen, "she is happy here and does not want to move away from her friends." Carmen remarked, "I would never sacrifice myself for my children like she does."

Julian's grandma said that most grandparents did not like moving away from downtown to east Toronto. Schools were not nearby nor were the markets; children would have to take a school bus. She would be like other grandparents who relied on their children to drive them around – or they must take a bus. Downtown, they walked to local Chinese grocery stores, made friends with other grandparents, and took grandchildren to school in strollers. They belonged to downtown and had a life there.

They thought about not moving but, she said, "My daughter cries when we say we want to rent a place and stay downtown." She felt sorry for her daughter and said she had to make another sacrifice and leave the neighborhood; otherwise, she and her husband would prefer to return to China.

I felt sad as she talked. She had given up her home in China to come to downtown Toronto. Now she was giving up a place where she felt a sense of home to move to a place that was a barren landscape in her mind. It was a place where she lost her independence, as well as her sense of home and daily life. I wondered if she could, again, search for a sense of home in Canada.

Interlude

The Ongoing Story

The grandma moved with her daughter's family in November. In early December, Freeman called and gave me the new phone number the grandma asked him to pass along to me. Hui Lan said she wanted to call the grandma, but was afraid that it might make her even sadder. She said we should wait until she was settled. One day in September, before the move, Julian's grandma told me that another grandmother who moved to Scarborough talked to her over the phone. That grandmother had cried and cried for over two hours as she talked about her life in Scarborough. So, I waited until the Christmas holidays. When I called, Julian's grandma was alone with Allen and Julian. The boys' parents and grandpa had no holidays and were at work. Julian's new school was nearby. But there was no Parent Centre, and Allen cried and told the grandma that he wanted to go to school, too. It was winter, cold and snowy, and the days were short. Grandma said she came to downtown one day, but was hardly able to get back home before dark. It took over three hours to make the round trip. So, she had no time to visit friends.

She also said that she could not go to her ESL classes any more, nor could she continue her weekend job at the elderly granny's home. She also badly missed tutoring Freeman's grandsons. As a former teacher, this had given her great pleasure. Instead, she cleaned the big house, made meals, did the family laundry, looked after Allen, and picked up Julian from school. She had no time for anything else.

As she talked, I realized that life was unfolding as she had feared.

点评: *Shi Jing's Reflection*

We live in moments of life. As a researcher, no matter how often and how long we are together with our participants, we can only glimpse life's fragments in the lived moments in which we are privileged to participate. I spent many hours, over many days, over several years, in a research relationship with Julian's grandma. But all I have are glimpses of her life, scenes in a series of episodes. Still, routine and fragmented as they seem to be, these episodes of lived moments help me connect a grandparent's cross-cultural understanding of schooling, with her concept of learning and her way of teaching and educating young children.

Change is the most changeless thing in the world. While the younger generation makes sacrifices as they came to a new world for a better education and a better life for their children, the older generation makes even greater sacrifices in their personal and social life. On landscapes in transition, young people must adapt to rapid changes and new life challenges. When these adaptations amount to the adoption of what they perceive as a Western way, their elders, the grandparents in my study, who hold dear to traditional Chinese values, feel in conflict. There is a schism, a discontinuity; a generational rupture in the narrative stream of values. The older generation's care and support for the younger generations is no longer as reciprocal and interdependent as once it was in traditional Chinese family, a structure guided by Confucian values. Still, as Grandpa Jiang put it, "It is worth it." Grandparents perceive their self-sacrifice as an important contribution to the harmony and growth of the larger family and of society. They reach across cultures and countries to realize their values, and they help their daughters and sons in Toronto and Scarborough while sending money to relatives in China.

In this chapter, I recounted some family stories from Chinese grandparents' perspectives. The stories reveal perceived differences between China and Canada in terms of learning, schooling, child discipline, and childcare;

their self and family values in a Confucian tradition; and their sacrifice and contribution to the harmony and growth of the family and society. The stories suggest more questions than answers, and refinements rather than solutions for the broad question of immigrant education governing my inquiry. In the following chapter, my inquiry into immigrant education is taken up with a family narrative of Hui Lan's, a story about mother of sons.

Note

1. I have kept the colloquial way to refer to the grandparents/parents as Grandma, Grandpa, or Mom. I kept the colloquial way both in my field notes and research texts so as to keep the authentic flavor of Chinese parents and grandparents' daily lived experience in the Parent Centre and the school community, which reveals the close interactions and relationships among the families, between Carmen and the families, and between the families and myself.

CHAPTER 4

A Mother's Hope: Hui Lan's Family Stories

母亲的心愿: 惠兰一家

PRELUDE

Hui Lan 惠兰, the main character in Chapter 4, is a stay-at-home mother of three children. Her husband works at a Chinese restaurant in downtown Toronto. Hui Lan and her husband first left China in 1997, looking for new opportunities for their life in a Spanish-speaking country in South America. They ran a small restaurant in the neighborhood next to the president's residence. A political crisis in the country affected their business and they moved to Canada.

Hui Lan and her family would not have become the major characters in this chapter if I had not developed a sense of inquiry during my research. With their background, this family did not seem to fit into my initial criteria that participants should be *independent immigrants/skilled workers* with university degrees and professional skills according to the ranking criteria of Citizenship and Immigration Canada (CIC). The evolving sense of inquiry has led me along a narrative path into people's lived experience in their own terms, instead of mine. This perspective not only challenged my initial bias, but also helped me keep an open mind for surprises in my inquiry as life has been, and is forever, ongoing and evolving in its own way.

Yong Sheng 永胜 and Yong Ming 永明, Hui Lan's younger sons, are important characters. It was the two cute little boys who drew my immediate attention when I first saw them at the Parent Centre. I did not meet Yong Chang, the eldest son of Hui Lan, until the next summer of when I visited their home. Quite surprisingly, I found Yong Chang, who I thought was in a regular Grade 8 class, was actually in the LEAP program. LEAP programs are offered in selected Toronto schools. They provide "an opportunity for accelerated literacy and numeracy development to students aged 11–16 who have gaps in their prior schooling" (Toronto District School Board 2005).

I discovered that Yong Chang was in LEAP II (Level Two of the Literacy Enrichment Academic Programs) in September when I followed up some newcomer students from the Newcomer Support Class to the LEAP programs.

When I saw Yong Sheng at the Parent Centre, I always wondered what was going through his little head as he looked like a deep thinker, with a pair of glasses on his tiny face. He seldom talked, so I was pleased to see him in Grade 2, as one of the little frogs, singing in the school Spring Musical choir. Later, I was shocked to learn that the quiet little boy got the family into trouble with the police by accidentally dialing 911.

I met Hui Lan's husband and his friend's family when Hui Lan helped to take care of Xiao Feng, the friend's boy, while the boy's mother returned to China. During his mom's two-month absence, the seven-year-old boy created drama in Hui Lan's life, getting her family involved with the police as well as with the Children's Aid Society.

In this chapter Carmen and Freeman continue to be important characters. Julian's Grandma also reappears, as she was a regular visitor to the Parent Centre and became friends with Hui Lan, with whom she attended evening ESL classes.

When I was first located at the Parent Centre to start intensive participant observation, I saw Yong Sheng and Yong Ming playing with the puzzle pieces on the carpet. I did not realize then that I was walking into people's lives that were proceeding before me just like intriguing puzzle pieces. However, unlike the puzzle pieces laid out all in front of the children, the puzzle pieces in people's ever-evolving lives were initially invisible to me until they seemed to come together into a meaningful shape all by themselves over time.

Episode One: Two Little Brothers and the Buddy Reading Program

Scene I: *Yong Sheng and Yong Ming, Hui Lan's Younger Sons*

Fall, the 1st Year, at the Parent Centre
I met the two little brothers, five-year-old Yong Sheng and three-year-old Yong Ming, during my first week of observation at the Parent Centre.

After I checked in with the Main Office of the school, I went to the Parent Centre. Carmen greeted me and asked me to feel at home. My attention was drawn to two little boys working on a large puzzle of *Dinosaurs in a Jungle* on the carpet between the two couches. I wondered if they could understand my *Pu-Tong-Hua* 普通话 (Mandarin) as I only heard *Cantonese* spoken among mothers and grandmothers chatting on the couches.

"How old are you?" I asked in English. "I am three. My brother is five." The three-year-old replied quickly in English. The five-year-old leaned forward, adding pieces to the puzzle. I was amused by this older boy who looked so serious, wearing his dark-framed glasses on his tiny face. The two boys' hair was neatly cut, but a strand of hair stood up above the five-year-old's forehead in a tiny curve that gave him a very cute look. While the five-year-old was busy with his hands, the three-year-old was busy with both his hands and his mouth. "Here, here. Put it here," he said. The five-year-old held a puzzle piece in the right hand. He pushed his glasses up with his left hand. With an assured look, he ignored the little one's instructions and added the piece to its right spot. "Yes!" The little one cheered and passed more pieces to his brother.

"Tidy up! Tidy up time!" Carmen called out by the sink where she was preparing snacks for the children. Adults got up to take their children to the sink to wash their hands for the snacks. A few women came to pick up toys, books, and puzzle pieces scattered on the floor, carpet, and couches. "Yong Sheng 永胜! Yong Ming 永明! Go to wash your hands!" said a woman who looked like the two boys' mother as she helped pick up the puzzle pieces. She spoke *Pu-Tong-Hua*, although I heard her talking with other mothers and grandmothers in *Cantonese*.

After Snack Time, the two little brothers sat at the table drawing on a large piece of paper. We got acquainted.

"Who is Yong Sheng? Who is Yong Ming?" I asked in English.

"I am Yong Ming. My brother is Yong Sheng. And my BIG brother is Yong Chang," said the three-year-old, making his big brother sound really big.

"Oh? How big is he?" I smiled.

"He is..." the little one scratched his head, thinking hard.

"Twelve," Yong Sheng, the five-year-old, said calmly.

This was the first word I heard him speak.

"Twelve?! So he is really a big brother to you."

"Yeah!" Yong Sheng said with a rising tone. "My big brother teaches me English. I can write my name." Yong Sheng spelt his name in English letters and showed me his neat handwriting.

"My big brother teaches ME English. I can write MY name." Yong Ming said to me eagerly. He showed me his name in staggering English letters.

"Very good. Wonderful! Can you also write your Big Brother's name?"

"Yes, I can." The five-year-old wrote, "Yong Chang."

"Thank you. You are very good. You can read and write English."

"My big brother can speak Spanish!" Three-year-old Yong Ming announced in a loud proud voice.

"Oh? Where did he learn to speak Spanish?"

"I don't know." Yong Ming shook his little head with a shy smile.

Before I met Yong Chang the next summer when the mother invited me to their home, the big brother was in Yong Sheng and Yong Ming's conversations and in their mother's stories about the family.

Scene II: Buddy Reading Program

Fall, the 1st Year, Parent Centre

I saw Yong Sheng and Yong Ming on almost every visit to the Parent Centre. They were favorites of the adults. Ms. Liang, the Cantonese teacher, would wink at their mother and say, "Yong Sheng and Yong Ming are my children. They are my favorite students. I really love them." The boys and girls in Mr. Anderson's Tuesday afternoon Buddy Reading Program class for Grades 7 and 8 newcomer students fought to have Yong Sheng and Yong Ming join them when they broke into small groups.

Depending on the small groups, the two brothers had quite different experiences. Three-year-old Yong Ming sat quietly by the table, listening attentively to the four girls taking turns reading Snow White in Chinese to him. They giggled and laughed at one another as they spoke Pu-Tong-Hua with strong accents. Mistaking me for his mother, the girls asked if Yong Ming could follow them. Yong Ming looked like he understood, although I had never heard him speak Chinese.

Later I asked Yong Ming's mom if the boy could understand Pu-Tong-Hua. She said:

> I speak Cantonese to them at home. They watch Chinese VCD movies (Video CD, popular before DVD in Asia) and listen to Chinese children's songs in Pu-Tong-Hua at home. Yong Sheng says, "We can speak Cantonese already. We need to learn Pu-Tong-Hua." I don't know how he developed this view.

The mother was proud of the boys and said, "Yong Ming enjoys reading by himself." She hugged the little boy, who was left alone at the table when the girls finished the story.

Five-year-old Yong Sheng, however, was in a small group of boys who did not read to him as they were supposed to in the Buddy Reading Program. They teased him with toy animals, snakes, dinosaurs, and crocodiles, which he tried to dodge as the bigger boys put them on his head or in his arms. He was surrounded by four bigger boys who were the loudest and naughtiest of the class. Yong Sheng's little face was tight, as he sat there quietly in the middle of the boys' group.

"Oh, he is so cute."

"He looks unhappy." A skinny boy winked as he touched Yong Sheng on the cheek with a toy crocodile.

"Ouch! He punched me on the nose!" The skinny boy cried out and fell over on the carpet with his hand on his nose. The boys roared into laughter.

"No, Yong Sheng!" The mother rushed to pull him aside, and Mr. Anderson tried to reason with the bigger boys.

"Good for you!" one grandma said loudly. I did not know whether she meant the skinny boy, or Yong Sheng.

"Time up. Line up!" Mr. Anderson called out.

The Parent Centre felt so quiet when Mr. Anderson's students finally left the room. Carmen looked at the rumpled room, shrugging her shoulders and shaking her head. Julian's grandma smiled weakly and said in Pu-Tong-Hua, "They were not here for learning. They were just playing around and making trouble."

Yong Sheng told his mom he did not like the bigger boys. His mother hugged him as he burst into tears.

Scene III: A Child Who Loves Learning

After the New Year of the Goat, Parent Centre
The Buddy Reading Program carried on into the new semester. Mr. Anderson believed the newcomer boys' misbehavior reflected cultural shock. The Buddy Reading Program was intended to help with their transition to a new country. The program, however, had an unexpected effect on the Parent Centre. Donald's mom told me that parents and grandparents were avoiding Tuesday afternoons because they feared that their little ones would learn bad behavior from the bigger boys. Only three or four families now came on Tuesdays while, on other days, there were often more than a dozen. But Yong Sheng and Yong Ming and their mother came regularly. So did Julian's grandma who brought Julian and his little brother Allen.

Over time, as with Freeman, I became a major helper in the Parent Centre, assisting Carmen with Chinese translation for flyers and notices and helping newly arrived families in the Parent Centre and at the school. Perhaps because I was a teacher in China, I was able to establish rapport with the Buddy Reading Program boys and girls, and Mr. Anderson and Carmen often put me with the group of naughtiest boys.

One Tuesday afternoon, Carmen, with a bad cold, asked me to read to the children. I read a dinosaur book to the little ones while we waited for the bigger children from the Newcomer Support Class. When they arrived, I asked which book they would like to read.

"Farmer Joe," Yong Sheng and Yong Ming said.

I told the bigger boys and girls I would read this story very slowly and they had to listen attentively. I said I would ask questions to make sure that they were listening. It worked. Nobody talked as I read and explained the story. But, it was always the little ones like Yong Sheng and Yong Ming who responded to my questions.

"What was Farmer Joe looking for?"
"A present for his wife."
"What did he get for his wife?"
"A red computer!"

At the end of the storytelling, the children and the parents applauded, to my surprise. Then Mr. Anderson asked if they remembered what he had read last week.

There was a silence in the room.

"It was about a magic..." Mr. Anderson suggested.

"Magic Key!" Yong Sheng responded. Freeman put up his thumb and exchanged a look with Julian's grandma.

As Mr. Anderson read, it was always Yong Sheng who responded to questions.

"He is a child who loves learning!" Julian's grandma exclaimed in admiration.

Episode Two: Hui Lan, Mother of Sons

Scene I: An Indispensable Parent Centre Helper

Spring, the 2nd Year, at the Parent Centre

Over time, I observed that Yong Sheng 永胜 and Yong Ming's 永明 mother, Hui Lan, 惠兰, like Freeman, was an indispensable Parent Centre helper. For instance, Sally's grandma often talked loudly and cheerfully with other grandmas or grandpas in Cantonese during Circle Time. Carmen would pause her reading and look at Sally's grandma and then at Hui Lan. Hui Lan would smile and speak to Sally's grandma in Cantonese and Carmen would continue with her reading. When Danny and Julian hit one another with their elbows in the Circle, Hui Lan took Danny in her arms and calmed him. Hui Lan always swept the floor and cleaned the dishes after Snack Time. As we tidied the room and washed the dishes together, she told me how much Carmen had to do. She said she was happy to help, so that Carmen would have more time to teach the children.

In May, Freeman and Carmen invited Hui Lan and me to participate in a fund-raising activity. This involved a field trip by bus to a casino in a nearby city. Freeman bought our tickets saying it was a treat for our hard work at the Parent Centre. Hui Lan and I felt it a bit odd about this fund-raising activity. Carmen said that it was just for fun, not really gambling or anything. Hui Lan and I said almost simultaneously to each other, "If you go, I will go; if you don't, I won't, either." We both laughed. The next day Hui Lan said that her husband encouraged her to go as she had been a stay-at-home mother taking care of their children, never having any time for herself. But it had to be on Sunday because her husband studied English on Saturdays and worked during the week. We decided to go.

Scene II: Hui Lan's Large Backpack

June, the 2nd Year, the Morning Before the Trip to the Casino
When I arrived at school to catch the bus on the morning of the trip, Hui Lan and Freeman were already there. Hui Lan carried the large backpack she carried during the weekday. "Why do you carry your large bag?" I asked.

> Oh, my three children were more excited than I was about the trip. I have never gone anywhere by myself without them. Everyone helped me pack last night. Yong Chang asked me to bring a jacket and a T-shirt, saying that I could put on the jacket if I felt cold, and change to the T-shirt if I felt hot. Yong Sheng put an umbrella into the bag saying that it might rain and it would block the sun if it was a hot day. Yong Ming said I should bring drinks and snacks. I didn't want to carry so many things, but my husband said that since the children had prepared the bag, I might as well carry it. The boys said that it was my first trip and asked me to enjoy myself and to make sure I went with others so as "not to get lost". The little ones woke me up early to make sure that I would not miss the bus.

I smiled, thinking how much the boys were influenced by the mom's daily care for the family and others.

Scene III: Hui Lan's Family Values and Educational Approaches

June, the 2nd Year, on the School Bus to Casino
The bus left the school at 9:30 a.m., when everyone had arrived. Hui Lan and I took the seat behind Carmen and Freeman. It was a gray day, but I enjoyed Hui Lan's stories about herself and her family during the two-and-half-hour drive.

Hui Lan grew up with her grandmother, a school teacher in Guangzhou, the capital city of Guangdong (Canton). The grandma was so strict with Hui Lan that she forbade her to wear anything new. Hui Lan's parents bought her new clothes, which the grandma would store in a wooden trunk saying that the clothes she had looked fine. When the clothes came out of the trunk a year or so later, they no longer looked new and were too small. Hui Lan said she remembered being unhappy because she had to wear "old" new clothes and shoes that were too tight throughout her school years. She said her grandma wanted to make sure that she would concentrate on her study, not on clothes or makeup. So, Hui Lan said, she grew up with an attitude that clothes were important only to the extent they were clean and tidy.

Hui Lan took a decent "iron-bowl" job 铁饭碗 (Chinese slang for *a secure job in state-owned business*) in a big department store in Guangzhou upon her graduation from high school. She worked there for 10 years. Her husband was an accountant in a local business. He was the eldest son of a large family. His mother always urged him to take care of the family, and as the eldest son, he felt this obligation. Hui Lan illustrated how this worked in the family by saying that when they bought a TV, they were also expected to buy one for her parents-in-law. Her mother-in-law would then remind her husband that the second son did not have a TV. His youngest brother, the third son of the family, lived with Hui Lan and her husband until he married. He asked for a color TV as a wedding gift. Over time, she said, the expectation to care for the extended family became so demanding that her husband decided to leave his home and possessions to his parents and siblings and follow "the currents of going overseas". They started a new life by running a restaurant in a South American country.

However, the mountains and oceans could not block the mother's expectations. Thinking they were making good money abroad, the mother requested that money be sent home. Hui Lan said that her husband was annoyed and felt his mother did not understand the hardship of beginning a new life in a new country. But Hui Lan urged her husband to send money, even on their tight budget. Hui Lan said that she told her husband that his sons were watching how he treated his mother. "If you ignore your mother now, your sons will learn to ignore you when you are old." Hui Lan said that her mother in-law was a mother of sons, and she, herself, was also a mother of sons. "You must do to others what you expect others to do to you, right?" Hui Lan said that she wanted to make sure that her sons grew up to be caring toward one another and respectful of their elders.

As a Chinese woman, I understood what Hui Lan said. Still, I was impressed at how much Hui Lan, as a typical Chinese wife and mother, kept the traditional moral and family values that are getting lost in China nowadays. During the trip, she told me more stories about her family and her educational life outside of China. Hui Lan said:

> Our eldest son used to think that we had a lot of money as we owned a restaurant. He asked us to buy him things. My husband and I decided to teach him a lesson. This came at a time when political tensions in the South American country began to influence our business. For one week, we had only plain rice or noodles at dinner. Our son wanted more and at first refused to eat. I told him that our business was down due to the political crisis and we might soon run out of money. We wanted him to understand the hardship of life.
>
> In Toronto, sometimes the two little boys would cry for McDonald's on our way home from school. I would buy what they asked for, but close to the end of the month, I served only rice, noodles, or bread. I told the boys that because I spent money on McDonald's early in the month, I had no money for groceries at the end of the month. Five-year-old Yong Sheng argued that their father earned a lot of money, "$800 a month." But my eldest son, now 12 years old, had learned the lesson when we were in South America, and he said to his little brother, "$800 a month is not a lot of money as Mom has to pay rent, buy clothes, and other daily necessities for the whole family." Since that time, the two little boys have never cried for McDonald's. Sometimes, on the wage day, my husband would suggest getting McDonald's. The boys would say in chorus that they did not like McDonald's any more.

Hui Lan said the family lived in a house basement. Their eldest son said that he would work as soon as he turned 16 so that his father could save money to buy a house. Hui Lan said that she and her husband said to the boy, "We are pleased that you are such a good son, but we do not want you to worry about making money. We want you to concentrate on your studies and go to university."

Episode Three: The Family's Priority

Scene I: One Home, Many Languages

Summer, the 2nd Year, at Hui Lan's Home
In the summer, Hui Lan invited me to visit her home. We met at the intersection next to the school and walked to her home. I finally met her eldest son.

We stopped in front of a two-story redbrick house. The front lawn was paved with bricks. There were low iron bars making a fence around the house. We went into the basement apartment from a side door. Yong Ming appeared, smiled, and ran away. Yong Sheng and his elder brother were watching TV.

"Say 'Hello Teacher!'" their mother said in Chinese.

Yong Sheng and his elder brother said in English, "Hi, Teacher."

"Louder!" the mother requested.

"Hi, Teacher!" the boys repeated in a much louder chorus.

The boys were watching a Japanese cartoon movie of blond, blue-eyed characters, dubbed in Cantonese. This caused me to ask what languages they spoke at home. Hui Lan said the boys often spoke English together. She and her husband spoke Cantonese with the boys, but they would respond in English. Their eldest son sometimes spoke Spanish with them.

Hui Lan turned off the TV and asked the eldest son to get a chair for me from another room at the far end of the basement. She said that that room was a cool storage room for the house. She used it as a study for her eldest son. The kitchen was in between the living room and the "study room". There was a closed door nearby the table where we sat. Beside that were a fridge and the TV. The three brothers sat quietly around the table.

"What's your name?" I asked Hui Lan's eldest son.

"Yong Chang," he said, in chorus with the little boys. Yong Ming chuckled.

Yong Chang was in Grade 7 and was as tall as his mother. Hui Lan said he did not like learning Chinese. "Why not?" I asked. "It is too difficult," Yong Chang replied.

Remembering our conversations on language last fall (*Episode One, Scene II*), I asked Hui Lan if she taught her boys Chinese at home. She said she did. Hui Lan said it was very difficult to find appropriate learning materials and exercise books in Toronto. She brought many books and VCDs (video CDs) from China for the boys to learn Chinese. She also bought a series of TV programs developed by a Taiwan publisher for children to learn English. Our conversation on language learning was revealing. I said, "Yong Chang's English is good. He can help with his brothers."

"His English is not good. The other day, his father asked him to read an English letter and to explain it in Chinese, but he couldn't. Eventually he explained the letter to us in Spanish." Hui Lan shook her head.

"That doesn't mean he has a problem with his English. He can understand the English letter, but he cannot explain it in Chinese. So his Spanish is better than his Chinese, isn't it?" I commented.

"Yes, he likes to go to the Spanish class. He finds Chinese too difficult."

I am amused by the situation. The boy is handling four languages, but the mother is not happy since he knows English best, Spanish second, Cantonese third, and *Pu-Tong-Hua* (Mandarin) the last. She would prefer her boys to be good at both English and Chinese.

Yong Ming picked up something on the floor, and commented, "I found something in the floor." "On the floor, not in the floor," Yong Chang said. They talked with each other in English while Hui Lan talked with me in *Pu-Tong-Hua*.

The boys talked to the mom in Cantonese. As the boys left the room, the mom called out, "5." The boys said, "5:30," while running away. Hui Lan said she wanted the boys home no later than 5 p.m., for she had heard that there were drug users in the park. "The park is a complicated place. You don't know who uses drugs or who sells drugs."

Scene II: Hui Lan's Dilemmas

Summer, the 2nd Year, at Hui Lan's Home
Hui Lan talked about her life and her dilemmas. She said:

> I want to go to work. I feel bored staying at home as a housewife. My husband said, "The boys are still too young. What's the point of earning more money if the boys are not brought up the right way? The money I make is enough. The boys' education is the most important." He works at a restaurant. His boss had cancer and the boss's wife asked my husband to take over the business. I thought it was a good idea. My family could stay on the top floor over the restaurant. But my husband said no because it would affect the boys' studies.

Hui Lan had other reasons for wanting to move. She said that her home was turned into a "pub" after dinner during the summer when the owners, their two boys, and the second floor tenant would come to the basement, saying it was cooler. A neighborhood relative often came as well. They stayed late, sometimes until midnight.

"The place must be very noisy. How can the boys sleep?" I asked.

"I close the door of the 'study room' when my eldest son needs to do homework and I make sure nobody moves beyond the kitchen area. The little ones go to the bedroom and close the door."

"Can you tell them not to come or not to stay up so late?"

"What can I do? They are either my landlady, landlord, my neighbors, or my relative. I can't tell them not to come. It is fine as long as their boys do not break anything at my home." Hui Lan sighed.

> We are looking for another place. Carmen suggested a neighbourhood apartment building, but my husband said, "People move in and out. You never know where they are from, who they really are and where they go. It is not a good environment for the boys." Someone else suggested another street, but we did not think it was good for the boys' safety. So, after all, the basement home is best. At least, we know the people: where they are from and who they are.

> We talked about going into debt to buy a house. But Yong Chang said that it would be too much for his father who would have to work day and night to pay the debt. Yong Chang said when he turned to 16 he could work part-time to help. I told him, "It is good that you think this way. Now we just want you to study well."

Scene III: Values in Life that Hui Lan and Her Husband Hold On To

Summer, the 2nd Year, at Hui Lan's Home

Though Hui Lan missed working and wanted a better living situation, she said the boys were always the family priority. "They are at a crucial period and I must watch over them to make sure they are not misled, especially my eldest son, as he is entering his teenage years." Hui Lan said they lived in a complicated environment and needed to be careful and watchful of their sons. She told me a story about computers to illustrate her point.

> Yong Chang wanted a computer. It would be good for his studies. But we said no. He could use the computer at the library. The library is better because it limits computer use and the boy would not have time to play video games or get into bad things on the Internet. Also, we want the boys to live a simple life and concentrate their minds on their study, not on spending money.

Hui Lan told me more stories about her family that revealed the values about life that she and her husband held on to. Hui Lan said her brother found her husband a better-paid job in Scarborough where housing was less expensive.

> He would be paid $600 a week. But my husband declined the offer, saying that his boss gave him the job when he was most in need. He said, "Now the boss is sick and in need, it is not nice to leave him. I must stay when my boss is in need."

The pressure to send money back to China continued when the grandma called. Hui Lan said that she sent money to her mother-in-law, and her husband thought they should also send money to Hui Lan's parents, to be fair to both families. But Hui Lan said no, since her parents never asked for money.

Episode Four: Hui Lan's Family with the Police and the Children's Aid

Chinese families tend to avoid involvement with the police since, for them, "the police" often carry criminal connotations. Unfortunately, after the summer for a whole year, Hui Lan was confronted twice by the police for seemingly serious circumstances.

Scene I: *Yong Sheng, the Little Caring Soul of the Family*

Summer, the 2nd Year, at Hui Lan's Home
Yong Sheng, now a six-year-old, was a tiny boy, not much taller than Yong Ming, his younger brother, but he looked older than his big brother, Yong Chang. He wore a pair of tiny glasses with a black frame. He seldom smiled or talked. He looked like a deep thinker.

I was somewhat surprised to learn that it was always Yong Sheng who answered the phone at home. This six-year-old boy, quiet at the Parent Centre, would talk with his grandparents, uncles and aunts in China, sometimes for two hours. Hui Lan said he especially cared about his great grandma, his father's grandmother. She was over 80 years old and lived at his grandma's home. Yong Sheng first met his great grandma last summer when the family visited China. Hui Lan told me that during the visit, every day Yong Sheng would go outside of his grandma's house to pick up banana skins dropped by passers-by. "Great Grandma would fall if she slipped on the banana skins," Yong Sheng told his mother. "Why do people drop garbage on the street?" Back in Toronto, Yong Sheng always asked about his great grandma when he talked on the phone to his grandmother in China asking whether the great grandma ate and slept well, and so on.

Scene II: *Yong Sheng and 911*

Fall, the 2nd Year, at the Parent Centre and at Hui Lan's Home
When the new semester began, Yong Sheng started Grade 1 and Yong Ming went to morning kindergarten. In the afternoons, I saw Hui Lan and Yong Ming in the Parent Centre. Yong Chang was now in Grade 8. I thought he was in a regular class, so I was surprised to find him in LEAP II. I seldom saw Yong Sheng, now a Grade-1 student, only catching glimpses of him when he came to the Parent Centre to find his mother to go home after school. He seemed even quieter. One day he looked at his toes and did not respond when I asked him how he liked his new class. His mother smiled and told me Yong Sheng was worried, for he got the family into trouble. Here is how she told the story:

> This happened in the first weekend of the new semester. I went out for less than 10 minutes to buy groceries from a nearby store and asked Yong Chang to look after his younger brothers. They were reading together at a table and a glass of water spilled on the books. Yong Chang took the books into the backyard to dry them in the sun. Yong Sheng decided to talk to a cousin in the United States about his new class. The area code was 912 but he dialled 911 instead. In less than three minutes a police officer was at the door and all he found was my two little boys in the basement. Later Yong Sheng told me he was very scared although the police officer spoke nicely and asked them what they were doing and where their parents were. Young Chang tried to explain the situation but the police officer asked him to phone his father. When I came home a few moments later, I was shocked to see the police car in front of the house. My husband arrived a few minutes later. The police officer said that he was patrolling in the neighbourhood when he received the call. He told us that we should not leave young children unattended and that they should be taught not to dial emergency numbers like 911 for fun. But it was a mistake. Yong Sheng learned about 911 in kindergarten and knew it was very serious. Besides, at age 13, Yong Chang can take responsibility for his younger brothers when my husband and I are not home. I told the policeman that I never left the boys alone for more than half an hour even with Yong Chang looking after the two little ones. But the police requested that my husband and I attend classes to learn

precautions that need to be taken to prevent young children from dialling 911 when there is no emergency. We didn't mind. We have to do what is right.

Hui Lan went on to tell me that this mistake had a strong effect on Yong Sheng and that was why he seemed so shy and would not answer my questions. She said that Yong Sheng was so worried that he kept crying and would not eat. He kept asking, "Why do you and Papa still have to go to the police class if everything is ok? They will take you and Papa away from home, won't they? They will take me away from you, won't they?" Hui Lan said she comforted him and reassured him saying, "Uncle Police won't take you away from Mama and Papa." She explained the necessity of learning the lessons and told him not to worry. "I didn't do it for fun. Why do you still have to go to the police class?" Yong Sheng asked. No matter how reassuringly Hui Lan told him that everything was all right, he continued to cry and worry.

Scene III: Unexpected Drama in Hui Lan's Life

Fall, the 3rd Year, at the Parent Centre
I learned that Hui Lan was, again, helping her husband's friend taking care of Xiao Feng, the friend's son, while the boy's mother visited China. A year ago Xiao Feng's mother was injured in a car accident. While recuperating, she took her two little daughters to China, and left them with her parents, while Xiao Feng, who was very naughty and who also had to go to school, stayed with Hui Lan in Toronto. Xiao Feng's father and Hui Lan's husband were childhood friends. I had helped Hui Lan talk with the principal to have Xiao Feng transferred to Bay Street Community School from East Toronto. Xiao Feng's parents moved downtown and rented a place close to Hui Lan's home before the mother left for China, so that Hui Lan and her husband could help. Hui Lan helped look after Xiao Feng and took him to and from school. The boy stayed at Hui Lan's home until late in the evening when his father picked him up after work.

Last semester I saw Xiao Feng's mom at the Parent Centre after she returned to Toronto. I noticed that Hui Lan and Xiao Feng's mom raise children differently. Xiao Feng appeared to be a difficult child, but his mother paid no attention to the boy's misbehavior. I often heard Hui Lan say to Xiao Feng's mom at the Parent Centre, "Look what he is doing. You've got to stop him." But Xiao Feng's mom would not say anything and simply ignored the boy's misbehavior. She also told Hui Lan how seven-year-old Xiao Feng talked back to his uncle and told him to, "Mind your own business, or, I will ask you to leave my home!" when the uncle disciplined the boy. Xiao Feng's mom laughed at the uncle, for he said, "What did you say? I am your father's eldest brother. Your father calls me Big Brother, you know!" She did not seem to think her husband's brother's "big uncle" status in the family should apply in Canada.

Hui Lan, however, disagreed. Later she told me that she was not pleased with Xiao Feng's mom's attitude and way of parenting. Still Hui Lan continued helping the family, especially when the boy's mom went back to China again to pick up her daughters. She said:

> I cannot stand by watching when the family is in need. Now the boy's mother is back in Beijing. She wanted to stay for 3 months. I said I couldn't handle her boy for that long. He is too naughty.
>
> I always give my sons homework. I also give him homework, but he won't do it and he misbehaves so much that my sons can't do theirs.

Hui Lan sighed. As we talked, Xiao Feng's father came to the Parent Centre. He worked in a Chinese restaurant from morning to late evening, often seven days a week, like Hui Lan's husband. He said he was off today. Hui Lan talked with him in Cantonese, reminding him to make sure his son had breakfast at home and also to remember to have him bring a food container and spoon so that Hui Lan could share lunch with him. The father smiled gently and nodded his head. He sat down and asked me how to help the boy with his math. He said his boy seemed to have a poor memory and could not remember anything he learned at school.

I did not see Hui Lan as often in the fall of 2004 since I was going to the Parent Centre less frequently. I was, however, attending School Council meetings as a volunteer interpreter. At a Council Meeting in mid-October, Freeman, who regularly attended as a Council member, updated me about the Parent Centre.

> Oh, Hui Lan got into serious trouble. The school, the police, the Children's Aid... Xiao Feng told his teacher that Hui Lan asked him to do work at her home and also would not give him lunch to eat. So the teacher called the Children's Aid. Chinese grandparents and parents, myself, and Carmen, we signed a letter stating that we witnessed that Hui Lan brought lunch to the

Parent Centre to the boy and her own boys and she was not mistreating Xiao Feng. So, the boy was not taken away by the Children's Aid.

"That boy, you know how naughty he is!" Freeman shook his head.

When I saw Hui Lan, I learned more about the incident from Hui Lan's point of view.

> One day two serious-looking people came to the Parent Centre and wanted to take Xiao Feng away without showing me who they were. I grabbed the boy and wouldn't let him go. "Who are you? Where are you taking him?" They said they were from Children's Aid. I asked them to show their identity. Then they showed me their identification card. They questioned the boy and me in separate rooms with the translation of interpreters. The people from Children's Aid and the police asked me why I would ask a 7-year-old boy to work every day after school at my home. I said I didn't. They asked, "What did you do after school at home?" I said, "'I asked my boys to do homework. I also gave Xiao Feng homework, but he wouldn't do it.' At the same time, the boy was asked again what work I asked him to do, work or homework. He said, 'Homework.'"

Hui Lan recounted the incident to me in *Pu-Tong-Hua* with a code-mixing of English words such as *work* and *homework*. So, it seemed that the issue was caused by Xiao Feng's confusion of the words *homework* and *work*. The teacher thought Hui Lan was forcing a seven-year-old to work. There was more to the story. Hui Lan said:

> Then they asked me why the boy complained to his teacher that he was hungry in the afternoon class and he did not have lunch. I told them I brought lunch to the Parent Centre every day for the boys. I treated Xiao Feng the same as my own boys. They all had the same home-made food for lunch, but Xiao Feng was picky on food and often refused to eat the lunch I made. I said, "When his mom was around, the boy would ask for McDonald's, or other fast food. I did not give in to his request for special food, so he was unhappy. He told his teacher that I mistreated him and wouldn't give him lunch. He is unhappy with me, for I always stop him from misbehaving and I ask him to do homework after school. So he lied to the teacher." But the Children's Aid people said that they would rather believe the boy, for studies had shown that a seven-year-old child wouldn't tell lies. Mr. Wong and other Chinese parents and grandparents, including Carmen, all stood by me and signed a letter to prove my innocence. They proved that they saw me bring lunch to the Parent Centre every day to the boy and my own sons. Finally the Children's Aid and the police were convinced.

Hui Lan said she felt badly hurt in this incident. She said:

> The teacher often came to the Parent Centre for coffee. She could have checked with Carmen before she made the phone call, even if she couldn't trust me. Sometimes, she came to talk with Carmen during lunchtime. She should have seen us having lunch at the small table.

Hui Lan shook her head. I asked Hui Lan if she was paid by the parents for taking care of Xiao Feng. She shook her head again and said, "We are friends. We just help when friends are in need. We never ask for a single penny, even though the boy often stays and eats with us."

Episode Five: Beyond Languages

Scene I: English Is Difficult to Learn

Spring, the 2nd Year, at the Parent Centre
Hui Lan said she and her husband found English difficult to learn. She said her husband said he "would rather do heavy labor work than learn English." They learned some Spanish and knew a few Portuguese words from the time in South America. But, she said:

> English is more difficult. I often confuse English with Spanish. I cannot read English. When shopping, I look at the English labels, but read them in Spanish and guess what they are. For example, I can tell which shampoo is for dry hair. I cannot read an English word, but I figure out the meaning of English labels by reading them in Spanish... Sometimes in chatting with my neighbour, I respond in a mixture of Chinese/Cantonese, Spanish, English, and even Portuguese. She got confused and said, "Wow, you speak so many languages. I only speak English." But I am confused, too. Even though we do not really understand each other, we like chatting together and try to figure out what each other are saying by guessing with gestures.

I was amused, imagining the two women, one of Chinese origin and the other of Portuguese origin, chatting over the fence between their houses with flying hands and a mixture of English, Cantonese, Mandarin, Spanish, and Portuguese. "You learned Spanish and I am sure you will also learn English," I encouraged her.

"Tidy up time, tidy up." Carmen called out while preparing snacks by the sink. Hui Lan stood up and asked Yong Ming and Yong Sheng to help. The two little boys were good at helping their mother. They knew which toy should go to which box.

Scene II: The Boys' Language Preferences

Summer, the 2nd Year, at Hui Lan's Home

Language learning always seemed to be on Hui Lan's mind and involved matters not easily seen in the formal school system. During the summer, Hui Lan's boys went to the Christian Community Centre for various activities. The center provided ESL support, math tutoring and sports. When I visited Hui Lan's family again a couple of weeks after my first visit, Yong Sheng and Yong Ming were watching Chinese children's songs on DVD. Hui Lan said that the captions would help the boys learn to read Chinese characters.

Yong Chang was on an outing with the Christian Community Centre. Hui Lan said she was not so sure about Yong Chang's involvement with the center because one day Yong Chang told her that the center people encouraged him to believe in Christianity. He said his mother was a Buddhist. The center people said that he was in Canada and he should make his own choice. Hui Lan sighed. She said, at least she knew they were nice people and Yong Chang was learning English and math there and was not learning anything bad. So she did not discourage Yong Chang from participating in their activities.

We talked more about the boys' learning language. Hui Lan said:

> Yong Chang doesn't like learning Chinese and dropped his Chinese class at school, switching to the Spanish class. Yong Ming turns out to be even more reluctant to learn Chinese. He responds in English when I speak to him in Chinese. The four-year-old says to me, "What's the point in learning Chinese? I am not going to China. I am in Canada. I don't need to speak Chinese."

> Yong Ming said that he wanted to be a policeman. "You can't become a policeman if you don't speak Chinese. There are so many Chinese in Toronto." I teased him. He said, "I don't need to talk. I can just put bad people into the police car and drive them to the police station."

> Yong Sheng, however, loves learning Chinese. When I asked him what he would like to be, he said, "A doctor." I told him, "You have to learn Chinese to be a good doctor to serve the Chinese community here."

Scene III: Hui Lan's Efforts to Learn English

Fall, the 2nd Year, at Bay Street Community School
With the boys in school, Hui Lan wanted to take a morning ESL class. She found one at a nearby library. However, she was told that she was not permitted to leave the class at 11:30 a.m. when she needed to come to the school to give her boys lunch. I told Hui Lan about the LINC program, a federal government-funded ESL language instruction program for adult newcomers. I knew the classes were located in the basement of Bay Street Community School and the registration was at a nearby Community Centre. I gave her the center's address and was happy that both Hui Lan and Julian's grandma registered for an evening ESL class. Since then, they had often told me about their ESL classes and I helped them with their ESL homework.

EPISODE SIX: LEARNING FROM LIFE AND "SCHOOLING" AT HOME

Scene I: Learning from Life: Yong Chang's Options for His Future

August, the 3rd Year, Hui Lan's Home
I visited Hui Lan's home again in the summer of 2004 in order to see some of her children's schoolwork and homework. I was interested, and impressed, by Hui Lan and her husband's educational views and practices.

I arrived sometime after 2 p.m. Hui Lan met me and we walked to the back of the house where Yong Chang, Yong Sheng, and Yong Ming had their heads squeezed together. Yong Chang was playing with a palm-sized game player while his little brothers watched intently. Hui Lan's hand washed laundry was drying on a string along the fence. We went downstairs. The TV was on. It was the second day of the Athens Olympics.

I gave Hui Lan pictures I took of Yong Chang at his June graduation from Bay Street Community School. "He looks handsome," I said. Hui Lan laughed and said he was reluctant to dress up. She went outside for a second and came back with the boys.

"Look at the pictures, Yong Sheng. Who is this young man?" I asked.

"My big brother!" Yong Sheng exclaimed cheerfully in English.

"Who is this young man holding two awards?" I showed him another picture.

"My big brother!" Yong Sheng said in a louder reassuring voice.

"Would you like to get awards like your big brother?"

"Yeah!" He responded with an emphasized tone while nodding his head.

Hui Lan said,

> Yong Sheng also won awards for being kind and working hard in his Grade 1 class. He showed the awards to his dad who said, "These awards do not count. You have to get 10 awards like the ones your big brother got." "Ten? That's too hard. Impossible!" Yong Sheng replied. His dad said, "If you try hard, you can get five awards a semester, right? Then in one year you can reach the goal of 10 awards."

Hui Lan's husband was home. He joined us to watch Olympic swimming. Hui Lan commented:

> It is a kind of invisible discrimination the way the games are shown by CBC (Canadian Broadcasting Company). They focus on USA, Canada, and Australia. The athletes are all White. We seldom see Chinese athletes perform although China is ranked # 1 for medals. Chinese swimmers are always put at the 8th lane. This is obviously a kind of discrimination. The athlete would have no chance to win as the waves from swimmers in the middle lanes would make it more difficult.

But Hui Lan's husband disagreed, saying, "No, it was randomly selected by the athletes. It is a matter of luck in the draw."

Hui Lan replied:

> I don't think so. How come the Chinese athletes always chose the 8th lane in the draw? Also, the camera is always focused on Canadian or American athletes. You barely have a chance to view how Chinese athletes won the medals although they were ranked high in the first two days. Anyway, we can't really complain this is discrimination, can we? They do sometimes show a little of other countries' athletes.

The boys joined us as we watched the games. Hui Lan said, "Just now I went to take their game player. I only allow them each to play video games for half an hour a day. The three brothers put their individual time together and play one hour and a half." Hui Lan laughed. Hui Lan's husband picked up the discrimination theme in our early conversation and said:

We Chinese have no easy life. We are not only discriminated against by others. We are discriminated against by other Chinese. Chinese people discriminate against Chinese people. Eh! For example, I work in a restaurant. My Chinese boss discriminates. When business is not good, his wife complains and blames me for the bad business. When business is very good, I work very hard. I feel pain in my back but never complain. When she complains, she forgets how hard I have worked.

I felt a little confused, for last summer they told me his boss was nice to him. It turned out that the restaurant was sold a while later when Hui Lan and her husband declined to buy the business at a very low price offered by his former boss when the man became sick. Both Hui Lan and her husband repeated how much they worried that running a restaurant as a family business would interfere with their children's education because it would take up all their time and energy; also, the boys would end up working in the restaurant to help with English.

Now working in another downtown restaurant and being treated unfairly, Hui Lan's husband sighed:

What can you do? If you do not have good English, you have to put up with this. So I urge Yong Chang to study hard so that he won't live the kind of life we live. We do not mind the labour work as long as the boys study hard and do well. My boss asked Yong Chang to come to the restaurant to help in the summer. We agreed. He works 3 or 4 hours a day. Today he works from 6-9 in the evening. It is a learning opportunity for him, to learn how to meet people and talk with people. He can speak Cantonese, Spanish, English and French. So he has an opportunity to speak different languages with different people. It doesn't matter that he is not paid as a regular employee. We just want him to learn that life is not easy so that he understands and can make a choice – whether to do the kind of labour work I am doing or study hard for a better future.

Hui Lan added:

Yes, we do not want him to earn a living. When I ask him to do his homework, he says, "It is summer holiday. I don't want to do homework." So I said, "If you do not want to study, that's fine. Then you go to work." He came home and said it was too hard to work. He would rather study.

Hui Lan laughed. I asked Yong Chang what he thought of working in the restaurant. He said, "It is hard and very busy." I asked him what language he spoke most with the customers. He said he mostly spoke English, sometimes French and rarely Spanish.

"It is a good learning experience for Yong Chang," said the father. "Eh, it is four o'clock. Time for me to go to work." He stayed for a few more minutes, musing on his situation.

> What can you do? You are a labourer. You just have to work hard. So that's why I keep telling the boys to study hard. I say to Yong Chang, "If you do not study hard, you will have to do the same labour work as I do." I didn't do labour work in China. I was an accountant in a company. It was a comfortable office job. Now, we are here. We have to start from scratch.

"You can get a certificate here to become an accountant again," I said.
"No, no, my English is not good."
"There are supporting ESL programs at colleges or universities."

> I've been taking ESL lessons. Still my English is not good enough to take academic courses. I work every day. If I also took classes, I would not have time to review the lessons nor have time to sleep. I feel tired after work. Whenever I have time, I need to sleep.

The father smiled, with a little guilt. "I don't mind doing hard labor work as long as the boys study hard. I hope they will have a better future."

"Your sons are good kids. They study hard. Yong Chang is a good student."

"Mm, they are not." The Mom shook her head. "They always want to play video games. We limit their playing time."

I was reading Yong Chang's report card and asked why Yong Chang's math was so low. The father responded, "I tutor Yong Chang at home, but I can only teach him in Chinese. Yong Chang is learning math in English. There is a mismatch." I agreed with this, saying, "I understand the mismatch. I learned math in Chinese. When I count or calculate, I do it mentally in Chinese and speak the results in English."

Yong Chang's father thanked me for coming and said that next time I should come early to have dim sum with his family. I thanked him and said goodbye.

Scene II: "Schooling" at Home

August, the 3rd Summer, Hui Lan's Home

I commented that the washroom was so damp that the toilet paper was moist. Hui Lan said, "The landlord's family also uses our bathroom to shower. That's ok."

There were piles of books and exercise books on the table in the "study room". I picked one of Yong Chang's exercise books with English and Chinese words. Hui Lan explained that she asked the boys to copy three pages of English and two pages of Chinese and do five pages of math every day during the summer.

"Yong Chang's Chinese handwriting is not as neat as Yong Sheng's," the mother said.

"How come? I remember Yong Chang's Chinese handwriting was good last summer," I said.

"He doesn't like writing Chinese. Yong Sheng is better. He likes studying Chinese. The little one is the worst. He says we are in Canada. We have to speak English."

I laughed and wondered how come little five-year old Yong Ming had such strong opinions about language issues. In a corner of the study room, a table was piled with books which, Hui Lan said, were old books given away by Carmen and teachers in the school. "Mm," I said, thumbing through some books, "very good. You can read them, too." Hui Lan said, "I sometimes read to the boys. They laugh at me, saying my pronunciation is not correct. So I let them read the books themselves."

I was pleased with Yong Sheng's language progress since last September. His workbook last year showed that he wrote English sentences with no obvious distinctions between words as he printed the letters in a scattered way. Now his workbook showed clear and tidy printing with a good sense of the written language. Hui Lan kept all of Yong Sheng's report cards, awards, schoolwork, and homework. I was somewhat surprised at the low marks on his Grade 1 report card. His mother said that Yong Sheng did not like his teacher asking him questions. The teacher told Hui Lan she knew Yong Sheng was quiet and often would not speak up even though he knew the answer. The teacher said she could tell that because Yong Sheng would say it under his breath. So, when other students could not answer, the teacher would ask Yong Sheng, but he would be silent. The teacher would urge him by saying, "Think hard" or "Give it a try." Yong Sheng told his mom he thought this was unfair because other students were allowed to sit down when they could not answer. Hui Lan said that the teacher told her Yong Sheng's marks should be in the A range but, because of his quietness and reluctance to speak in class, they were lowered.

Yong Sheng's grades were a puzzle. From his schoolwork and homework, I could see Yong Sheng's rich imagination and his ambitious dreams of the future. He wrote, "I want to be an astronaut, for an astronaut can fly." He wrote often about going to the big library. He wrote about his big brother and little brother, his mom and dad. He appeared to be a very thoughtful child with deep and sensitive feelings, and a rich inner self.

There were piles of summer homework papers on the table. Hui Lan marked the children's work, so they took it seriously. She used recycled paper as long as it was blank on one side. She made use of used papers, flyers and even her old calendar. I said that I would bring her some used paper with a blank side.

Hui Lan photocopied some lessons from the Chinese Grade 1 math textbook. I borrowed some copies to compare the math textbooks in China and Canada. Hui Lan pulled out two big boxes containing Yong Sheng's and Yong Ming's schoolwork and homework. Yong Sheng's teacher taught him to keep his grade 1 work in files according to different subjects. He had folders for social science, arts, math, science, and language. I looked at his math schoolwork and compared it with Hui Lan's summer homework and saw that what Yong Sheng learned at home was one year ahead of what he learned in his Canadian class. The Chinese math textbook shows that Chinese Grade 1 students, to certain extent, learn Canadian Grade 2 math. Hui Lan had Yong Ming, who was in kindergarten, do Yong Sheng's Grade 1 level math. This meant that Hui Lan tried to have the boys follow the progress of children of their ages in China.

Because their cousins in China wanted to know what the boys were studying in Canada, most of Yong Sheng's kindergarten work was missing. But now, Hui Lan was saving his work and only sent photocopies to Yong Sheng's cousins. She was pleased with Yong Sheng's progress and said that even he himself noticed his improvement when reviewing his workbooks and was proud of himself. Now he wrote neatly and kept his work organized. He felt bothered when Yong Ming put his schoolwork in Yong Sheng's folders. So Hui Lan had a separate box for Yong Ming who was learning to organize his own box.

Hui Lan said that she created five math worksheets for each boy every day. They also had to copy three pages of English and two pages of Chinese daily. I asked Hui Lan if it was too much since it was summer. She said, "I do not ask them to finish the work all at once. They can take breaks by playing in the backyard or watching TV, and I take them to the library. The boys also work after dinner. So, it is not a lot of work over the whole day."

Coming back to the puzzle of Yong Sheng's report card, it was clear from the work in the basement home that he had a high level of math and language achievement this year. More importantly, as his mom said, he seemed to have a passion for learning and he was the most self-motivated of her children.

> Yong Ming is different. He is more active and talkative than Yong Sheng. Whenever I ask them a question, it is always Yong Ming who wants to answer. But when I ask him, he smiles and says, "Oh, I forget".

Hui Lan said that Canadian schools favored actively participating children like Yong Ming. Yong Sheng, she thought, was disadvantaged due to his quiet nature.

For the purposes of my research, I wanted to look more closely at the boys' work. Hui Lan gave me a large shopping bag to carry their papers. I left around 5:30 p.m.

EPISODE SEVEN: COMMUNICATION BETWEEN SCHOOL AND HOME

In the fall of my third year in the school, Yong Ming started Grade 1 and Yong Sheng Grade 2. At lunchtime I often saw Hui Lan at the Parent Centre having lunch with the boys. Julian's grandma also brought lunch to the Parent Centre as Julian had started Grade 1. Yong Chang was in Grade 9 at a different school. Sometimes I saw him at Bay Street Community School in the afternoon when he came to pick up his little brothers. When I asked, he said that he liked the new school and was doing well. Hui Lan kept me informed of her boys. Sometimes we went to school events together – School Council meetings, Curriculum Night, and Spring Musical. Hui Lan was very pleased to tell me that Mr. McCarthy, Yong Sheng's Grade 2 teacher, and Mr. Wiseman, the music teacher, had Yang Sheng participating in the musical, singing as one of the little frogs in the *frog choir*. She believed that it would help him become more active.

Scene I: Communication Barriers and Expectation Discrepancy

September, the 4th Year, on the Phone with Hui Lan
Hui Lan was worried about Yong Chang's high-school progress and felt frustrated because she was unable to get information. She wanted to meet with Yong Chang's new teachers, but was concerned that she might disrupt the school as she believed different schools must have different rules. At Bay Street Community School, she could ask the boys' teachers about the boys whenever she met the teachers in the hallway or Parent Centre. At the end of the first semester, Yong Chang told his mother that his high-school teachers thought he was doing well and there was no need for her to go to the parent–teacher interviews.

So, for his entire first year of high school, Hui Lan did not meet Yong Chang's teachers. She was worried and talked with me over the phone several times. For the entire summer, she had her three boys attend the Christian Community Centre summer programs, and she continued giving homework. But there was little she could prepare for Yong Chang, who would be entering Grade 10 in the fall.

At the beginning of the fall semester, Hui Lan, Freeman and I decided to meet for dim sum at a Chinese restaurant. This was the fourth year that I had known them. When we phoned each other to schedule the date, Hui Lan told me more of her concerns over Yong Chang who was now in Grade 10, the second year away from Bay Street Community School. She explained her concerns:

> I asked Yong Chang several times to ask his teacher if he could be upgraded to a regular class, but his teacher said he had to wait and see. I have tried to meet with Yong Chang's teacher since he first went to this high school a year ago. I asked someone who could speak English to call for me. I was told there was no need to see the teacher since Yong Chang was doing fine. Once, later in the year, the teacher asked why I wanted to see him/her (Hui Lan did not know whether the teacher was a man or a woman, for the communication was made through a friend who phoned the teacher for her). I said I wanted to know how my son was doing, but the teacher said everything was fine and there was no need for me to see him/her. The teacher said if there was a need, s/he would send a letter or notice to me. No mail ever came, and I don't think they have School Council meetings because I did not get any notices.

Hui Lan thought the teacher should at least have met her at the end of last semester when Yong Chang finished Grade 9. She said she had not even seen his grade 9 report card because the teachers were working to rule. She hoped that Yong Chang could be moved from the LEAP program to a regular class because she was concerned he was getting further behind regular class students. Aware of the gap between the curriculum for regular class and the curriculum for the LEAP program, she said:

> Yong Chang is now going to Grade 10. He ranks Number Two in his current class (LEAP), but he is behind a regular class. I would like him to be put into a regular class so that he will get more pressure to study harder. I am worried that he will simply finish the homework as requested in the ESL class and be satisfied without knowing how much harder he needs to study to catch up and excel in a regular class.

Hui Lan believed that Yong Chang needed to excel in a regular class, not an ESL class, to get into university. She said:

> But the teachers just look at the present. They are not so much concerned about your future. If they think you are doing well for your level of language, they don't think about how you might not be able to do what you want in the future.

When I encouraged her to take the initiative and go to the school to let people know her high expectation and the family dream, she said:

> First of all, I don't speak English. So there is a barrier. Second, I do not want to make the teacher feel that I am making too much fuss. If I push too hard, I might offend the teacher. It would affect the child badly. I don't want that. I understand every school has its own way to run the school. At Bay Street Community School, I could talk with his teacher any time I wanted. At this high school, I have no chance to meet with the teacher at all. But I can't make a complaint. I might offend him/her. That would be bad for my child. I want him upgraded to regular class, but I don't know what to do.

Hui Lan talked about differences between teachers and parents in their expectations of children from her perspective.

> In Canada, teachers think differently from us. They do not care how good or how bad you are academically. As long as you listen to him/her, or you are not making trouble, then you are good. They don't care about your future, or what

> works best for you. Yong Chang is a good child. He does his homework. He listens. He never makes trouble. So the teacher thinks he is good. But I would like him to be more challenged by studying in a regular class.

I said, "I understand many Chinese parents would like to see their children go to a good university. That's why they've given up so much to come to Canada."

I asked if it was possible that Yong Chang did not want his parents to meet his teachers. Could he have misled Hui Lan? I wondered. "No, he dares not," Hui Lan said with confidence.

> I also know other students who are studying in the same school. I talked with those students. They said the same thing. Also, I asked others to call the school. The response was always the same: "They said they would send you a letter if there is a need."

I said that in high school, a student is expected to do well not just academically, but also socially. I wondered if Hui Lan encouraged Yong Chang to participate in school activities.

She said that the boy often went to the Christian Community Centre and he played basketball. She said, when he went out, she often went to the playground or gym to see who was there. She was worried that he might hang around with misbehaving boys. She said she kept a close eye on him.

"It is very troublesome." She sighed. "He is going out. He is growing up. You don't know what kind of people he might bump into. I need to make sure he makes good friends."

Scene II: Communication Breakdown between School and Home

September, the 4th Year, at a Chinese Restaurant
Hui Lan and I set the dim sum date with Freeman on Wednesday, the second week of the new semester. At lunch, Freeman told me that his grandson, Stephen, was happy in his new French immersion school. Hui Lan said she finally got Yong Chang's Grade 9 report card. It had his marks but no teacher comments. She asked Yong Chang to tell his teacher that his mom wanted a clear answer to her question as to why he could not be moved to a regular class. Yong Chang was told that, in Grade 9, he was

making up what he would have learned in the regular Grade 7 and 8 classes. Now, in Grade 10, he is learning Grade 9 curriculum in the first half of the year and he will be learning Grade 10 curriculum in the second half of the year. Then, in Grade 11, he will be a regular class student.

Hui Lan was not satisfied with this and told me that she was thinking of moving Yong Chang to a regular class in another school. The lack of communication continued, and this concerned her.

Her thoughts on moving were still much as they were when we discussed this last year. She did not want to move out of the downtown neighborhood because she thought it would not be good for the children. She liked the downtown community with its nearby library and community centers.

> There are many programs for children to learn and have fun. I bring Yong Sheng and Yong Ming to the library every day. Yong Chang goes to the library alone by himself. In another 5 years, Yong Sheng and Yong Ming will be able to go to the library or the community centres to study by themselves. It will be easier for me then. Now I have to keep a good eye on them.

Interlude

Life Moves On

Life moves on, unfolding in somewhat unexpected ways. The new school year began with a new principal at Bay Street Community School in September, the fourth year of my fieldwork in the school. Last semester, Stephen, Freeman's grandson, who liked French, decided to transfer to a French immersion school. Hence, Freeman, who had volunteered at Bay Street Community School for over a dozen years, could no longer serve as a School Council member at the School as no child of his family was attending the school. He still came to Carmen's "rescue" whenever she called, especially in difficult situations. Carmen almost cried when talking with Freeman's wife because the number of Chinese families visiting the Parent Centre had dropped. She was worried that she would lose her job if the numbers kept dropping. She asked if Freeman could come to the Parent Centre more often. Chinese families felt more at home at the Parent Centre when Freeman was there helping Carmen with communication, as well as in organizing programs and activities. The new principal also appreciated Freeman's support to the school community and hoped he would continue visiting the school. Hui Lan still came to the Parent Centre to help Carmen clean up, but she could not stay for the whole day as before because Yong Ming had begun Grade 1. With all the boys at school, she was able to have time to attend Citizenship Class to prepare for her Canadian citizenship application. She felt that in this class she not only learned about Canada, but also learned more English than in the ESL class. Hui Lan planned to have Yong Sheng attend the French Immersion Program like Freeman's grandson when he attended Grade 4. She believed that it would be good for Yong Sheng to have an additional language, like his big brother who could speak Spanish.

On a November Sunday morning, I was napping after a conference trip. The phone rang. It was Hui Lan. She told me she had finally met with Yong Chang's teachers at the high school the week before, but it was a disquieting visit. She said the teachers of four subjects said the same thing: "Yong Chang is doing well. There is nothing you need worry about." Hui Lan asked the teachers to be stricter, for she was concerned that he might think too highly of himself and forget to work hard. One teacher said, "How would you like me to push your son? Make him as good as me?"

Hui Lan said she did not know how to respond. I understood how she felt. I could see the gap in communication and the differences in terms of expectations and approaches between the parent and the teacher. The teachers did not understand why Yong Chang's mom seemed unsatisfied with the boy who was a good student in every teacher's eyes. Hui Lan, however, quoted a Chinese saying: "There are higher mountains outside of this mountain 山外有山". She insisted on the necessity of pushing the boy to study harder, in the hope that Yong Chang would go to medical school.

> You work with people. You help others as well as yourself. I don't want him to be an engineer or a researcher. You work with machines or numbers. Your knowledge can be out-of-date. Being a doctor, you accumulate your knowledge and skills with day-to-day practice. And you have to move around. Sitting in front of computer too long is not good for your health.

Hui Lan said she pushed her eldest son hard because of her beliefs:

The eldest son is the most important. He will set an example for the younger brothers. If he does well on his way, the other two will follow. So it is not always a good idea to leave it up to the boy to decide what he wants to do. He might choose something of current interest, but which is not necessarily really good for his future. It is important for parents to guide the direction and make sure the boy is heading toward a good future.

Yong Sheng still holds on to his goal to become a dentist. He had a bad tooth a couple of years ago. It was pulled out by a dentist. Since then he has made up his mind to become a dentist. So, when he is reluctant to do his math, I say, "You have to do your math if you want to be dentist." "Why?" he asks. "You would pull out a wrong tooth if you are not good at math. You've got to be good at math to be a good dentist." So, that keeps him working harder at math. I also say to him, "You also have to work hard at your language. You have to explain to people what is wrong with their teeth and also write a report about the patient." So, he listens when I ask him to do additional homework, in both English and Chinese.

Hui Lan told me all this with a laugh. She went on:

Yong Ming had wanted to be a policeman. However, when he watched the news and heard that four RCMP officers were killed on duty, he changed his mind. He didn't know until then how dangerous a police officer's job could be. He had only thought how great the police officers looked in their splendid uniforms.

Hui Lan said that she was also attending classes.

My English is not good enough yet for me to take the Citizenship test. It may take me two terms to reach the level. I will keep learning until I pass the exam. I want to show my boys that although English is difficult for me, I will not give up. If I can keep learning, there is no reason for them not to study hard.

点评:

SHI JING'S REFLECTION

Hui Lan and her husband only finished high school in China. They thought of me respectfully because I taught at university in China and I did my PhD studies at University of Toronto. They saw me as a role model for their sons. As a matter of fact, I learned a great deal from them, during the three years of my fieldwork, in their ways of educating children, in terms of schooling, learning, and parenting. Although these parents did not articulate their views in cultural terms as explicitly as Grandpa Jiang did in his reflections, I can see that the Chinese traditional education and family values influence them strongly when they educate their children, not only in terms of how to be a good learner, but also in terms of how to be a good human.

Like hundreds and thousands of Chinese families who immigrated to Canada for the sake of their children, Hui Lan and her husband hold on to their belief that education plays a crucial role in the future of their boys and of the family. They have no regrets for the sacrifices they make as long as it contributes to a better future for the boys. They see the importance of school education as well as the importance of family education. They keep tutoring and modeling for their boys to push them to achieve academic success at school, and at the same time to make sure that they are growing up as good citizens with traditional Chinese humanity and family values. They are aware of the challenges in the new land, but they hold on to their dreams and make Canada their home with hope, determination, and effort. They represent Chinese families in Canada who bring to their new country important traditional Chinese values of education and family. These are the values to which the family holds dear in their search of home and a sense of belonging in Canada. Chinese as they appear to be, these family stories are told to foster communication and understanding so that people of diverse ethnic sociocultural backgrounds may identify and resonate with many common values and also can come to understanding those that appear different.

Chapter 5

Life in Transition: Newcomer Boy Zhi Gao

生活在变迁: 广东男孩志高

Prelude

Zhi Gao[1]志高, a newcomer boy from Guangdong 广东, China, is the major character in this chapter. I initially hesitated to perceive him and other newcomer boys of his class as potential participants for my study for reasons mentioned in Chapters 2 and 4. My attitude toward Zhi Gao, as well as some other Chinese newcomer families, changed from my early hesitance to my full support of the newcomer boys and girls and their families through working closely with the school, the teachers, and the families. This change reveals the process of my evolving sense of inquiry as I "lived" in the stories that these people under study lived by in between landscapes of schools in transition.

Zhi Hui 智辉, a newcomer boy from Fujian 福建, China, is also an important character in this chapter. *Zhi Gao* 志高 and *Zhi Hui* 智辉 were like two inseparable twin brothers, for when one was in trouble, the other was surely involved.

Zhi Hui and other newcomer boys "jumped" into my attention and everyone else's at the Parent Centre in the autumn of my first year at the Bay Street Community School when the Newcomer Support Class came to the Parent Centre for a Buddy Reading Program and the newcomer boys turned the Parent Centre upside down. Zhi Hui was never quiet in the Parent Centre and in class. He made fun with other boys by giving people nicknames. Partly because of these boys, my narrative path at the school was expanded beyond my early expectations to other classrooms, field trips, parent–teacher interviews, School Council meetings, school events – Multicultural Night, Curriculum Night, Transition Night, Spring Musical, Winter Concert, TRIBES Day – and home visits.

Zhi Hui and other newcomer boys seemed to be setting up a stage and acting in a prelude of their intercultural and cross-cultural life in transition in bilingual and multicultural Canada before Zhi Gao, the major character, came into the picture.

Zhi Gao arrived in the Newcomer Support Class from Guangdong, China in May, the second year. The first time he came to the Parent Centre with his class, he "flew" into everyone's attention as he threw a book at Zhi Hui before he walked into the room. Lin Lin 琳琳, a girl in the class, told me on the first day of his arrival, Zhi Gao 志高 had a fight with another boy in class; Zhi Gao often swore in Chinese with a word that insulted one's mother. Zhi Hui 智辉 cautioned other boys and girls that they had better not talk with Zhi Gao if they did not want their mother to be insulted. Unlike Zhi Hui who was cheerful and fun making, Zhi Gao appeared solemn and angry, wearing a look that even made me uneasy. I wondered what made a boy of his age carry such anger in his eyes.

Because of his behavior and my concern that he would not be cooperative, I did not, initially, think of Zhi Gao as a potential participant. To my surprise, he was more willing to participate than was Zhi Hui. He seemed to listen when I stopped him from swearing and misbehaving. Later, during a home visit, Zhi Gao's mom urged me to talk with him as she believed that,

> One word said by you is worth 10 words said by me. Zhi Gao listens to you. He often comes home and tells me about you. He said, "We have a teacher in our class who speaks Chinese. She is a woman, but she is a doctoral student!"

I observed and talked with Zhi Gao in class, at math tutorials, on field trips, in the library, at the Parent Centre, and even as I escorted him to the Main Office. I wondered what accounted for his behavior. I discussed this question with his English teachers, Chinese teachers, the vice principal, the settlement worker at the school, with his mother and stepfather at their home, and with other Chinese parents and grandparents at the Parent Centre. Zhi Gao crept into the mind of everyone with whom he was involved.

When it was time for the newcomer students to move to a high school or to a LEAP program in September of the new school year, Zhi Gao and Zhi Hui remained in the Newcomer Support Class. Ms. Corter, the new Newcomer Support Class teacher, made special efforts to work with the two boys. However, they continued to argue and fight with each other and with other boys. Nevertheless, it appeared that Zhi Gao and Zhi Hui were also friends. They hung out together, often playing video games at a Chinese shopping mall after school. One day I saw Zhi Hui came to school with a black eye. He said that he had a fight with Zhi Gao over the weekend. Zhi Gao said Zhi Hui initiated the fight. They talked about it casually and neither seemed to take it seriously. Later that spring, Ms. Corter showed me a journal Zhi Hui wrote in Chinese about a dream he had.

> I had a bad dream last night. In my dream Zhi Gao 志高 *told me that he hated school, he hated teachers and he hated the students at the school. He did not want to come to school any more. I cried and said to him, "No! You cannot drop out of school. You must go to school. It is important for you to go to school." I was so relieved to wake up and find out that it was only a dream.*

But when the two boys graduated from Bay Street Community School and went to different high schools in the third year, the dream became reality.

Episode One: Newcomer Boys on Landscapes of Schools in Transition

In previous chapters, I told stories of my early contacts with the newcomer students especially boys who were misbehaving, often as a group, in the Buddy Reading Program at the Parent Centre. In this episode, I back up in time to show what this class was like before Zhi Gao arrived. I want to provide the overall picture of the newcomer students' cross-cultural school life in transition, which, to a great extent, created the context for Zhi Gao's behavior. I also want to show how central this class was to the eventful path I followed on the home–school–community landscape.

Scene I: "Do you like milk?"—Language and Culture Dissonance

March 25, the 2nd Year, Buddy Reading Program at the Parent Centre
The Buddy Reading Program was carried on into the new school year. Many months had passed since it was first initiated, and the boys, if anything, had become more unruly.

Carmen prepared to read. She asked if anyone from the Newcomer Support class would help her to hold the large-sized book. "No!" said the boys in chorus. "Won't anyone hold the book for me?" "No!" said the boys in a louder chorus. They were laughing and making strange noises. Freeman said in Chinese, "Carmen asked you to help her to hold the book". "Oh?" said some boys. A girl stood and held the book. Later when the newcomer class left the Parent Centre, Freeman said that the children did not know enough English to understand Carmen's request.

When reading was over, Mr. Anderson and Carmen mixed the newcomer students with small children and put them into small groups with the help of Freeman and myself. I was asked to work with a group of boys. I asked them to read a story in turns, sentence by sentence. "Ye Long can't read," Jack said. "He cannot read English and he even can't speak Chinese. He can only speak Fujian dialect." Ye Long 叶龙 told me he did not learn English in China. He was more attentive than other boys and would repeat words and sentences as I read. I pulled Peng Fa 彭发's chair closer to the table as he was spinning on it. "How old are you, Jack?" I asked in English. Jack looked at me. I asked again in Chinese. This is how it went. I talked mostly in Chinese since they could not understand simple English such as, "Do you like milk?"

"Um, yummy!" Carmen commented when she came over to get something from the fridge and heard us reading about a little boy who mixed cornflakes with jam, milk, sugar, and other ingredients. The boys made rude noises to indicate their dislike of the food. Peng Fa said he had never eaten cornflakes for breakfast. Zhi Hui and Jack said they did not have milk for breakfast. They could not connect with foods in the story. We then read a book, *The Dream*. When I asked the boys what the story was about, they dragged on in a loud chorus, "D-R-A-G-O-N!!", so loud that everyone in the room looked in our direction.

I learned that these newcomer boys were 13 years old and in Grade 7. They would attend high school in a year. I wondered how they would make it in high school with so little English and so little apparent interest in learning it.

Scene II: *"Democracy wouldn't work here"*

May 6, the 2nd Year, Buddy Reading Program, Parent Centre
Carmen read a fairy tale about the prince and the frog. Zhi Hui with other boys was not listening. Mr. Anderson disciplined them constantly. Yong Sheng 永胜, Yong Ming 永明, and other little children listened attentively. When Carmen asked, "Did she...," the little ones would respond, "no-no-no-no." The bigger boys were amused and started mimicking and responding in chorus, "No, no, no, NO!!!" They answered loudly this way regardless of the question. When Carmen corrected them to say "Yes" for one answer, they chanted, "Yes, yes, yes, YES!!!" and laughed.

Mr. Anderson read another story and explained antonyms, such as *high-low, quiet-loud, good-bad, tall-short*, and *young-old*. "We have good behaviors and bad behaviors," he said. "Yeah, we have some very BAD behaviors." Carmen smiled and winked at me.

"Look at the baby. Is she young or old?" Mr. Anderson asked.

"Young!" they all answered.

"Is Mr. Anderson young or old?" Mr. Anderson pointed at himself.

"Old!!!" the bigger boys answered with no hesitation.

"O-oh!" Mr. Anderson made a funny face. We adults laughed. Mr. Anderson appeared to be in his late 30 s.

"The library is quiet. Room 48 (Newcomer Support Classroom) is very..."

"Noisy!" some big boys responded loudly.

"Loud," Mr. Anderson said. "*Loud* also means *noisy*."

Mr. Anderson asked the newcomer boys and girls who would like to come forward to read. "No!" said the boys. He asked Zhi Hui. "Not me!" Zhi Hui said. Suddenly Mr. Anderson's cell phone rang. He looked at me, "Could you please..."

I asked the bigger children what they would like to read. Someone said "Sui Bian 随便 (Do whatever you like)." Zhi Hui and Peng Fa started, "Sui Bian La 随便啦 (Whatever). Bian 便- Da Bian 大便 (Shit)." They laughed loudly. "Do you behave like this in China?" I asked in Chinese. "They did not come from the same school," a girl said. I began to read a story about a magic key. I said, "In the story the boy had his key on his neck. Ye Long has his keys on his neck." Carmen pointed to herself. I said, "Carmen has her key on her neck." Many boys took out their keys. Zhi Hui threw his into the air. "Zhi Hui, would you like to put your key on your neck, too?" I said. He didn't get it. Peng Fa said in Chinese, "She asked you to put your key on your neck." Mr. Anderson returned. It was time for the class to leave. He told me that their class was going to a show on Thursday and asked me if I would like to come.

After the class was gone, Freeman said, "Mr. Anderson is too nice." "Yes," said Hui Lan, "The boys are not well behaved. They need to be disciplined." I said, "The teacher is teaching them in a respectful and democratic way. He asked the students to decide who wanted to read. In China, you do not have such choice." "Respect and authority are important between the teacher and students. Democracy wouldn't work here," Freeman said. "What would you do with these kids in China?" Freeman asked Julian's grandma. "You would ask them to stand at the back of the classroom," she replied.

Episode Two: Diverged Path from Parent Centre to Room 48

Scene I: What Language Do You Speak?—Meeting the New Boy Zhi Gao

May 7, the 2nd year, Newcomer Support Class
It was almost 1:30 p.m. as I entered Room 48. "*Lao Shi Hao* 老师好 (Hi, Teacher)." Lin Lin 琳琳 and other girls and some boys greeted me in Chinese.

Mr. Anderson raised his voice to settle the boys. After a review on punctuation, he said there were 40 minutes for reading and then a birthday party for Liang Liang 亮亮 and Peng Fa. Peng Fa murmured in Chinese that he did not want a party with Liang Liang. Mr. Anderson sat by the desk near the door and worked one-on-one with students. Most girls started reading, but the boys talked and moved around the room. I talked with Liang Liang. I was puzzled why this boy from north China, who had not finished Grade 5 in China, was placed in Grade 7 in this mixed grades 7/8 newcomer student class. Liang Liang spoke Pu-Tong-Hua/Mandarin 普通话 with a strong northern accent. He seemed to be singled out and was often made fun of by Zhi Hui, Peng Fa, and other Fujianese boys. He would talk back when provoked and was often caught by the teacher. I asked Liang Liang to read. He managed the whole story. I was impressed. His English appeared to be better than some others in the class. I encouraged him to study hard and not use bad names. "But they nickname me and call me bad names," he replied.

Peng Fa wandered around and wrote something on a desk. I walked closer. It was in Chinese, "天才是我 (The genius is me)." I smiled and asked him to return to his seat and read. He did. I praised him and asked him to repeat after me several words he mispronounced. I noticed the note he recorded: he had finished 35 books.

As some boys talked in nasty words to one another, I said, "Both Chinese and English are beautiful languages. Why do you pick up bad English words so quickly while you can hardly say a complete English sentence?" "That is what we hear most." "Where do you hear them?" "On TV."

Zhi Hui 智辉 and the new boy, Zhi Gao 志高, asked me what language I spoke. I said, "I speak Chinese and English." "What *other* Chinese language and dialects do you speak?" they asked. "Why do you ask? You think I cannot understand your Cantonese and Fujian dialects and you can play tricks on me as what you do to Mr. Anderson, don't you? I understand every word you say!" They walked away with a defeated look.

Scene II: Marching along Toronto Streets

May 8, the 2nd year, Newcomer Support Class Fieldtrip
Mr. Anderson asked the children to line up and behave themselves as they walked to Ryerson Theatre. We walked fast with Mr. Anderson at the head of the line and me at the end. Mr. Anderson kept calling, "Hurry up! We are going to be late." I tried to keep order as the boys pushed one another and bumped into others on the street. A girl jumped to grab a leaf. A boy followed her. As we walked noisily along the street, I felt like a mother trying vainly to keep her exuberant children in good manner.

At the intersection of Dundas and Yonge streets, Zhi Hui remarked, "That building is the Eaton Centre." When we talked, he asked if I had a child. I said if I had one soon after I was married, the child would be as old as him. "Ah, I am your son," he teased with a smile. "If you were my son, I wouldn't mind too much you being naughty, but I would make you study hard and go to university."

He became quiet and walked faster. Later, I learned that for 10 years Zhi Hui grew up in his grandparents' home in Fujian China while his parents worked for a better life for the family, first in Japan and then in Toronto. Now, his mother had to leave home again to work in the United States, for she lost her Toronto job during the SARS crisis.

"Could you do me a favor, Zhi Hui? Could you please count how many students are in the line?" I was at the end of the line and needed to make sure that no one was left behind. We were walking through a narrow passage by a construction site. He said, "Teacher, I can't make it." He could not see everyone. "Try again, Zhi Hui."

"You have to move forward," said one boy. "Why should I go to the front? I do not want to..." "Move forward, Zhi Hui. I know you can count for me."

He walked faster, jumping while counting. "Teacher, 20!" he shouted.

"Very good! Thank you, Zhi Hui!"

We stopped in front of a building. "Oh, we have been here before. It was boring. I don't want to go," Peng Fa said in Chinese as he tried to back out. We entered the theatre and were led upstairs. The show had already started. As we just walked in from the bright sunshine, we could not see our steps. Getting settled was a noisy process. Finally we all found a seat. The show was about high-school life: Four girls were loudly arguing about something on the stage. It was a musical in English, which, of course, the newcomer children could not understand. Soon a girl beside me fell asleep. The boys became restless. Qin Li 秦利 left his seat and used the faint aisle light to view a stack of picture cards. Zhi Gao 志高, the new boy who just arrived this week, grabbed his cards, and almost started a fight. I stopped them. Qin Li put the cards in his pocket and moved to the front row. In a few minutes, he was again looking at his cards. Zhi Gao blocked the light and again tried to grab the cards. In a while, Peng Fa, Qin Li, and Jack said they wanted to go to the washroom. Mr. Anderson asked them to go one by one.

I watched the children sympathetically. The idea of the field trip was to help these newcomer students to learn about high school life and to learn the new language and culture in a more engaging way. However, it was obvious that they looked forward to getting out of the theatre.

On our way back, we passed by a hot dog stand where the children gathered for a drink. "$1? It is only 50 cents near our school," I heard Peng Fa say. Many children got a coke, but I noticed that Peng Fa, Liang Liang, Jack, and Zhi Gao bought nothing. Peng Fa had said he was thirsty on our way to the theatre, so I spoke to him, "I notice that you didn't get a drink. You said you were thirsty long ago. Did you bring money with you? Would you like me to get you a drink?" Peng Fa replied, "No, I have 50 cents. Near the school a drink is only 50 cents." "I can give you another 50 cents to get a drink right now." "No, I can get a drink from the place near our school," he insisted. The children stopped again at an ice cream car. When we started walking, I asked Zhi Hui to count the students for me again; this time there were only 16. He said Peng Fa, Jack, Liang Liang, and Zhi Gao "are far ahead of us." I wondered if they were running for the 50-cent drinks near the school, or if they felt uneasy when other children bought expensive ice cream and icy drinks.

Scene III: Zhi Gao, the Angry New Boy

June, the 2nd year, Newcomer Support Class
Nancy, a volunteer in the Newcomer Support Class, applied for a teacher education program. After spending two days with the class, she said she now wondered if she wanted to be a teacher.

"Where are the kids?" I wondered. Just then the students burst into Room 48 as they returned from the Chinese class. The formerly quiet room seemed to boil. Zhi Hui and Liang Liang called each other names. "Where is Jack?" Mr. Anderson asked. "Jack no no," Peng Fa called out. Zhi Hui shouted, "Jack not here." Other boys joined him in the shout. "Was Jack in the Chinese class?" Mr. Anderson asked. "No!" several boys chanted loudly.

Jia Ming, a newly arrived boy from Shanghai, asked me why these students spoke English so badly.

Suddenly Ke Ling and Zhi Gao started calling each other names. They kicked each other and banged on their desks while shouting in Chinese. Mr. Anderson vainly tried to stop them. He asked if I could take the two boys, along with two forms he handed me, to the Office. I looked at the forms: they were behavior reports.

Zhi Gao became furious, banged his desk, swore, and then angrily left the room. Ke Ling was quiet on our way to the Office. I wondered where Zhi Gao was. When we arrived at the office, Zhi Gao was already there sitting in a corner. He immediately started shouting and Ke Ling shouted back. I tried to stop them. "You are in the Main Office. How could you still talk like that?" "I don't want to talk to you! I am going home." Zhi Gao walked out.

Michelle, the secretary, said that the boys had to fill out the forms. I said they did not know enough English and asked Michelle if I could help Ke Ling to fill out his form while he explained to me in Chinese what had happened. She said I could. Ke Ling explained, "I was copying the sentences from the blackboard. He rocked the table and I couldn't write. So I kicked him and he kicked back."

Mr. Wilson, the vice principal, asked me if I would go with him to Zhi Gao's home to find the boy. He was not there. Through me, Mr. Wilson talked with the parents. That afternoon, Zhi Gao returned to the class. Mr. Anderson asked me to interpret while he talked with Zhi Gao. The boy did not say anything.

EPISODE THREE: LOCATING ZHI GAO AND NEWCOMER STUDENTS ON DIVERGING PATHS

In June of the second year of my fieldwork in the school, 8 of the 20 newcomer children graduated from Bay Street Community School. Jia Ming, like most of those remaining, moved on to LEAP programs. Mr. Anderson, who left the school for an administrative job, was replaced by Ms. Corter, a first-year teacher, in September when another school year started. Zhi Hui, Zhi Gao, and Jack, however, stayed with Ms. Corter, partly because of their English and partly because of their behavior. I lost track of Liang Liang and Ye Long, who, I later learned, were placed in Special Ed Programs. In order to follow up with the students formerly in the Newcomer Support Class, the principal introduced me to Ms. Campbell in the LEAP Programs. I met Ms. Corter, the new Newcomer Support Class teacher, at Curriculum Night in mid-September. Ms. Corter welcomed me to her class, saying she heard of me from Mr. Anderson and Freeman. Since I wanted to meet all the Chinese newcomer children in one location, I arranged to visit Ms. Tan's Mandarin class. She and I knew each other through Freeman at the Parent Centre. Thus, as the newcomer boys' and girls' paths diverged, so did mine on the school landscape.

Scene I: Zhi Gao Taking the Leadership Role

October 16, the 2nd Year, Newcomer Support Class
At 12:40 p.m., I said goodbye to Carmen and went to the Newcomer Support Class. I saw Jack and asked him about their afternoon class. He said they would have one session in class and then go to the library for computer lessons. The girls came back. I asked if they had lunch in the cafeteria. They said they had lunch at home.

In the math class before going to the library, Ms. Corter demonstrated how to draw and cut out a pattern. The girls stood behind Ms. Corter observing closely, but the boys, mostly initiated by Zhi Gao, were talking and paid little attention. Following the demonstration, students were told to return to their own desks to draw and cut out a pattern. When Zhi Gao said he did not know how to do it, I said, "Tell your teacher and she will help you." He kept talking with other boys. I told Ms. Corter that Zhi Gao needed help. She sat with him and helped him. Many students finished their work, but some boys were fooling around and did not finish. Ms. Corter lined them up for the walk to the library.

Ms. Corter asked Zhi Gao to take a leadership role to make sure everybody walked quietly along the hallway. It was amazing to see how seriously he took it. I said to Ms. Corter, "It seems that giving Zhi Gao responsibility makes him feel important, and valued." She replied, "Sometimes it works; sometimes it doesn't. Yesterday he was very bad, but today he is behaving much better."

Zhi Gao stopped the class outside the library and made everybody stand in line. Most were quiet. Zhi Gao said to me in Chinese, "Teacher, the door is open. Should I close it?" I said, "Okay. Good." He closed the classroom door opposite to the library to prevent the class from being disturbed by the hallway noise. Both Ms. Corter and I praised him for keeping the class orderly on the walk. Zhi Gao said "Thank you" and looked pleased.

There were not enough computers for everybody. Ms. Corter paired Zhi Gao and Zhi Hui respectively with a newly arrived boy and asked them to show the new boy how to operate the computer properly according to the librarian's instructions.

Before I left for the Parent Centre that afternoon, Ms. Corter told me that her class was to make a lunch for the staff meeting next week. She also invited me to take part in the school field trip for senior grade students in November.

Scene II: Math Tutorial for Newcomer Grade 8 Students

November 19, the 2nd Year, Newcomer Support Class
Mr. Feng 冯伯, Jessica's grandpa, was a retired secondary school principal and math teacher in China. I got to know him as a School Council member. He volunteered as a math tutor, first in Jessica's

Grades 3 and 4 classes and later in the Newcomer Support Class. He often told me of his concerns about discipline. He especially worried about the newcomer Chinese boys who showed little interest in their studies. He would begin a Newcomer Support Class lesson trying to establish order, much as he might have done in China. But the boys kept talking. Behind his back, they called him *Deng Xiao-ping*, because of his resemblance to the former leader of China. Mr. Feng was pleased when I visited the class at his tutorial time and helped keep order.

Mr. Feng was in the classroom when I arrived. His lesson was on trigonometry. He used a large sheet of paper on which he demonstrated. He asked students to figure out the area and side length of a triangle. The boys talked and Mr. Feng stopped frequently to discipline them. Zhi Hui put his right cheek on his right arm on the desk. He was quiet, but apparently daydreaming. Mr. Feng, a Cantonese speaker, spoke Pu-Tong-Hua with a strong accent. The Fujianese boys like Zhi Hui seemed to have some difficulty following. Zhi Gao sometimes responded in Cantonese. Other boys would say, "No Cantonese!" Still, Xiu Hua, a recently arrived girl from Fujian, understood immediately. Some of the boys asked her for help.

In China, students are often asked to come to the blackboard to demonstrate for the class. Since the boys were talking, I suggested, "Let's have someone come up front." "I don't understand, yet," Zhi Gao, who had been talking, exclaimed. "Ok," I said, "let's listen to Mr. Feng again. Pay attention." He listened, asked a few questions and then exclaimed, "Oh, I understand now. I get it!" I checked his exercise book. He had the right answer. "Good for you, Zhi Gao! You are very smart. When you listen carefully, you get it very quickly." I encouraged him. Jack was talking to other boys. I said to him, "Jack, don't talk. Listen. Look, Zhi Gao got it by listening attentively." Jack stopped talking. Zhi Gao was quiet.

Before observing Zhi Gao closely, as I did today, I thought he was academically slow. I was impressed by his math exercise book. He must have done well in math in China. His response to Mr. Feng's lesson suggested he was quick-minded. Both Mr. Anderson and Ms. Corter thought the boys' misbehaviors were expressions of culture shock. Ms. Corter also observed that upon returning to school after weekends, the newcomer students tended to forget everything they had learned in the previous week.

Scene III: Parent–Teacher Interview

December 4, the 2nd year, Newcomer Support Class
Since September of my second year at the school, I had, at the principal's request, translated flyers and interpreted at School Council meetings and parent–teacher interviews. As all but one Grades 7/8 newcomer students were from Mainland China, I usually worked with Ms. Corter and Ms. Campbell at the time of the parent–teacher interviews.

This evening I was with Ms. Corter. We phoned parents who missed their appointment. I called Zhi Gao's home and spoke with his mom. In a few minutes, Zhi Gao's mom, Ms. Geng 耿女士, rushed into the classroom, out of breath and apologizing for being late. She said that she just got home from work and ran to the school immediately after hanging up the phone. We sat down, with me between Ms. Corter and Zhi Gao's mother.

Ms. Corter showed Zhi Gao's mom his report card and explained that the first column listed Zhi Gao's marks for each subject and the second column showed the averages of the Grade 8 students' marks. "Zhi Gao has great strength in math. His marks in subjects that require a lot of language are not bad, but he can do better if he works harder."

Zhi Gao's mother carefully studied the report card. She asked what the top score was in the class. Ms. Corter said, "The top score in math is 90. Mr. Feng, the math tutor, said Zhi Gao could do better in math if he worked harder." Ms. Corter said that Zhi Gao's behavior was much improved, especially in the recent two weeks. "He got a *Mutual Respect* award from the school. A boy from another class was beating him, but he controlled himself and chose not to fight back as he usually would. He made a very mature decision." Ms. Corter said that she felt very proud of him.

"Oh, I see. I see," his mother said. "I have noticed changes in recent weeks. He usually called bad names and cursed in dirty language. Now he seldom uses dirty language." Zhi Gao's mother was a Cantonese speaker, but she could speak Pu-Tong-Hua, which helped me with the translation. When she talked, her voice was full of care about her son.

> I know Zhi Gao is hot-tempered. Please tell the teacher to be stricter with him and discipline him. I often talked with Zhi Gao, but he wouldn't listen to me. So, please ask the teacher to talk more with Zhi Gao. He listens to the teacher and respects what the teacher says.

Ms. Corter laughed, and said:

> Almost all kids of this age tend to listen to their teacher more than to their parents. Zhi Gao is a good boy. I am working hard with other colleagues to help him. I have also integrated him in the regular class for a half day to push him to learn more English.

As the discussion continued, Zhi Gao's mother and Ms. Corter tended to emphasize different things. When Ms. Corter suggested that Zhi Gao watch English TV and listen to English radio at home, his mother responded by referring to Zhi Gao's marks and repeating that she wanted him to study hard. The mother attributed Zhi Gao's misbehavior to his temper, which she did not seem to think was a serious matter. Ms. Corter, however, tried to emphasize the importance of disciplining Zhi Gao's behavior, especially his temper, because it was affecting both him and the rest of the class. Other parents arrived, so Zhi Gao's mother signed the report card, thanked us, and left.

Episode Four: "Why was Zhi Gao frustrated?"

From this episode on, answers to my puzzle over the anger in Zhi Gao's eyes arose to the surface as I came to know him better and pieced together fragmented stories of his school and family life in China.

Scene I: Getting Ready for High School

January 24, the 3rd Year, Newcomer Support Class
I got to school around noontime. I checked in at the Main Office and met Ms. Corter there. She said she needed my help to act as an interpreter for a few things in the afternoon: Ms. Nelson, the guidance teacher, was coming to help the Grade 8 students choose high-school courses; Yang Yang, who was returning to China, might come to say goodbye; Zhi Gao had behavior problems this week and was sent to the Main Office several times.

> He had been great. Suddenly he became wild. I wonder what happened. Is there anything at home that upset him? Or did I say or do something to upset him? Or is it because some of the students, but not Zhi Gao, moved to LEAP? Can you be the translator when Mr. Wilson (the vice principal) talks with him? Maybe you can find out why he is so upset.

It occurred to me that moving Zhi Gao to the LEAP program might be good for his self-esteem. When I raised this possibility with Ms. Corter, she said that it was behavior and not ability that prevented the move.

I visited Carmen in the Parent Centre, and then went to Ms. Corter's newcomer class. "Hi, Teacher!" Students greeted me, "Which class are you going to today?" "Yours," I said. "Yeah!!" they cheered. I was impressed when Ms. Corter showed me the morning's artwork, a teapot drawing. Ms. Corter regularly integrated art into her daily curriculum.

Ms. Nelson arrived for the session on choosing high-school courses. She explained the forms in front of each student: "Family name, given name, birth date, address, phone number.... The first line is your family name. Zhi Gao, what is your family name?"

A Grade 7 girl interrupted and asked me to sign a card the class had made for Yang Yang. Zhi Gao said, "Oh, when *Toaster* comes, I will give him this." He showed a little toy dog with a Santa hat. This was a gift given to him by the librarians during a high-school visit, and one that Zhi Gao treasured. There was a discussion about Yang Yang before the class returned to Ms. Nelson's activity.

Ms. Nelson explained the core and optional course choices. One of the options gave students a choice of music, with band, string and vocal as alternatives, or visual art. The boys showed no interest in either music or visual art. Zhi Gao 志高 walked away, saying none of the courses interested him, but Ms. Nelson called him back. I said, "Why don't you choose music? You can learn to sing English songs and improve your English pronunciation." Xiao Qiang 小强 agreed, but Zhi Gao responded, "Oh, you idiot. If you choose that class, they will put you on stage and you will have to sing in public." Ms. Nelson asked me what Zhi Gao said, and said, "No, you will only sing together in class." So Xiao Qiang chose the vocal. Wen Feng 文锋 decided to sign in with him. I asked Zhi Gao what he would choose. He checked the vocal class, saying, "Oh, since you two go, I will go with you."

When it came to language choices, Ms. Corter recommended ESL-A for Xiao Qiang, ESL-B for Wen Feng, and ESL-C for Zhi Gao, according to their English levels, which meant that the boys would have to be split up in high school. An even greater split occurred among these newcomer students because many of them were heading for different high schools. Zhi Hui was heading for a vocational school. Ms. Corter had discussed this with Zhi Hui's dad, with my translation. Zhi Gao, however, insisted on going to an academic one because most of the newcomer Chinese students went to this one. Ms. Nelson patiently explained the choices in each of the schools.

To a great extent, as this exchange shows, newcomer Chinese students selected their courses, as well as their high schools, according to their friends' choices.

When the forms were completed, Zhi Hui and Zhi Gao would normally have gone to Room 46 where Ms. Corter hoped to integrate the two boys into the regular class. But neither liked the class. Today Ms. Corter said that Zhi Gao was to go to the Main Office. Zhi Hui reluctantly left for Room 46 and Zhi Gao looked tense instantly.

Scene II: "Why is Zhi Gao upset?"

January 24, the 3rd Year, Main Office and Newcomer Support Class
"It is not a punishment to send you to the Main Office." As we walked downstairs to the Main Office, I said to Zhi Gao, "Your teacher is trying to help you. She wants to understand what is happening. Both your teacher and your mom said they were pleased with how good you have been and how much you have improved in your behaviour."

We went into the office. Zhi Gao seemed to know the route well and went directly to Mr. Wilson's office, but he took a corner seat away from Mr. Wilson. I sat between Zhi Gao and Mr. Wilson. Mr. Wilson briefed me, saying that Zhi Gao's behavior had improved greatly and everyone was happy. However, all of a sudden this past week, he became unruly again, and had even insulted his teacher. He did this in Chinese and, because of Zhi Gao's tone of voice in his frequent use of the word, Ms. Corter, at first, did not realize that he was swearing. But when she asked, the Chinese teacher and other students explained that the word was a swear word insulting one's mother. Ms. Corter was upset and wanted to know what made Zhi Gao change his behavior. Mr. Wilson mentioned Ms. Corter's speculations discussed with me earlier. I asked:

> Is there anything that upsets you, Zhi Gao? Everyone says you've been very good. Your mother and your teacher all feel so proud of you. Why all of a sudden do you become upset and angry again? What happened? What is wrong? The teachers do not mean to punish you. They are just trying to figure out what is wrong so that they can help you.

Zhi Gao said that during the holidays, he played video games with other boys. The boss of the Internet Café got angry at them, saying they messed up the system, so he turned off the computers and drove them out. That made Zhi Gao upset, for he lost the points saved in the machine by winning games. He was in a bad mood, he said, and so he became somewhat nasty in class.

Mr. Wilson asked me to explain that the name he called his teacher was insulting and hurt her. She was caring and supportive of him, and felt very proud of him. She put her heart into working with him, and therefore felt especially bad when Zhi Gao swore at her.

I told Mr. Wilson that my sense of Zhi Gao was that he tended to use vulgar language habitually to show his frustration, rather than using it to attack a person. Mr. Wilson said he understood that, but Zhi Gao needed to learn to express his frustration politely, not offensively. "He is not allowed to do so. He could be suspended from school." When this was explained to Zhi Gao, he looked worried and asked, "Am I going to be suspended from school?" I could tell this thought bothered him. I said:

> Your teacher can forgive what you've done. You can tell yourself, "I am not going to say the word again today." I know it is hard to get rid of the habit since you have had it for a long while. When you say the word, you are almost unaware that you are saying it. It just comes out of your mouth so easily. But, eventually, you can get rid of the habit. You know your teacher has been so nice to you. She really likes you to be good. You are very smart. You have lots of potential. Your teacher wants to help you succeed. Your mother also told the teacher how good you've been at home. You make breakfast and you've been helping her. Your teacher also told your mom how good you were at school. Can you try to change that habit, and not use that bad word?

Zhi Gao nodded his head and wiped tears from his eyes. I was pleased that he was listening, and also a little surprised, for he always appeared to be so tough.

I asked him what other things frustrated him. "When there was too much homework, or when I couldn't understand the homework and didn't know what to do, I would swear. But I was not swearing at anyone. I was just swearing because I was frustrated."

"Why didn't you ask classmates like Xiu Hua who have more English and who understand the homework?" I asked.

"I did, but I was teased by the girls. 'Oh, how come you are such an idiot? How come you cannot understand this?' So I didn't want to ask them again."

"Yeah. That's not good," I said. "So, you see, you felt hurt by that. You should understand how others feel when you call them *idiot*. If you want others to treat you nicely and respectfully, you should treat others nicely and respectfully yourself. Right?"

Zhi Gao nodded his head. We walked back to the classroom with Mr. Wilson.

Scene III: Learning How to Play

January 24, the 3rd Year, Newcomer Support Class
Ms. Corter was playing a vocabulary card game with the students. She asked me to take her spot while she talked with Mr. Wilson in the hallway. Zhi Gao joined the game, saying, "Oh, I know what this game is about. I play it on the computer." He picked up a card and reached for another. This disturbed the group. "No, it is Xiao Qiang's turn." Other boys tried to stop him from messing up the game. Zhi Gao spit out the swearing word. "Zhi Gao, not again," I said. "You promised me that you would not say that word again." He stepped back and went to the tap to drink some water.

"Hey, 烤炉 *Toaster*! 烤炉 *Toaster*!" The children exclaimed when Yang Yang and his aunt arrived for his party. "Why are you leaving? When are you going back to China? When are you coming back?" (Yang Yang is a boy from Fujian. The following chapter tells more detailed stories about him.) I stayed for the party. At 3:30 p.m., Ms. Corter held the vocabulary cards in her hand and asked each student to read a word before leaving the room. I returned to the Parent Centre and then left the school.

EPISODE FIVE: ZHI GAO TELLS HIS STORIES

I knew Zhi Gao for almost a year before interviewing him. The purpose of my interview was more heavily shaped by what I observed in the class and my discussions with Ms. Corter over what might be helpful for working with Zhi Gao than it was by my research agenda. We sat by Carmen's desk in the corner of the Parent Centre while grandparents and parents talked loudly and played with their children. Carmen's desk was near the Baby's

Corner where Julian and several little boys were playing and banging something on the floor. It was noisy, but the sounds provided cover for our talk.

Scene I: "Life is so unpleasant"

February 26, the 3rd Year, Talk with Zhi Gao, at the Parent Centre
I began by talking about his strength in math and, as I had done many times before, encouraged him to be more attentive in class. His attitude continued to puzzle me, and I asked, "Why do you often look annoyed? Children your age should be very cheerful. Why do you often look unhappy?"

Zhi Gao told me incidents that were seemingly unrelated but helped trace the narrative roots of his behavior and his defiant attitude toward teachers. At one point he said, "Life is so unpleasant." He told me he was harshly disciplined by his teacher in China when he did not do homework. Once he fought with a teacher when the teacher spanked him with a broom. I asked him what would make for a positive teacher–student relationship.

> Don't give us too much work. The teacher should treat us sincerely. If we boys fight with each other, the teacher could talk with us and make us say sorry to each other. Or he or she could tell the parents to discipline the boys.

Zhi Gao noted differences between Chinese and Canadian schools.

> In China, we couldn't go to the washroom whenever we liked. We had to ask permission first. Also, in China, we were punished if we didn't hand in our schoolwork/homework. I had to copy the textbook... Oh, XXX (swear)! It made me tired to death. Here if we don't finish our work, the teacher helps us and doesn't scold us.

Zhi Gao said he liked his Toronto school and his Toronto teacher better. Also, he said, in China he was spanked by his mother when he played truant from school or threw things at home, and his mother disciplined him more harshly than his father. But here

> She never spanks me except once when I came home at 4 o'clock in the morning. My father is harsh here. I asked him for $100 to buy a computer desk. He banged on the table and said I spent too much money. Wow, he looked fierce.

Scene II: "太白了... *At school a minute is like an hour to me*"

February 26, the 3rd Year, Talk with Zhi Gao, at the Parent Centre
I asked Zhi Gao what he did after school in Toronto, he said:

> I go to the Internet Café to play video games after school at 3:30. I stay there until 6, or 7 or 8 o'clock. Sometimes I go to Li Gang 李刚's home to play video games. My mom scolded me, and Li Gang stopped playing with me. I was upset with my mom, so I ignored her.

Zhi Gao stopped talking when I tried to speak on behalf of his mother by explaining that Chinese parents usually expect their children not to play, but to study hard for a promising future. So I changed the topic to ask about his father. Zhi Gao said:

> My father? My father is very good. When something was broken. I asked him to buy a new one, he would buy it for me. Last time the computer was broken. He gave me $20. I said it was not enough. I also needed to get some discs, so he gave me $100. My father is nice. My mom also gave me money, but she would ask me what I spent it on. She wants me to buy something for my studies. She asks me not to go to the Internet Café to play video games.

"She is right." I said. Zhi Gao continued:

> There is a computer at home, but it is too boring to stay at home alone. At the Internet Café, I played chess with Li Gang and other friends, like Zhi Hui, Ji An 纪安, and Deng Hai 邓海. *Do you still remember Ji An? We play together after 3:30. We often play video games until 2 at night. Many people there. It is a lot of fun. It is not so much fun if I play alone at home.*

When I asked, Zhi Gao said that it cost $5 per hour at the Internet Café. He was given a new account number to replace the one deleted by the boss during the Christmas holidays. (The conflict with the Internet Café boss had caused his puzzling behavior problems in school, as described in Scene II, Episode Four.) I asked him what else he did in his spare time. He said:

> We play cards and bubble gums, children's stuff, you know. We play the games. It is fun. I don't think it is a waste of money as long as we have fun. It doesn't matter. If you come to my home and eat everything at my home, and eat up everything in the fridge, it doesn't matter. My mom says, "As long as you are

happy, it is fine." My mom sometimes buys me food from a restaurant. So does my father. Li Gang is a good friend. Last time I was suspended from school, my father asked me to leave home. Li Gang let me stay at his home. The next day, I went back home. My mom didn't scold me. She just asked me where I was last night. I told her that I slept at a friend's home. She bought me a hamburger and fries. She said this should be the last time. If I were suspended again, she wouldn't care any more.

Zhi Gao said that he did not like to be suspended from school because "it is no fun." I said, "If you feel this way, why do you often say you don't like going to school?" Zhi Gao replied,

You know, the teacher speaks English. I can understand half of it and the other half I cannot understand. So I feel angry and swear. This teacher is 太白了 ... *Yesterday I was supposed to go to Room 46 at 12:45, but the teacher told me to go at 1:30. The Room 46 teacher asked me why I was late. I said because the teacher in Room 48 was an idiot.*

"You shouldn't call names. This is insulting," I responded. This led to a repeat of the conversation in which I reminded Zhi Gao of the teacher's caring and of his agreement to stop swearing and name calling. He was quiet. I went on to ask what he was doing to overcome the language difficulties that caused miscommunication. "I watch some English programs at home. My father asked me not to go out. He said he would hire a tutor for me." Zhi Gao said, "But, the thing I dislike most is learning."

Time goes so slowly when I am studying. Why does time pass by so fast when I am playing? Classes begin at 8:45. It is three hours. When I play for three hours at the Internet Café, I feel that I have hardly sat there long enough to warm the chair. In class, I feel uneasy. I feel uncomfortable all over. I look forward to the end of the school day. I feel that every minute at school passes by so slowly. A minute is like an hour to me.

Scene III: "太白了. 我太白了. 我是个白痴. **(I am an idiot.)**"

February 26, the 3rd Year, Talk with Zhi Gao, at the Parent Centre
Zhi Gao felt he had little English. Nevertheless, he said he would not like to work in Chinatown grocery stores in the future. He would rather find a good office job. He said he was not so interested in sports, such as soccer.

He liked ping-pong, but did not know where to play in Toronto. In addition to playing video games, he said he went out with his girlfriend. "Now I have a girlfriend as a teenager. Is it a bad thing?" I understood his concern. Chinese students of his age are expected to focus their attention on studies. Before the 1990s, even university students were perceived as having a lack of self-discipline and perhaps a questionable moral quality if they started dating.

"太白了 (Tai Bai Le)." He used this expression whenever our topic was on his schooling or studies. "What do you mean by 太白了?" I asked. He said, "太白了, 白痴. I am an idiot." He used this word when he meant he was *bored* or when something or someone was *boring* or *ignorant*. Although literally 太白了 (*boring; bored;* or *ignorant*), and 白痴 (*idiot*) were used by Zhi Gao as swear words, and often sounded insulting, the frequent use of these words seemed to reveal his personal frustration at not understanding English and the consequences of this for his school work and his social relations.

Zhi Gao told me that he did not have non-Chinese friends. I asked him how he liked his time in Rooms 46 and 47, the regular classes. He said:

> Students in Room 47 are 太白了 *(boring, ignorant, or idiot, according to his definition). They always talk about who likes whom. They ask me, "Are you gay? Do you like Zhi Hui? Do you like Deng Hai?" So I said to them, "Eat your shit! F-K!" Li Gang and Zhi Hui shouted at those boys with me. So they dared not fight with us. We do not like to go to Room 47. Every Wednesday, Thursday and Friday we have to go to Room 47. It is no fun. They sometimes throw glue at us.*

Zhi Gao said he read Chinese cartoon books, like *The Old Pedant* 老夫子, but he did not read any English. He said, "I asked Ms. Liang about Li Jia-cheng 李嘉诚 who liked playing video games and skipped classes. How come he became one of the richest people in Hong Kong?" Mostly, Zhi Gao said, he listened to Chinese songs though he heard English songs in Room 47. "Sometimes those English songs use swearing words, so I don't listen."

When I asked him how he felt about being sent to the Main Office, he said it was better than the Chinese way of discipline.

> Here the vice principal only chats with you. He wouldn't ask you to copy anything. If you are asked to copy something, it is not too much. In China, I had to copy the whole textbook. Chinese words are so difficult to write, you

know, and I haven't learned much Chinese. In Cantonese class (here), I even couldn't write my own name. I didn't know how to write my family name in the traditional form. Ms. Liang said it was wrong that I couldn't write Chinese.

Zhi Gao seemed to feel close to Ms. Liang, the Cantonese teacher, who spent much time working with him. Whenever I met Ms. Liang, our conversations were mainly about Zhi Gao.

Ms. Corter also worked hard with Zhi Gao but the relationship was different. I wondered why he seemed to resent her.

> Sometimes I am angry with her. Once it was Zhi Hui who made Kai Li 凯丽 upset. It was not my fault. I asked Kai Li who upset her. I said teasingly, "Who upset you? Who upset you?" Kai Li cried. The teacher asked me what was wrong. I said, "I don't know." The teacher asked me to sit at a side desk, alone. Zhi Hui was not blamed at all even though he made Kai Li cry. I just asked her who upset her.

I commented, "You and Zhi Hui often make trouble in class. And you speak Chinese, so your teacher can't understand and doesn't know who initiated the argument." I reminded him again that Ms. Corter cared about him and wanted him to be good. "Mm," Zhi Gao nodded his head.

Scene IV: Zhi Gao's Narrativization of His Childhood in China

February 26, the 2nd Year, Talk with Zhi Gao, at the Parent Centre
We talked about his life in a rural area of Guangdong (Canton). In his story, his grandparents were not part of his childhood. His paternal grandfather worked in Shenzhen 深圳, a new city, with his father, and his paternal grandmother and maternal grandparents died before he was born. He did not tell me that his parents were divorced, though I knew this from other parents. In his story, the father in China and the father in Canada sounded like one person. I did not fully understand the understated meanings of his somewhat contradictory and confusing accounts until a few months later when I talked with his mother. I understood then how and why Zhi Gao had actually narrativized a childhood that he wished for, with a mixed picture of the actual harsh and lonely childhood he had lived. The following are the excerpts of the interview.

When I asked Zhi Gao to tell me something interesting about his childhood, he looked cheerful and said, "Interesting things? Fireworks! In Chinese New Year, I liked to bomb up fish with fireworks." I commented, "That was bad. How could you do that?" He said:

> The fishpond belonged to my dad. He would take me fishing. Sometimes I asked friends to come home fishing. The pond was a dozen meters deep. When it was hot, we went swimming. Then my dad made a springboard for us to jump into the pond. Once a friend broke the board. I told my father that I broke it. My dad didn't blame me. When they drained the pond, they caught big fish. One fish would be a dozen kilograms. They would share it with the villagers.

"Your father was very nice." I commented. "Mm," Zhi Gao said. When I asked about his home in China, he said he lived in his aunt's one-story house.

> My father came to Canada long ago. He didn't build a house in China. How could he have the money to build a house there? He didn't want to build a house there, my mom said. It was my aunt's house, free for us to live in. My father gave money and built a big house. It had seven stories, the tallest in the village. My cousin 表哥 *was my good friend. He took me to Guangzhou on his motorbike. In the countryside, we had a big house there. There were many workers in my home. The door was very big. We had to press the doorbell. If you bang the door, no one would hear. Many people were in my home. I liked it. I liked the countryside. I had many people to play with. I didn't like Guangzhou. Guangzhou was annoying to me. The air was not fresh and everything was expensive. Last time we went to the countryside, my father bought me many things before he went back to Guangzhou. I said I didn't like Guangzhou. In Grade 5, I fought with the teacher and dropped out of school. So my father sent me back to the countryside to attend school. I felt better there although the friends in the countryside spoke a Cantonese dialect, and I couldn't understand their accent.*

When it was close to 3:30 p.m., I had to wrap up our conversation. I asked Zhi Gao if he usually had breakfast as he looked so skinny. He said he did not because he got up too late in the morning, often at 8:30 a.m., and he went to bed at 11:00 p.m. I told him to go to bed at 9:30 p.m. and explained that 10 p.m. to 2 a.m. was said to be the golden time for sleep. "Go to bed at 9:30?!" Zhi Gao exclaimed. "I can't fall asleep so early. Can I go to bed a little later? I can't fall asleep that early."

I said, "Give it a try. Go to bed early. If you sleep well and eat well, you will feel well and be less restless. Don't lose your temper and try not to get upset with your teacher. OK?" "Mm," he nodded.

EPISODE SIX: FINDING ZHI GAO IN-BETWEEN LANDSCAPES OF SCHOOLS IN TRANSITION

I had wanted to have an in-depth talk with Zhi Gao's mother when he was at Bay Street Community School. Zhi Gao said she worked in a restaurant seven days a week and came home late. So I had only met and talked with her briefly when she came to the school for parent–teacher interview, Curriculum Night, Transition Night, and other school events. Before Zhi Gao graduated in June of my third year in the school, Ms. Liang and I shared our worries about Zhi Gao's life in high school. Ms. Liang said:

> It is as if Zhi Gao were walking along the verge of a cliff. If you pull him back, care about him, he will stay upright, but if you let it be and push him out, thinking he is a bad kid, he will fall off.

Our concern was that a push and fall might happen in high school. His new teachers would not know his background and in high school teachers appear to be less involved in students' lives than in schools like Bay Street Community School. Nor did Zhi Gao seem to be prepared for life in a new school. His behavior was still cyclical and volatile. Two weeks before Zhi Gao began high school, I arranged to visit his mom at her home.

Scene I: The Parents' Worries

August 16, the 3rd Year, visit to Zhi Gao's Home
I had been to Zhi Gao's home once with Mr. Wilson a year ago. I found the house easily. Zhi Gao's mom greeted me and said she had just cleaned the house, a Chinese gesture of hospitality.

A long hallway led to the kitchen. Zhi Gao's mom offered me a coke. Her husband, Mr. Chan, Zhi Gao's stepfather, joined us and we shook hands. I did not have a very good impression of him from my first visit because he asked Mr. Wilson to tell the boy not to come home if he ran away from school. Mr. Chan told me that Zhi Gao was not home. He spoke Cantonese and a little English. Our conversation proceeded with a mixture of Cantonese and English on his side, a mixture of Mandarin and English on my side and, with the help of Zhi Gao's mom's translation and clarification between Cantonese and Mandarin.

The parents told me that over the summer Zhi Gao was never home for supper. They were worried and did not know what he was doing. When asked, he said he was playing with classmates. They were concerned that he might get into trouble. The mother said, "We don't know what he eats because he leaves home in the morning and comes home at 9:00 or 10:00 at night. He looks so thin. He is picky with food and doesn't eat much." The father said, "I told him not to stay out too late, but he would not listen to me. If he did come home earlier, he would watch TV until midnight, sometimes even 2:00 a.m." The mother noted that, "Zhi Gao said it was holidays, so he could sleep in. When it is school time he will not watch TV too late because he knows he has to get up early." Mr. Chan said, "He watches Chinese movies all the time. It is no good for learning English. I suggested that he watch English TV programs, but Zhi Gao wouldn't listen and said that I bothered him too much." The stepfather shook his head when talking about Zhi Gao. The mom said:

> Zhi Gao has always had a hot temper but his behaviour has changed since he came to Canada. He listened to me in China. I lived with him alone. He doesn't remember much about his own father. His father was a very... bad person ... he gambled ... often beat me ... So we were separated and divorced when Zhi Gao was very little. Zhi Gao was good and listened to me. He went to bed at 9:00 and got up early before 6:00 a.m. with me. He did well in school, especially in math where he often got 90. His marks stayed within the range of 80. He would do homework after supper. After he came to Canada, I never saw Zhi Gao do homework. When I asked, he said he didn't have homework or that he finished his homework at school.

> When Zhi Gao was little, I took care of him with some help from my sister. I didn't know he could go to school at age 5, so he started at age 7. So he was behind by two years. He confused the numbers of 6 and 9 because they looked similar to him. He couldn't count over 20. I asked him to look at the calendar and explained to him, "From Day 1 to Day 30 or 31". Look, 1 and 0 together become 10; 2 and 0 put together is 20. So every day I taught Zhi Gao to count by reading the calendar, and I taught him how to make the distinction between 6 and 9 and also showed him that 6 together with 9 is 69. Gradually Zhi Gao got a sense of numbers and learned quickly how to count from one to one hundred.

I was amazed by the way the mother taught the son. I asked her about her education. She said she only finished Grade 7 in China. She continued:

> Zhi Gao is a good kid. I often talked with him about his temper and about his being rebellious. But sometimes when I was very tired from work, I became impatient. I would scold Zhi Gao. He would become annoyed. I knew it wouldn't work if I shouted at him. I have to talk with him, not scold him. Zhi Gao was understanding of my hardship when we were in China. Every day he boiled water and put it in my thermos for me to take to work. I left him with my sister during the day, which usually was from early morning to 9:00 in the evening. I did some small business, selling things at a vendor, to make a living. My sister's daughter, Zhi Gao's cousin 表姐, *did well in school and has just graduated from university. In China, Zhi Gao listened to his aunt and his sister (the cousin) and to me. He was also naughty, but his teacher was very understanding. She said she knew Zhi Gao was naughty, but a naughty boy tended to be brighter. She said she would rather teach a child who was naughty and bright. She knew how to discipline Zhi Gao and he excelled, especially in math, and he got awards. The teacher was with Zhi Gao for four years.*

I tried to fit his mom's account with what Zhi Gao told me in the interview about being with his father, and about being transferred back and forth between a city school and a rural school. The mom explained that the understanding teacher was in the rural school in her hometown. She avoided talking about Zhi Gao studying in the city. Taking into account what Zhi Gao told me earlier, it appeared that consistent teacher support and understanding could make a positive difference. However, negative impact emerged when language and cultural barriers came in the way when the boy was placed on landscapes of schools in transition, even within China, and worse after coming to Canada. I was also puzzled. According to the mother, Zhi Gao had not seen his father again since he was two, and the father did not leave China. Mom's account made me ponder the inconsistency in Zhi Gao's story about his father: At one point he had talked about the father's presence in his childhood, such as fishing with him and sending him back to the country school, but at another point he said that his father was not with him when he was spanked by his Grade 5 teacher because the father was in Canada. During the interview, Zhi Gao's contradictory accounts made me sense the boy's unwillingness to reveal the broken family situation when he made it sound as if the father in China and the father in Canada were the same person. But I did not realize how much the boy had narrativized his childhood experience until

I listened to the mom's story. It is apparent that Zhi Gao, who had suffered from complete absence of a father in his childhood, had narrativized repeatedly a happy childhood imagining what he dreamed of as true. In his narrativization, a father who often gambled and beat the boy's mom became a nice person who was capable of building a seven-story house, the tallest one in the village and was generous with the boy and the villagers; many people lived in the big house; and a cousin was like a big brother to him. Mom's story, which countered the son's narrativization, revealed the actual lived experience of the boy: having to live with his mom at his aunt's home with no male role models such as a father and a big brother, and being lonely and discriminated against.

When her husband left the room, Zhi Gao's mom told me:

> My husband is a nice person but he is an old type, disciplining the child in a traditional way. He does not seem to know that the child needs to be disciplined in a caring way. When Zhi Gao asked him for money, he would not give it to him because he was afraid Zhi Gao would spend the money on video games. But I know Zhi Gao felt hurt when his stepfather said no to him.

Some parents and school staff thought that mistreatment at home might account for Zhi Gao's behavior, but this did not appear to be an issue based on my visit. The tensions between Zhi Gao and his stepfather were of different nature. Also, Zhi Gao's mom said, her husband's adult daughters "get along well with Zhi Gao, buying things for him and taking him out." Nevertheless, it appeared that Zhi Gao was unwilling to stay at home and might not have had a sense of belonging.

I did not know if Mr. Chan was still working. His age suggested that he must have retired long ago. Zhi Gao's mom said her work at the restaurant was harsh. She worked 10 hours a day, 7 days a week, washing dishes in a Chinese restaurant kitchen. She earned $300 a week. She said she could not bear the hardship. Her legs were swollen, so she took a few days off. That was why she was home today. Her situation illustrated something Hui Lan's husband had said: "Discrimination also occurs within the Chinese community. Newcomers are mistreated and discriminated against by some better-off, established, Toronto Chinese."

Hui Lan's husband took Yong Chang to work with him in the restaurant for the purpose of letting the boy experience a laborer's job (Chapter 5). So I asked Zhi Gao's mom if she thought it might be an idea to have Zhi Gao work with her at the restaurant during the summer. She replied indirectly by saying,

> In China, Zhi Gao knew life was not easy for me, so he was very good. He did his laundry and often made meals. Here it is different. I keep telling him that he should be a good kid, and not to do anything bad. He becomes annoyed and impatient, saying, "You tell me this every day. I am not doing anything bad. I am not going to be bad. Why do you keep telling me this?" He loses his temper, like his father, though he has not been with his father since age 2.

I could tell Zhi Gao's mom was a typical Chinese mother. She kept saying the same thing again and again because of her concern about her son. However, as she repeated the words every day, Zhi Gao became very annoyed. I could sense her frustration at not knowing how to discipline Zhi Gao. She had a Chinese mother's traditional concern and tried to keep Zhi Gao focused, but his behavior, her work life, and her unfamiliarity with the Canadian system made it difficult.

I wondered aloud if the family breakup was a factor. She mused:

> When we were separated, Zhi Gao was little, so he didn't know much. But now he is 14 years old, so he understands things. I know Zhi Gao was not happy that I came to Toronto and married this man. I understand why Zhi Gao has changed so much. But this man is a nice person although he is an old type. He doesn't show his care in a loving way. He shows it in a harsh way and always tries to discipline the boy. Although he means to be really good for Zhi Gao, Zhi Gao takes it as a rejection and becomes rebellious...

This thought resonated with similar things some parents at the Parent Centre had said about Zhi Gao overhearing others gossiping about his mom's re-marriage when he played in the park.

Mr. Chan rejoined us and asked for my phone number. He asked me, "Please call me and let me know how Zhi Gao is doing at high school." I told him, "I only do my work in his elementary school, but if you want, I will go to the high school with you to talk with Zhi Gao's new teachers." Zhi Gao's mom said, "You understand Zhi Gao very well. You know his personality, his strengths and weaknesses. Zhi Gao always said Canadian teachers, English or Chinese, were very good, nice to him." I said, "Zhi Gao's homeroom teacher was very nice to Zhi Gao. But there is a language barrier, and you cannot communicate directly with each other." She said,

"I know. In China, we could talk with the teacher directly, but here we can't. Also the teacher isn't able to come to our home and talk directly to us like you are."

Our conversation turned back to Zhi Gao's habits. The mom wanted me to know he was still a good boy and said he often did his own laundry. She said he picked up the habit of showering every day, but she was worried about his eating habits, saying, "He eats very little, and looks so skinny." Her concern was valuable to hear because some teachers had been concerned about the boy's thinness and wondered about his family situation. I also remembered the boy told me that he seldom had breakfast, or if he did, it was a coke and bread.

It appeared that there were different tensions between Zhi Gao and his mom than between him and his stepfather. This showed up when we talked about how to divert the boy's attention from video games. She said Zhi Gao liked fishing. "The other day he brought two fish home. I was worried he was taking something he shouldn't have and asked him if the fish were his. He said, 'If you don't believe me, you can ask my teacher.'"

I said, "Oh, I remember that. I was with them when their teacher took them fishing at the Community Centre. Their teacher told the students to take the fish they caught home to show their parents."

We talked about the importance of trust and the value of an activity like fishing when so many boys were into games at the video parlor. I even suggested that she and her husband go fishing with Zhi Gao. At that point, Mr. Chan left to answer a knock at the door. Zhi Gao's mom said, "I know he likes fishing, but he does not like to go out with his stepfather." Mr. Chan returned and heard me saying that I lived near High Park. He said, "Oh yes, High Park. People go fishing there." "If you come to fish with Zhi Gao, we can go together," I responded.

The mother said that Zhi Gao's nature was such that, "If you show that you understand him, he listens; but otherwise, he becomes rebellious. You understand Zhi Gao. I appreciate that."

Scene II: Zhi Gao at High School

Fall, the 3rd Year, on the Phone with Zhi Gao's Mom
In September, two weeks after the new semester began, I called Zhi Gao's mom to see how he was doing in his high school. She was pleased to tell me that Zhi Gao was doing fine at the new school. He went to school on

time every morning and came home early. He did not stay out late in the evening. I asked her if there were any teachers in the high school who spoke Chinese. She said there was a Mandarin-speaking guidance teacher originally from Taiwan and a Cantonese-speaking social worker originally from Hong Kong. I also heard from other Chinese parents and students that students of Chinese origins were the majority in the school.

Zhi Hui had gone to a different high school. Late in the summer, before the new semester began, I visited Zhi Hui and his dad at their home. Zhi Hui was surprised when I gave him a glass of bubble tea, something he had asked me for many times in the past two years. "This is a reward, Zhi Hui. You have proved you are a good boy and you have made big progress. Here, I kept my promise!"

That fall, Zhi Hui returned to Bay Street Community School a few times to visit Ms. Corter, but Zhi Gao never did. Ms. Corter told me that once she bumped into Zhi Gao on the street and asked him how he was doing in high school. He didn't respond. As I had reduced my school visits, I did not meet Zhi Hui when he visited Ms. Corter. I phoned him in late November. He said he was doing fine in his high school. I asked him if he still hung around with Zhi Gao. He told me that he had not seen Zhi Gao for a long time, but had heard from other boys that Zhi Gao had stopped going to school. I was puzzled, for every time I phoned, Zhi Gao's mom told me that he left for school on time every day.

In the first week of December I called Zhi Gao's mother. She told me that she recently attended a parent–teacher interview and learned that Zhi Gao had been truant since early October. A social worker was working with him. I told the mom that she could give my phone number to the social worker in case he wanted to know about the boy's behavior in elementary school. She said it was the same social worker who had worked with Zhi Gao at Bay Street Community School. Zhi Gao's mom talked with me about Zhi Gao:

> He said the school was challenging and the schoolwork very difficult, so he didn't like going to school. He always left in the morning and came back home in the afternoon as if he were in school. Until we were called for the teacher-parent interviews, we thought he was in school every day. I am very worried. I don't know where he goes. This morning, he left early as usual, but now I don't know if he went to school or somewhere else. When I tried to follow him to see if he went to school, he shouted at me, saying, "If you follow me, I won't go to school. I will absolutely not go to school!" He has become more hot tempered and talks nastily back

to me when I try to discipline him. I am very worried that Zhi Gao will become a bad boy by wandering around and playing on the street.

I asked her how Zhi Gao behaved when the social worker talked with him. She said, "He was fine. He listened, but afterwards he said the schoolwork was too difficult, so he didn't want to go to school." She went on to say that, "His teachers in the high school are not as patient as the teachers were in his elementary school, so he felt he 'couldn't catch up'".

Following this new information, I called Zhi Gao's home several times, only to find more bad news. Zhi Gao was becoming increasingly bad tempered. He slammed the door on the social worker and would not let him in when he came to talk with Zhi Gao at home. The mom also found cigarettes in his room. During one of my calls, Zhi Gao's mom asked if I could talk with the boy as she believed he might listen to me.

Scene III: "No shame from the family should be made public 家丑不可外扬"

January 6, the 4th Year, Zhi Gao's Home
It was snowing heavily as Zhi Gao's mom answered the door. "Oh, Teacher. He is not home. Come in. It must be very cold outside." She looked upstairs nervously as she led me into the house. I wondered why. Later she explained that their upstairs tenant was "nosy." The tenant always asked about visitors, thinking that the visitor was there because Zhi Gao was in trouble again. The mom found this upsetting. There is a Chinese saying that, "Family shame should not be made public家丑不可外扬". The mother was shamed by Zhi Gao's difficulties.

The mom gave me a pair of slippers. As she led me to the kitchen, I noticed that the house appeared to have been cleaned for my visit. After shaking hands with Mr. Chan, we sat around the table exactly as we had on my first visit. Even the parents' worried facial expressions were the same. The mom showed me two sheets of paper listing Zhi Gao's attendance record. He had not been in school since November 20, 2004. She said:

> Now it is worse. He goes out around 10 o'clock at night and comes back about 5 o'clock in the next morning. I do not know where he goes and who he is with. He shouts at me and asks me not to follow him. He used to ask me for $2 or $3 for lunch money. Now he often asks for $20. He says he wants to fix the

computer. First it was $20, then $30 and then $75. If we refused, he would become really nasty, swearing at us with F-words. When he first asked for lunch money, I told him that I could bring him lunch to school. Zhi Gao said, "If you dared to come to my school, I would call a group of people to beat you up!" He is very rude to me. He says I am stupid and fussy.

She looked confused, saddened, and depressed. She said she did not know what to do. "I know he is not going to school. I know he is playing video games, but I don't know what to do about it." "Did he tell you what happened at school? Did he get into a fight with others?" I asked. She said:

Yes, I suspect he got into a fight with someone. In the middle of last semester, he came home and asked me for some medicine to put on his legs and arms. It looked like he had a bad fight. I asked him if he was involved in a fight, but he wouldn't tell me anything. Since then, he has refused to go to school.

She was sobbing. The stepfather shook his head and said, "Zhi Gao was nasty to his mom when she talked with him and asked him to go to school." Almost as if talking to herself, she sadly responded:

I asked him for the reason. It was not because of my remarriage that made him ashamed. Students used to make fun of him. He didn't want me to go to his school and said he would have me beaten up if I went to his school. I don't know why…

It was 5 o'clock. We had talked for over one hour, but the boy was not home yet. "He usually comes home around five. He came home yesterday a while after five." The mom said when she saw me looking at my watch, I could sense that she was afraid that I might leave before the boy got home.

I felt cold and put on my scarf. She noticed and said, "The roof is broken." I looked up and saw a large piece of ceiling over the stove was torn off. "Oh, you have to have someone fix the roof. It is getting colder because of the snowstorm." "No, we have to wait until the springtime when it is warm. Now it is too cold," she said. The parents were both wearing thin cotton shirts. "Don't you feel cold?" I asked. "No, we don't," they both said.

I wondered why they were not cold when I needed to put on my coat. Perhaps their worries overshadowed everything else. I also wondered if it was because of their tight budget that they could not have the roof fixed immediately, as the mom told me that she was no longer working.

Scene IV: Why Was Zhi Gao Unwilling to Go to School?

January 6, the 4th Year, Zhi Gao's Home
Two hours had passed and Zhi Gao had not come home. I asked for a piece of paper so that I could leave him a message. At that moment there were loud noises. Bang! The door to the kitchen was pushed open and Zhi Gao walked in. He looked surprised to see me. He wore a new black winter coat and a shiny left ear stud. His hair was dyed red. "Hi, Zhi Gao. Long time no see. How are you?" I stood up and greeted him. "Ok." He said casually and turned to leave. I held his arm. "Hey, Zhi Gao. Come and take a seat. I want to talk with you." "I am busy," he said impatiently. "Busy?! What are you busy about? Don't you tease me. What are you busy about?" He smiled. I said, "Come on. Don't tease me. How can you tell me you are busy and do not want to talk with me? I walked in the snowstorm all the way to your home and waited for you for over two hours. Come and sit here." I pulled him to the seat by his mom. "Is it cold outside? You look handsome in your nice new coat."

His parents left us alone. "Do you remember the song *Mom Cares About Me Most* 世上只有妈妈好?" I asked. "Yeah!" he replied. Though I knew it might irritate him, I reminded him of his parents' care and concern. I then asked him about school. "It is all right." "All right? How do you like your teachers?" "They are okay." "How are the students? Are they friendly and nice?" He didn't say anything.

"Were there students who were unfriendly to you? A girl told me that her sister was in the same high school as yours. Her sister didn't know what homework they had after each class. No one told her or help her. She cried a lot. How about you? Do you have any such difficulties?" I asked.

Zhi Gao played with his Walkman.

"Did you fight with other boys in the school?"

"Yes." Then he told me the story.

> We were playing basketball. The group came and grabbed our ball. We asked for our ball. They wouldn't give it back. Not only did they not give the ball back, they also beat us. So, I also went to find some people to fight with

them. But they had more people. They have a big gang, several dozens of them. They called their Big Brother from another gang to beat us. So...

So, that was why he stopped going to school. When asked, he told me that the gang who initiated the fight were Chinese students in the same school.

"Did you tell your teacher?" I asked. "Huh, teachers! Will they care?!" he said with a look of anger and mistrust.

I asked if he would like to change schools. He said yes and said that he would go to school if he was transferred to Zhi Hui's school. "That's good. It would be such a waste if you stopped going to school. You are very smart. You can study well. I know you can." I encouraged him. "No, I am not smart. I am stupid." He put his forehead on the table. "Ha, I know why: you've played video games too much. If you do not have enough sleep or do not eat properly, you will become really dumb," I teased. He sat up and smiled.

"It is all right to play video games. Almost all boys of your age play video games. But you've got to have a limit. You cannot play it the whole night. Kids at your age need sleep to grow tall and healthy. Stand up. Let me see how tall you've become." He stood up. "Mm. You are almost as tall as me, but you want to grow up into a tall man, right? You've got to eat more and sleep more. Don't go out at night. It is not safe. At your age, you don't know who are the bad guys." "What shall I do at home? It is so boring at home," he said.

"You are a smart boy. You are not going to get yourself involved in gang fights. You will study hard and get into university. You can make a difference in your life. Okay. Let's be clear. You will go to school after you are transferred to another school." "Okay," he said. "And you won't stay out late at night." "Okay," he said, seeming to listen.

"Good!" I got up and prepared to leave. His mom returned and thanked me, saying she was glad to hear he wanted to change schools. Zhi Gao spoke in Cantonese and his mom responded. He exploded, shouting at his mom. I pulled him aside. "What's wrong? Why are you upset?" Mom said he asked for $25 for a cable connection to the Internet, but she would not be able to check his time on cable as she could on the phone line. Hearing this, Zhi Gao shouted, "The telephone line is so slow. You stupid!" "Zhi Gao!" I intervened, "You can't talk to your mom like that." He became quiet and sat with his head lowered. His stepfather came in and said something in Cantonese. Zhi Gao jumped up, shouted, and ran out. I ran after him and blocked him by the door. "Zhi Gao, don't talk to your mom and dad like that." He shouted, "He is not my father! I call him Uncle for the sake of my mom. He is stingy when I ask him for two dollars. He is a niggard!"

"Why should he give you money? How would you feel if I shouted at you and talked to you nastily?" I spoke quite severely to Zhi Gao, "Your parents are not rich. Look, they live a simple life. You've got to understand that they are doing their best to care about you. Now get inside. It is too cold outside. Don't go out at night."

Zhi Gao returned to the kitchen with me. Again his mom said something in Cantonese. Zhi Gao shouted and ran out, slamming the door.

I walked home in the chilly snowy night, wondering where Zhi Gao had gone and when he would come home. When he did come home, it seemed that the lines of communication with his parents were so badly ruptured that I wondered what would happen.

The parents appeared desperate, not knowing what to do, waiting anxiously at home, fearing a visit from the police. Meanwhile, though the argument I witnessed was over money, it was apparent from Zhi Gao's new coat, Walkman, and ear stud that the parents had tried their best to meet his requests. The family's desperate situation urged me to develop thoughts of a Parents' Aid organization, complementing the Children's Aid Society.

Scene V: "Children's Aid did not come"

January 7, the 4th Year, on the Phone with Zhi Gao and his Mom
After an almost sleepless night, I called Zhi Gao's home in the morning and asked if he came home last night. The mom said:

> Yes, he did. He came home early last night and didn't go out again. You told him not to stay out. He listened to you. I washed his clothes and asked him to help make supper. He did. After we watched TV, he went to bed. Thank you, Teacher.

I called again in the evening. The mom said she talked with Zhi Gao's high-school teacher, who told her to call the police if Zhi Gao stayed out all night or did something bad. When she talked to the teacher about transferring Zhi Gao to another school, she was told that it was difficult to change schools midterm and they might have to wait until next

September. We wondered what would happen during the eight-month wait. She went on to say that Zhi Gao fell during the day and hurt his hand. She took him to the hospital emergency, but there was such a long line-up that Zhi Gao became impatient and they returned home without seeing a doctor. He was now in bed. I suggested she see a family doctor but she said that would take two weeks. This reminded me of another parent's lament about how slowly things worked in Canada. Moreover, she said the Children's Aid did not come because they had too many urgent cases.

When I hung up, I reflected that even when the parents took initiatives rather than merely waiting helplessly at home, little was accomplished. I also wondered how successful a move to Zhi Hui's school would be, even if the move occurred quickly. I heard from other parents that the school had a high dropout rate.

Interlude

At the Verge of the Cliff

Aware of their urgent need for professional help, I obtained contact information for local community centers and services for Zhi Gao's parents. Carmen recommended several organizations and schools. Freeman drew a map for the mom to find a center with Cantonese speaking service. I accompanied her to another community center to help her find the Cantonese service there. But Zhi Gao's mom continued to call me, sometimes late at night, telling me her worries and frustrations. She did not follow up on all the leads. Also, there were no follow-ups from the services I helped her to make contact with.

From January to March, with three to five messages left on my home phone by the mom almost every week, I continued to search for professional help for the family. I also contacted the local school board trustee for help. The trustee, a former community-oriented principal, understood the boy's problem and recommended a special All-ESL school. Zhi Gao would normally need to have an assessment before being admitted to the school. After discussing Zhi Gao's situation and the likelihood he would resist an assessment, the trustee negotiated an appointment with the school without the normal assessment. He asked me if I could translate for the family as the family had to find an interpreter themselves.

I called Zhi Gao's home in mid-afternoon of March 8, with this good news. "What? What's up?" an irritated male voice greeted me. "XXX (Swear)! I am sleeping. You woke me up!" It was Zhi Gao.

"Oh, Zhi Gao. Sorry. Sorry to wake you up. Why are you sleeping at this hour of the day?" "太白了(Bored)! Nothing to do." "How is everything?" "Nothing. Boring."

We talked for over one hour. Mainly he complained about his parents and I tried to counter his views. "Stinger. XXX (swear)! He won't give me any money." He said he recently lost his new coat when he was out all night. "Ask my mom to buy me another coat. Ask my stepfather to buy me a ticket to go back to China. I will go back to school after I come back from China." The reason for his willingness to transfer to Zhi Hui's school came to light when he said, "Over 200 students at Zhi Hui's school dropped out of school and no one bothered them." He complained about being "bugged" by the social worker.

I asked him what he wanted to be in the future as he said he "would rather die than going to school". He said he wanted to be a hooligan 流氓. I said, "You are a smart boy, a good boy. Why do you want that?" He said, "Those who became hooligans had no choice. They are not necessarily villains."

My heart sank. "No one is forcing you to become a hooligan. Everyone is trying to help you. The social worker, your teachers, your parents, and myself keep talking with you because we care about you and want the best out of you."

I told Zhi Gao about the All-ESL school. He said childishly, "Is it fun? You go there first to find it out for me."

Later that evening I talked with Zhi Gao's mom about the All-ESL school, and also with the social worker who phoned me. He said Zhi Gao was not his responsibility as the boy had left Bay Street Community School, but because he thought the boy could be saved, based on what he knew of Zhi Gao in elementary school, he was helping. Now he was disappointed and exhausted and felt like giving up. He said, "I have been a social worker for 20 years and have never seen a child as rude and hot-tempered as Zhi Gao. I have eight schools to cover. I have spent much more time on Zhi Gao than is expected." I understood how the social worker felt. I also felt sad and exhausted. Others had been telling me that his helpers could do little unless Zhi Gao decided to change.

That evening, Zhi Gao's mom told me that she saw a note the boy put on his door saying, "I am going to listen to my parents and go to school. So please don't bother me." He had another note posted over his bed, saying. "Don't get addicted to video games." We both felt these notes showed Zhi Gao's struggle: He wanted to be good, but did not know how to face the challenges in his life and he lacked role models and self-discipline to make positive changes. We ended our conversation with our hope that Zhi Gao would come home early that night for the next morning's appointment. Although I agreed to accompany the family for the appointment, I also phoned the social worker to see if he could go together with us to provide professional support and make connections between the two schools. I only reached his voice mail.

I woke at 6:30 the following morning after an almost sleepless night. I wondered how Zhi Gao was and how this day would unfold. My phone rang at 7 a.m. It was the social worker who said he could not go to the school with us until next week due to his packed schedule. I explained that this was the only appointment we could get before March Break. I called Zhi Gao's mom. She said the boy left home last night and was not back home yet. The day wore on. Zhi Gao's mom and I called each other, back and forth. The boy did not return for our trip to the morning appointment. The appointment never did take place, and eventually Zhi Gao left school altogether.

When it became clear that Zhi Gao would not make his appointment, Zhi Gao's mom was deflated and said she felt depressed. She said, "Everyone has tried their best to help him, but he does not listen. It is his choice not to be a good person. He wants to be a bad person. He made friends with bad people (desperate sigh). It looks like there is no choice now: Either he dies or I die. I don't know what to do. I feel like I am going crazy..."

点评:

SHI JING'S REFLECTION

Zhi Gao's case gave me a strong sense of helplessness, frustration, and defeat. I wonder why the boy, at the verge of the cliff, seemed to refuse to take the many hands reaching out to him. Is the boy failing the schooling system or is the system failing the boy? Children's Aid works hard for mistreated children. Where is the help, I wonder, for despairing parents like Zhi Gao's mom, whose dreams of a better life and education for their children in a new country are shattered?

My work with Zhi Gao's family, and other newcomer families, led me to reflect on the many visible and invisible boundaries in a school system filled with well-intended programs and rich supporting resources. My reflections on these matters are presented in Chapters 8 and 9.

From a narrative point of view, Zhi Gao's fragmented school life and family life were further fragmented on the cross-cultural landscapes of schools in transition. When he went to high school, he lost the circle of new friends he had made at Bay Street Community School during his first years of arrival in a new country. Before he had made sense of the cross-cultural schooling in the elementary school, with little English, he was further challenged in high school, which to a great extent operates differently from the elementary school. The friendship among the newcomer boys and girls was special, as they had initially met one another on their first arrival in Canada at the Newcomer Support Class at Bay Street Community School. The friendship served as a special bond. As another newcomer boy Jia Ming explained (see Chapter 7), this was due to the fact that they were in the same boat and they helped and supported one another through difficult times in their lives. This kind of support disappeared when their life paths diverged in high schools. Zhi Gao's improved behavior at Bay Street Community School suggested that there were possibilities to prevent the boy from falling off the cliff. Teachers and supporting staff and community services could work together in a consistent and caring way, to weave an interrelated and interwoven net that could catch the boy whenever and wherever he was falling, and help and support the family with needs-based approaches. Of course, it is difficult to change the way the system operates as it involves so many people and factors. It also takes time for people to make changes in their habitual ways of thinking and doing things. However, I wonder what needs to be done in terms of the education of teachers, educational leaders, social workers, and community workers, as well as policymakers, to find ways to bridge the gaps in the somewhat fragmented system in order to prevent boys like Zhi Gao from falling in-between. I discuss these matters in more depth in Chapters 8 and 9.

Note

1. A small part of Zhi Gao's story was quoted in the discussion of ethical considerations in my cross-cultural studies in the following chapter: Xu, S. J. (2015). Ethical boundaries and considerations in cross-cultural narrative inquiry (Ch 10, pp. 136–151). In Sheila Trahar and Yu Wai Ming (Eds.). *Using Narrative Inquiry for Educational Research in the Asia Pacific*. Routledge, Taylor and Francis Group.

CHAPTER 6

Life in Transition: Newcomer Boy Yang Yang

生活在变迁: 福建男孩洋洋的故事

Prologue

Yang Yang[1] 洋洋 is a 14-year-old boy from Fujian 福建 China (Xu et al. 2007). I did not meet Yang Yang until the spring of the second year of my time in the school when he came to Bay Street Community School to attend Grade 7. Yang Yang had spent his first two years in Canada at another Toronto school, starting in a regular Grade 5 class. At Bay Street Community School, Yang Yang was located in the Newcomer Support Class due to his limited English. The Newcomer Support Class covered the regular curriculum at ESL standards for Grade 7/8 first-year newcomer students who have little or no English. Like most of the newcomer Grades 7 and 8 students at the school, Yang Yang came from Fujian China, a coastal province where, for centuries, people have had a tradition of making a living overseas. In the summer of the third year, during one of my home visits, Zhi Hui 智辉's dad, father of Yang Yang's classmate, told me this tradition could be traced back 600 years to the Ming Dynasty. At that time, Zheng He 郑和 (1371–1435), a Chinese mariner, set sail from Fujian on his seven journeys across the oceans to the West (郑和七次下西洋. It was recorded that Zheng He's first voyage started from Nanjing, with Fujian coast as his base for his later voyages, reaching as far as the Persian Gulf and Africa from 1403 to 1433). Zhi Hui's father said that Fujian men took pride in Zheng He and that a Fujian man would be at risk of not finding a wife if he lacked the courage to make a living overseas. Zhi Hui's father's story suggested an important cultural image that might be shared by the Fujianese. This seemed, to some extent, to answer a question that puzzled me: "Why did so many Fujian people try hard to leave China to make a living overseas, sometimes at the risk of their lives?"

As accounted in the previous chapters, I met Zhi Hui and other newcomer students in the fall of my first year at the Parent Centre when Mr. Anderson, the Newcomer Support Class teacher, brought students there for the Buddy Reading Program. As Zhi Hui and other boys always seemed to turn the Parent Centre and their classroom upside down, I became a helper first during the Buddy Reading Program, and then in the Newcomer Support Class.

Zhi Hui and other boys had nicknamed almost everyone in the class. Soon, Yang Yang was given a nickname. Whenever Carmen, the staff member of the Parent Centre, mentioned *goldfish, turtle,* or *monkey* while reading storybooks to the children at Circle Time, the boys from the Newcomer Support Class would roar in laughter. "What is the story behind the goldfish?" Carmen asked one day. The boys started vying with one another to tell us who had what nicknames including *Roaster* and *Bubble Tea,* names created to make fun of one another.

Unlike Zhi Hui 智辉, Zhi Gao 志高 and other boys, whose names were often listed on the blackboard or who were often sent to the Main Office by Mr. Anderson due to misbehavior, Yang Yang 洋洋 never got into such trouble. He was quiet and almost invisible among the noisy and naughty boys. He would smile shyly or dodge away when picked on by others. I never heard anything critical of him until I got to know his parents. I was surprised by unexpected stories unfolding in Yang Yang's life.

Episode One: Yang Yang's Father's Concerns

Scene I: *Yang Yang's Father Came to the School Council Meeting*

November 17, the 2nd Year, at the School Library
Early in the week Ms. Steadman, the school principal, asked me to help translate at the School Council meeting on Wednesday evening. At 6:00 p. m., I saw Yang Yang and his father come in with some Chinese parents. His father said that Yang Yang never told him what was going on in the school, nor showed him anything from the school. This was the first time Yang Yang told him anything about the school, and hence the father's first

time at the School Council meeting. At the meeting, a Community Representative presented fund-raising initiatives for after-school programs. Yang Yang's father, Freeman, Mr. Feng, Jia Ming's mom, and Hong Hong's mom volunteered to organize the fund-raising activity.

"Hi, young man, help us move the tables," Ms. Steadman said to Yang Yang when the meeting was over at 8:00 p.m. We helped to tidy the room.

I left the school together with the Chinese parents. I said goodbye to Freeman, Jia Ming's mom, and Hong Hong's mom as I decided not to walk together through the park with them as I usually did. I walked with Yang Yang and his father toward the opposite direction where I could still catch a bus to the subway. At the entrance to the school building, I bumped into Julian's grandma who came to the ESL evening class in the basement of the school. "Oh, you are still here?!" She was surprised to see me. I told her I had attended the School Council meeting. "Oh, are you alone? Do you have anyone for company? You'd better hurry. Go home early. Don't go home so late. Go! Go home early. Hurry!" I knew why Julian's grandma was so worried. There had been quite a few robberies last month in the neighborhood, with one incident taking place in the park and one on the very street I was passing by.

Scene II: *Yang Yang's Father's Expectations and Worries*

November 17, the 2nd Year, on the Way Home After the Meeting
I caught up with Yang Yang and his father. Yang Yang's father said that his boy was too quiet and never spoke to him about what was going on at school. I mentioned the after-school programs introduced at the meeting. I also suggested he check with community centres and register Yang Yang in some programs. The father said that his boy was only interested in playing video games at a local Chinese mall. He and his wife hoped that Yang Yang would learn English well, but felt that he was not studying.

The father said that they had warned the boy that if he did not study hard he would be sent back to China. He and his wife thought that it might be better for Yang Yang to attend school in China to at least learn something useful in Chinese. If he stayed in Toronto, spending his time playing video games, he would learn neither English nor Chinese.

Yang Yang's father said that it was his fault that Yang Yang did not study. He had left the boy in China with his grandparents for 10 years. At first I thought it was four years as *four* 四 and *ten* 十 in Chinese sound very similar especially in a southern accent. "Was it four years?" I asked. "No, ten years." The father said that he had been out of China for 11 years and had set up business in Toronto. I did not ask what business he was in.

Yang Yang's father said his English was bad, but he could manage daily conversation in his business, where, he said, he picked up some English. He hoped Yang Yang could learn English well so that the boy could have a better life and would not have to struggle as he had. Thinking of my conversation with Jia Ming's mom and Hong Hong's mom earlier before the meeting, I said, "Students have to do well in high school so as to get into university even though there are no entrance exams here". Yang Yang's father sighed.

> I do not have that high expectation of Yang Yang. I do not expect him to get into university, but I hope that he can learn English well enough to assimilate and survive in this society. But he doesn't seem to see the point. He just plays and doesn't study hard. He watches TV at home.

"Does he watch TV in English?" I asked. "He watches TV in Chinese." The father looked at Yang Yang. The boy was quiet, walking between us. "You might suggest he watch TV in English. That may help him with his English." I said, "You can talk with your wife about it."

"She is pregnant with the second child. I am out to work before six in the morning and back home after ten at night. I have almost no time to see him. He doesn't listen to his mom. She is due very soon. She cannot run after him."

The father said that he had little time to take care of the boy before. Now he wanted to pay more attention to him and his studies. That was why he volunteered for the fund-raising activity at the School Council meeting.

I asked Yang Yang why he did not get into after-school programs. He said, "Those programs are just sports. I do not like playing soccer or basketball." "What about those programs that help kids with math and English?" I asked. Yang Yang shook his head. He did not remember where he had put the flyers about those programs.

Episode Two: Yang Yang at School

Yang Yang was a quiet shy boy, never associated with any trouble making at school. Unlike Zhi Gao, Zhi Hui and some boys who often attracted a lot of attention by misbehaving, Yang Yang was invisible among the loud and naughty boys.

Scene I: *Yang Yang at the Math Tutorial*

November 13, the 2nd Year, Newcomer Support Class
The boys were sitting at the back tables. They could hardly be quiet for a second. Zhi Hui and Zhi Gao were fighting for a pencil. Other boys were talking to one another loudly in words that sounded very rude or nasty. Sometimes, someone got offended and started an argument, but in a minute they talked and laughed together again. I was totally confused by these boys.

Mr. Feng had some algebra questions on the poster such as "$-(-21+3) - (-16-5)*(15-13)=$ ". He explained the concept of the negative and the positive. Xiu Hua soon got it and figured out the correct answer in a minute.

The boys were still confused. They could not figure out that $(-21+3) = -18$. They got 24 instead. Jack went to ask Xiu Hua. She explained it to him. Xiao Qiang went to ask her, too.

I told Mr. Feng that the boys were still confused. He asked them to go back to their seats. It took Mr. Feng quite a few minutes to discipline the boys. Even the boys themselves got impatient. "All right. All right! Stop preaching to us. Just show us how to do the math."

"Then you've got to keep quiet. You are talking to one another and none of you are listening." I waved my hand to stop Zhi Gao and Zhi Hui from talking.

Mr. Feng said, "Let's imagine. You owe me $9 and you have only $5 in your pocket."

"Here is five dollars." Zhi Gao shouted. He pulled out a 5-dollar bill from his pocket and put it on the desk.

Eventually most boys understood how to do the math, but Yang Yang still did not understand. Some boys laughed at him.

Scene II: *Making a Bridge out of Straws*

November 21, the 2nd Year, at Newcomer Support Class
Ms. Corter engaged the newcomer students in a bridge-making project. She told me she was going to ask the students to make bridges across the gap between two tables and that the bridge should be sturdy enough to hold an egg. She divided the students into two groups and then she moved three tables to make two big gaps in between. The students said, "Wow, it

is so wide." Ms. Corter gave them several bags of straws and asked them to make bridges out of the straws. Ms. Corter gave them a few ideas as to how to connect the straws without supplements such as tapes and glues. She used scissors to cut a few holes on the straws and then connected them. She asked the students to work in teams. The girls started working together, but the boys worked individually and some fooled around, disturbing others.

A boy who had just arrived from China was sitting there watching. He had the straws connected into the shape of a big ring and hung the ring around his neck as he sucked another straw in his mouth with a boring look on his face. I said, "Why aren't you helping with the bridge-making?" He said, "What is the point of doing this? It is boring." We were talking in Chinese. He could not speak English.

Quite a few other boys got bored, too. They did not seem to get the point of making bridges out of straws, and it seemed impossible to them that the straws could be put together without the help of tape.

Ms. Corter said that she knew it was difficult for them to make bridges out of straws. She gave them this material just to see what they could make, and what ideas they could think of. Next week, she was going to teach them more concepts about how to make a bridge, and then eventually, she hoped they would understand the concept of a bridge, mathematically, and also in terms of language.

I could see that the students responded to the idea of making bridges out of straws differently. Quite a few boys, like Zhi Gao, Zhi Hui, and Jack, got very bored. Although Zhi Hui was not making the bridge in his own group, he was running around helping others whenever he thought somebody needed help.

Yang Yang told me it was too difficult to connect the straws.

"Yes, the straws are soft. You are not allowed to use tape, but the teacher gave you the scissors." I said, "Did you see how your teacher cut a hole in some straws and connected them together? You can think what kind of bridge you have in your hometown and how you can make your straw bridge strong and sturdy."

He said, "Oh, okay, I have an idea."

He started working by himself. He made holes in five or six straws and then he cut a straw into shorter pieces and sharpened the ends of the shorter pieces. After a while, he put the five or six long straws tightly together with the sharpened shorter ones in between. The first piece he made for his straw bridge looked quite sturdy.

I said, "Oh, that is a very good idea. Excellent!"

He was encouraged and pleased. Zhi Hui came and jumped to help. Yang Yang started to dissemble the connected straws. Zhi Hui insisted on not dissembling the connected piece, saying, "Oh, since you have connected them, don't pull them apart."

Yang Yang had tried out his idea with only one hole on each straw; now he wanted to disconnect the straws to cut more holes from one end to the other so that he could insert more short pieces in between the straws. The two boys had a disagreement about this. Yang Yang took the straws away from Zhi Hui and moved to a table near the window. Zhi Hui went to another table where the girls were working together.

Ms. Corter came over and said, "Oh, Yang Yang, you are doing a good job. It is a good idea. Do you want somebody else to come and help you? Would you like to work with the group?"

Yang Yang said, "No."

I explained to the teacher that Yang Yang moved to another table to do the work by himself because he felt Zhi Hui was more disturbing than helping. Ms. Corter let him do it the way he wanted, but once in a while she would go and talk with him to see how he was doing and to encourage him.

Episode Three: Yang Yang Back to China?

Yang Yang appeared to be unnoticed in class most of the time. However, his life out of school took people in school by surprise. The quiet boy became the major character of a home–school drama.

Scene I: Parent–Teacher Interview

December 4, the 2nd Year, at Newcomer Support Class

Zhi Gao's and Yang Yang's parents did not come to the Parent–Teacher Interview. Ms. Corter was not sure if the parents got the information from their boys or not. She said that she was especially worried about Yang Yang. She heard from other students that his parents wanted to send him back to China. Ms. Corter told me her heart went out to the boy when she learned that he had lived with his grandparents for many years in China before finally joining his parents in Toronto.

Understanding Canadian family values, I knew it was hard to imagine that Canadian parents would leave their children with their grandparents in another country for 10 years. On the other hand, because of my acquaintance with Chinese families who came to Canada with refugee status, I knew that it took many years for them to obtain legal status in Canada. They also had to work very hard for years in Chinese grocery stores, restaurants and clothing factories before being able to sponsor other family members. From my conversations with Yang Yang's father earlier, I understood that the boy's parents meant to be good to him, even if they sent him back to China. Part of their purpose in coming to Canada was to obtain a better education for Yang Yang; yet, he was doing little except playing video games.

Ms. Corter and I went downstairs to the Main Office. She pulled Yang Yang's files from a drawer. I called Yang Yang's home number. "Sorry, the number you have dialed is out of service." I tried the cell phone number, got voice mail, and left a message. I tried the business number. A woman answered the phone. I said I would like to talk to Mr. Zhao. 赵先生. "We have two Mr. Zhao-s, which one do you want to talk to?" "His child is at Bay Street School, Yang Yang." Then Yang Yang's mother came to the phone and said that Yang Yang had been sick, so they did not know about the interview. I explained that the teacher would like to report on Yang Yang's progress. Yang Yang's mom said she would come after 6:00 p.m. She didn't.

Scene II: Is *Yang Yang* returning to China?

January, the 3rd Year, Newcomer Support Class
After the winter holidays, I returned to school. Ms. Corter waved at me anxiously and said: "Shi Jing! They are sending Yang Yang back to China!"

"Really?! Maybe the family is taking him back to China just for the Chinese New Year," I said.

"I hope so, too," Ms. Corter sighed.

Ms. Corter asked me if I could call the family and ask if they would let Yang Yang come to school to say goodbye.

I went downstairs to the Main Office and called Yang Yang's home. His mother said that she had to go to China for a celebration of her new baby when she was 100 days old. Yang Yang's grandparents missed him very much and asked the mom to bring Yang Yang back to China.

I asked her if she would bring Yang Yang back to Canada or leave him at home with his grandparents. The mom said it would be up to Yang

Yang. She said that they would transfer him to another school even if Yang Yang decided to come back to Canada.

The mom sighed when she talked about Yang Yang not studying hard and playing video games. She said she had just had the new baby and had infections. She could not run after him.

I told Yang Yang's mother his teacher and classmates would like to say goodbye before he went to China. She said that she would ask Yang Yang to come to school tomorrow.

Scene III: Newcomer Students' Farewell Party for Yang Yang

January 24, 2the 3rd Year, Newcomer Support Class
Yang Yang came with his aunt. I went outside and talked with them. The students jumped up and jammed together by the door. "Hey, 烤炉 (Roaster)! 烤炉 (Roaster)! Why are you leaving? When are you going back to China? When do you come back?"

His aunt asked him to get his stuff from his locker. Yang Yang put everything in his locker into his bag without responding to his classmates' questions. His aunt said, "Now you go to the classroom. Everyone is waiting for you."

Yang Yang smiled shyly as everyone's attention was focused on him. His face went red. He came into the classroom.

"Yang Yang, so nice to see you," Ms. Corter said. "Remember to get your things from your desk." She found a plastic bag for him. Yang Yang emptied his desk. Ms. Corter asked him to sit at the teacher's desk in front of the students' desks that were arranged in a shape of horseshoe. Xiao Mei 小梅 gave him the card made by the class with everyone's signature and a gift wrapped nicely and tied with a red ribbon.

Yang Yang sat there quietly. He didn't seem to know what to say. He just smiled.

The boys and girls asked Yang Yang many questions:

"Where are you going?"
"Are you going back to China?"
"Are you going to attend school there?"
"Are you coming back?"
"When are you coming back?"

Yang Yang's aunt answered most of the questions as Yang Yang simply said, "Uh" or "Mm". The aunt said:

It will depend on Yang Yang. If he chooses to stay, he can stay and attend school in China. If he doesn't like it, he will come back, but he will go to a school in Brampton. His father has a new store there. He likes it there better. So Yang Yang will go to a school in Brampton instead of coming back to this school.

"Where is Brampton?" the boys and girls asked Yang Yang. Yang Yang didn't know where Brampton was. They were talking in Chinese. I explained to Ms. Corter what the kids were talking about. She said Brampton was only one-hour drive away from Toronto. It was not too far away.

"Oh, where is my important letter?" Zhi Gao suddenly exclaimed. "Oh. It must be in 烤炉(Roaster)'s bag." He ran to search for it in Yang Yang's plastic bag that held things from his desk. "Oh, yeah! Here it is." Zhi Gao found his letter in Yang Yang's bag. Other students laughed at him: "You misplaced your stuff into Yang Yang's desk, and you blame Yang Yang."

"Ah, this is a very important document. I will become a lawyer. You will be fined $1000 for your misbehavior." Zhi Gao talked in an authoritative voice that he thought made him sounded like a lawyer. "My letter is very important. I need to keep it well."

Zhi Hui suddenly came back from Room 46. "Hey, Brother Yang 洋哥! You are here." He looked very excited to see Yang Yang. Ms. Corter said he was supposed to be at Room 46, the regular class. Zhi Hui did not want to go back to Room 46. He sat there, talking and laughing with the other boys. He teased Yang Yang, "Hey, Roaster 烤炉. Go to 少林寺 (Shao Lin Temple)." Shao Lin Temple 少林寺 is a temple in China well known for martial art since ancient times. Also, in the old days, some people would become monks in temples located in big mountains when they felt disillusioned with the human world.

"Oh, yeah. Go to 少林寺 (Shao Lin Temple)!" Other boys followed and all the boys and girls laughed.

Ms. Corter didn't get it and asked me what the joke was about. Then she said, "Oh, that's good. When you are back, you could teach us all some martial art."

Yang Yang sat quietly and smiled shyly. He did not seem to know what to say when the boys kept asking him questions and teasing him. For a few minutes, no one was talking. The boys who had always had difficulty keeping quiet for a second in class seemed to have difficulty finding what to say at the moment.

"Ah, it looks like before a wedding when people don't know what to say," Wen Jun 文军 said.

"Yeah. It is just like that," Xiao Qiang 小强 responded.

The class fell into silence again. Yang Yang's aunt said if there was not anything else, she had to go back to work. Yang Yang stood up and said goodbye to all. Wen Jun and Xiao Qiang said, "Oh, Yang Yang, you can stay until the end of the school day." But Yang Yang left with his aunt.

When I saw them off in the hallway, Yang Yang's aunt said that Yang Yang's parents did not like the boy playing video games with other Chinese boys in the school. They would like him to stay away from the downtown neighborhood.

Episode Four: Yang Yang Working in His Family Store?

Nothing seemed to be noticeably changed in the Newcomer Support Class after Yang Yang left. However, he was not out of people's mind. Moreover, the climax of his life drama was yet to come.

Scene I: Yang Yang at His Family Store

February 25, the 3rd Year, Yang Yang's Family Bakery

"Teacher, I saw Yang Yang at his dad's store last week," a girl said.

"Really? Are you sure?" I could not believe my ears.

"Yes, I saw him, too. He was working there," another girl said.

"We will have to call Children's Aid if it is true," said a teacher who worked closely with Ms. Corter.

"Would you like me to talk with the mom again to see what happened before you talk to the office and call Children's Aid?" I asked.

The teacher thought it was a good idea.

I asked the girls which store they were talking about. Then I realized what they were referring to – the big bakery where I often shopped in the past five years.

I went into the store with which I was so familiar. I walked to the back of the store. I saw a boy behind a counter. Yang Yang was in a white uniform, which made him look somewhat taller than the Yang Yang in my memory. "Is it true that his family had him quit school and work in the family store for a living?" I watched Yang Yang from a distance with questions in my mind. I know it is not unusual for a child of Yang Yang's age to start working to help the family make a living in rural China. It is not rare for children to help their parents with light labor in the field during sowing and harvesting seasons. By comparison, working in a bakery was easy. Still, I doubted Yang Yang's parents intended to have him drop out of school to work in the bakery. I wondered why Yang Yang's parents seemed to have misled the school. Why did Yang Yang appear to be working in the store?

I returned to the school and told the teacher, "I didn't get a chance to talk with Yang Yang. I think we need to talk with the family to know what is really happening before calling Children's Aid. Would you like me to call his home to get an explanation?"

I knew I would immediately call Children's Aid if I were a non-Chinese teacher. But as a Chinese, the situation puzzled me. Hui Lan, a parent I knew at the Parent Centre, told me she and her husband planned to send their eldest son to work in a Chinese grocery store to learn about life. She said she had a friend whose son did not study hard. Her friend sent the boy to work in a fish store, telling him that he would end up there for the rest of his life if he did not study hard. The boy was asked to sell fish in the cold wind last winter for just one day. That was enough to teach the boy a lesson. Since then, he had been good at school. So, Hui Lan told her son if he did not study hard, he would end up laboring in grocery stores.

With this thought, I wondered if Yang Yang's parents were thinking the same way and if it was their way of pushing Yang Yang not to play video games and to teach him to study hard. I asked the teachers not to call Children's Aid until I talked with Yang Yang or a family member.

Scene II: Talking With Yang Yang's Mom

February 26, the 3rd Year, a Pay Phone
I called Yang Yang's home from my office. Nobody answered. I remembered that when I called Chinese parents for the principal, many parents would not answer. One mother explained that she would not answer when she saw the number appear with an English name as she could not speak English. Since I was calling from the office and an English name would appear, I went downstairs to the lobby and called from a payphone. Yang Yang's mom answered. I told her Yang Yang's teacher asked me to call because some of his classmates saw him working in the bakery.

"Oh, no, no. He only went to the bakery over the weekend. He is not working there."

"But, I saw him yesterday. He was working. The school said they were going to call Children's Aid. I told the school I heard you say that Yang Yang's father was opening a new store in Brampton. At Yang Yang's farewell party, Yang Yang's aunt also said that you were going to have Yang Yang go to school in Brampton. The school would like to know why Yang Yang was seen working in your family store."

The mother said that Yang Yang would not listen to her.

> He always went to the nearby Chinese shopping mall to play video games. One day his father went to the mall three times to catch him. I gave him money for food, but he spent it on playing video games.

Yang Yang's mom told me attached to the bakery was a store, also belonging to the family, where they sold Chinese magazines, household necessities, and stationery. What upset the parents most was that, last winter, the boy stole from the store.

> Some boys in his class said to Yang Yang, "It is your father's store. You can take anything you like." As he is the son of the boss, the staff couldn't say anything. He would sell the items at one dollar each to the boys in his class and then go to play video games with them. So, that's why we do not want Yang Yang to go to this school any more.

The mom said that she and Yang Yang's father wanted him to study in a boarding school in Mississauga. It would cost $20,000 a year. They bought a house in Brampton and were going to move. They were waiting for admission to the boarding school.

The mom said she could not discipline Yang Yang too harshly. She said that, in Canada, parents were not allowed to spank their children. But Yang Yang was stealing. The parents were very worried. Earlier they had threatened to send Yang Yang back to China to push him to study hard. But he no longer took their warnings seriously. So they took him out of school to show him they were serious. They could not allow him to develop a habit of stealing. "If he cannot be a good student, at least he should become a good man 不成材, 要成人, hard-working like his father," the mom said with a sigh.

Yang Yang's mom said that they hired a tutor for Yang Yang at $25 an hour. This amount of money meant a lot to many Chinese people who worked at grocery stores or restaurants at only $5 to $10 an hour. The tutor said Yang Yang was hopeless. He was not listening. He would not use an exercise book and instead wrote on napkins. It made the tutor very upset.

I said, "If you want, I could talk with Yang Yang. Yang Yang listened when I talked with him in his class. Yang Yang is a good boy. He is quiet. He is shy. That may be why he looks as if he is not responding."

The mother said that he was good in front of other people. At home he was quiet, but did not want to study. He would either go out to play video games or stay at home watching TV until 2 o'clock in the morning and then sleep until noon.

I asked why she let him watch TV that late. She said they didn't. But after they went to bed, he would turn on the TV and turn down the volume. This made the parents very upset. It was the reason why they wanted him to study at a boarding school.

"It is okay in China for you to have Yang Yang work in your family store," I said, "But in Canada you will get into trouble as children are not allowed to work until age 16. Yesterday I wanted to talk with Yang Yang and let him know about the legal restrictions here in Canada."

EPISODE FIVE: YANG YANG'S MOM'S CONCERNS AND HOPES

Scene I: *Yang Yang's Ups and Downs*

Spring and Summer, the 3rd Year, on the Phone with Yang Yang's Mom
Yang Yang eventually went to a public school in Brampton, close to his father's new bakery. Later his mom told me he was not admitted into the boarding school because of his limited English. Ms. Corter told me she called Yang Yang's new teacher and was pleased that she was a very nice, experienced teacher.

I also talked with Yang Yang's mom a few times over the phone and received good news that Yang Yang liked the new school and was no longer playing video games. He was doing well. The mom said that the boy cared for nothing before, but now he would call home and ask how everybody was. He would ask the mom to take care of herself as she was still not feeling well. She was very pleased. Yang Yang's teacher at his new school encouraged him to take swimming lessons and play basketball and soccer so that he was distracted from video games.

I was pleased with the good news. The mom thanked me for caring about Yang Yang and asked me to visit. I said I would like to come when Yang Yang was home.

In the summer I called Yang Yang's mom. She said Yang Yang became lazy during summer holidays and would not help with housework. He acted like he did before he went to Brampton. She said she and the dad worked late and got home after 10 or 11 p.m.

She said that she was strict with Yang Yang for the sake of being good to him. She wanted him to have a good education and be a good person. She said her own mother died when she was three and her father was sick. There were five children in her family. Her eldest brother, at Yang Yang's age, took on the responsibilities of raising her and her siblings.

Yang Yang's mom said that he had changed since they took him away from the downtown neighborhood and sent him to the Brampton school last spring. However, she was unhappy about his behavior this summer.

The mom said her husband was working very hard. She hoped that Yang Yang would be like his father and would help the father when he grew up. They had two stores, but were going to sell the Brampton store because of poor business. She hoped Yang Yang would become a real man even if he could not go to university.

Scene II: *Yang Yang's Family Store*

August 21, the 3rd Year, in the Chinese Neighborhood
It was 2 p.m. on Saturday when I arrived in the Chinese neighborhood. There were bustling crowds of people in addition to cars, buses, and other vehicles rushing north and south in the middle of the street. The stores were extended with outdoor stands of fruit and vegetables covering half the sidewalk. Grannies were sitting by the sidewalk selling garlic, mint, and other vegetables grown in their backyards. It was difficult to walk, but I finally found my way to Yang Yang's family bakery. As I walked in, I saw Yang Yang standing beside piles of moon cake boxes. The Mid-autumn Festival, an important Chinese holiday for family reunion and for good harvest, was to come.

"Hey, Yang Yang. I was looking for you. There are so many people in your store. You have a very good business."

He smiled and nodded his head shyly. I asked him where his mom was. He said his mom was home. "Shall we go to your home?" I asked. He nodded his head. I followed him. We went around the building of the bakery to the back street. There was a two-story building like a townhouse. There was a big backyard paved with bricks where a worker was piling boxes.

Scene III: *Yang Yang Back Home in Toronto*

August 21, the 3rd Year, at Yang Yang's Home
Yang Yang opened the door. We walked upstairs and I saw a living room full of baby toys, clothes, two TVs, and a glass coffee table with three bowls of lunch leftovers on it.

I asked Yang Yang about his school in Brampton. He said he liked it. He played hockey, something he did not do in Toronto. He said he lived with a relative, but the relative went to China and was not returning. I asked who would live with him in the new semester. He shook his head.

Yang Yang's mom came downstairs, apologized for the room's messiness, and said Yang Yang should have put his lunch away. She spoke about his bothersome habits. I sensed that she was going to repeat things she told me on the phone and I knew this would make the boy ashamed and embarrassed as I was a person he looked up to as his teacher.

"Yang Yang is very good," I said. "When he was at Bay Street Community School, he was well-behaved. I never heard him swear. He is taller than the last time I saw him. He is a young man now."

> Yes, he is taller. He changed so much since he went to Brampton. I told him that it wasn't good to take things out of the store, even though the store is ours. You still have to pay. Now he won't take anything...

The baby was crying upstairs. "Oh, sorry. My girl is crying. Yang Yang, listen to your teacher," she said and hurried upstairs.

I turned to Yang Yang, who looked solemn, and asked, "Yang Yang, have you been to the University of Toronto?" He said he hadn't. I asked him if he would like to see what a university looked like. He beamed.

I looked at the bowls on the coffee table and asked, "Who did the dishes when you were in Brampton?"

Yang Yang said he did.

I said, "Good, you are a big boy now. You know your mom has to take care of your baby sister and the store. She is so busy. You know how to help Mom with some housework, right? Let's help Mom to tidy the room before we go."

Yang Yang got up, washed the dishes and put them away.

"Very good", I smiled at him.

He tidied the room. Then I said, "Now the room looks much tidier. Let's clean the floor. The house will look nice and clean."

He cleaned every corner of the room.

"What about the staircase?" I suggested.

He hesitated for a second, went upstairs, and cleaned the stairs one by one.

His aunt came and said, "Oh, Yang Yang. Good boy! You should help me clean my floor." She smiled with a look that seemed like she hardly believed what she was seeing: Yang Yang doing housework.

Yang Yang's mom came downstairs with the baby in her arms.

Yang Yang cleaned the floor even harder. He redid parts he had already cleaned.

"Good, good," said the mom. "It is good that you help clean the house today. But you'd better do it every day."

Scene IV: Trip to St. George Campus of the University of Toronto

August 21, the 3rd Year, University of Toronto

We set off for the University of Toronto St. George campus. Yang Yang's mom gave him three loonies (Canadian dollars) to take the bus.

I asked Yang Yang if he would like to take the bus.

"No. Walk." He said he always walked in Brampton.

As we walked, we talked about what he wanted to do next school term. Would he return to Brampton or to Bay Street Community School? I knew that his parents were worried about this. When I talked to his mom earlier, she said that they had to make a decision about this. They had decided to sell the Brampton store and had been offered a good price.

Yang Yang had no one to live with because the relative he had lived with went back to China. Yang Yang told his mom he could live alone. The mom said he could not. Even if the law allowed it, she would not. She had told Yang Yang's Brampton teacher about their dilemma. The teacher offered to have Yang Yang live with her family. So the parents were going to meet the teacher and talk about the situation this week.

I said if they needed anyone to do the interpretation, I could help. I said I was interested in meeting the teacher. The mom said her husband had talked with Yang Yang's tutor. She would go with them. If she couldn't, they would ask me.

When we were at home, I asked Yang Yang where he would like to attend school in September. He said he would like to stay in Brampton.

I asked why.

"Because there are not so many Chinese around," he said.

"Were you bullied or discriminated against by any of your new school students?"

"No."

"Who were your friends at the new school?"

"Some Chinese, born here, and non-Chinese."

"What did you do together?" I asked.

Yang Yang said they played hockey together.

However, on our way to the university, I again asked him if he would like to return to Toronto or stay in Brampton next semester. He said he would like to come back to Toronto.

"Why?" I asked.

"I can stay at home."

"Why would you like to stay at home?"

"There are people at home."

I felt a clench in my heart and asked him who was with him in Brampton after school.

"No one."

"What about your friends? Didn't you play together after school?" I asked.

"They all went home after school."

We walked along College Street and passed the public library. I asked if he had been there. He said, "Yes." He came with his classmates when he was at Bay Street Community School.

"Is that building U of T's?" Yang Yang asked.

"Yes, it is the Department of Engineering. That is King's College Circle."

We walked to Hart House, a prominent building on campus.

"These buildings look so old," He said.

"Yes, the university is more than 175 years old. These buildings are over 100 years old."

When I asked what places he had visited, he said he had been to the CN Tower and Niagara Falls with his uncle. I knew from my work with the Newcomer Support Class that some children had never been out of the Chinese neighborhood, except for school field trips.

Episode Six: Yang Yang back to Bay Street Community School

Scene I: *Yang Yang Re-registered at Bay Street Community School*

September 7, the 3rd Year, Bay Street Community School
Yesterday was the first day of school. I wondered what happened to Yang Yang and his father's visit to Brampton. After school, I called Yang Yang's mom. She said that the dad was upset because Yang Yang could not remember the teacher's home address, nor even her name. They could not find the teacher. Yang Yang said that he did not want to stay in Brampton by himself, so the father had to take him back to Toronto. They decided to have Yang Yang go back to Bay Street Community School. I said that I would talk with Ms. Corter and help with the registration. Next morning when I got to school, I saw Yang Yang sitting on the steps in front of the school building. He told me his mom had to return home to get some required documents. I asked Yang Yang what document he held in his hand, and he said it was his report card from the Brampton school. I asked which teacher was his homeroom teacher who had been said to be very nice to him. He pointed at the name: It was his ESL class teacher. I wondered why Yang Yang told his father he had forgotten his teacher's name.

Yang Yang's mom arrived. I went to the Main Office with them. After registration, we went upstairs. Ms. Corter welcomed Yang Yang to the class and said, "Hi" to Yang Yang's mom. The boys and girls looked excited and curious. Yang Yang smiled shyly and did not say anything. All but one of the students that Yang Yang knew had either moved to the LEAP Program or had left for high school, such as Zhi Gao and Zhi Hui.

Ms. Corter apologized and said that she had to go back to class. Yang Yang's mom and I backed out of the classroom.

Scene II: *Yang Yang's Special Needs*

January 5, 2005, Bay Street Community School
After the New Year holidays, I was on my way out of school with Zhi Gao's mom to a Community Centre when we bumped into Ms. Corter. She was sorry to know about Zhi Gao's situation and helped us to find contact information of some high schools close to the neighborhood. She said she was just about to contact me to do her a favor. It was about Yang Yang. I said I would come back to school after I showed Zhi Gao's mom where the Community Centre was and helped her to find a community worker there who could speak Chinese.

When I returned to school, Yang Yang was standing in the hallway with his new classmates. Yang Yang smiled. "Hi, Yang Yang!" I greeted him.

"Hi, Teacher!" Ping exclaimed. She and Yang Yang were the only two students I knew well in this class now. There were a dozen more recently arrived students.

Ms. Corter showed me two forms for Yang Yang to get special help in speech and occupational therapy so as to keep him out of the high-school Special Education program. She was concerned about placing Yang Yang in that program. She wondered how accurate the test was that identified him for special education, given the year of his arrival in Toronto. This surprised me. I did not know Yang Yang had been identified as a learning disabled child in his first school. Ms. Corter raised this issue because it was time to consider which high school and which program would best fit Yang Yang.

Ms. Corter showed me a drawing Yang Yang did last semester. I was amazed at the picture's details. Ms. Corter said she found it difficult not to suspect the test results when she observed Yang Yang in her class, especially with his drawings. She said she would like to observe him more carefully before she decided whether Yang Yang should be placed in a Special Education program.

EPISODE SIX: YANG YANG BACK TO BAY STREET COMMUNITY SCHOOL 147

Scene III: Second Visit To Yang Yang's Home

January 5, the 4th Year, Yang Yang's Home in Toronto
I asked Yang Yang to wait for me after school so that we could walk to his home together. On our way to his home, I asked him if he was expected to help at the bakery. He said he wasn't, but he had to pick up his aunt's and uncle's children.

When we arrived at Yang Yang's home, I explained the forms that Ms. Corter needed to be signed in order for Yang Yang to have speech and occupational therapy help. When Yang Yang's mom asked him to fill out the forms, he could not spell his parents' names in English nor write his home address.

Yang Yang's mom said that life was harsh in the countryside where she grew up and she only finished Grade 4. She really wanted to go to school, but couldn't. She said, "I do not understand why children nowadays do not like studying. What good conditions they have!"

Yang Yang's father came home. I told him about the forms. His smile faded. He said Yang Yang had started playing video games again. Sometimes Yang Yang got up after midnight to play; sometimes he even got up at 5 a.m. to play video games with his cousin next door.

Scene IV: Yang Yang's Unseen Lives in School and out of School

February 21, the 4th Year, Newcomer Support Class
Ms. Corter said Yang Yang received a Valentine's card. She showed me Yang Yang's schoolwork: his 3-D drawing, acting in a videotaped class play, and work in math and language. I observed how Yang Yang helped Ms. Corter clean the messy desks after a school-wide activity. From his journal, it appeared that Yang Yang was helping with housework at home. Formerly shy and alone, Yang Yang had made good friends with recent newcomer children in his class. He acted like their big brother since he was now the tallest and eldest student in class.

Delighted, I went home from school. There I found a phone message from Yang Yang's mom. Given what I had seen and heard at the school, I was surprised to hear Yang Yang's mom complain that he was coming home late, was playing video games, and did not help enough at home. She said she and her husband had to intercept Yang Yang at the video parlor by entering the building separately and simultaneously from the front and back entrances in order to catch him. Yang Yang's mom wondered if they should really send Yang Yang back to China to attend a boarding school, as she was concerned about Yang Yang going to high school soon and she had heard about many dropouts in Toronto high schools, as well as other situations that really worried her. She said many of her relatives and friends in China said the Chinese school she was interested in was a good school. They had their children attend the school. It was located in a mountain. She said that she and her husband were in a dilemma, as they also understood that it might not work for Yang Yang to attend high school back in China without the parents' presence and support.

Interlude

Yang Yang's Graduation

Yang Yang graduated from Bay Street Community School in June of the third year of my time at the school. He had his hair done nicely at the hairdresser's and dressed up in a black suit. He looked happy and cheerful. The interactions between him and his classmates showed that he was popular among both boys and girls. He seemed to turn into a different person, a cheerful tall handsome young man, still with a shy smile on his face. What's more, he won two awards at the graduation ceremony. I was surprised that none of his family members were present at the graduation. I sneaked out of the gym and phoned his home. His mom said that she did not know about the graduation ceremony. Yang Yang had asked her for his dad's black suit yesterday evening without telling her what it was for. I wondered why Yang Yang did not seem to want his parents to know what he was doing at school, no matter whether it was good news or bad news. Yang Yang's mom was pleased to know that Yang Yang won two awards. In a minute, she came with her baby girl. The little girl started crying as soon as she saw the many people in the gym. The mom had to go outside and asked me to tell Yang Yang that she would be waiting for him outside of the school building.

I took pictures for Yang Yang and his mom and also for other graduating students. I wished them well in their new journeys to different schools.

点评:

Shi Jing's Reflection

I have presented many details of Yang Yang's life, but these are only glimpses from the set of field notes, which, in turn, are merely fragmented moments of Yang Yang's life in a three-dimensional narrative inquiry space. However, these glimpses reveal many aspects of Yang Yang's life that appeared to be unseen, either by teachers in the school or by his parents at home. Like many Chinese newcomer students, especially boys in my observation, Yang Yang has sometimes seemed to enjoy, but more often struggled in, his unseen life as he traveled in between home and school and in between landscapes of schools in transition.

Yang Yang's story raises many issues on cross-cultural school education, family education, special education, and adolescent education. The stories are told as such that communication can be enhanced among teachers, parents, school administrators, community workers, policymakers, and educational researchers. In face of changing and challenging situations, we need to reconsider, renegotiate, and reconstitute the roles of the school, the teacher, the parent, the learner, and the community in children and youth's education.

Yang Yang's life has continued. Yang Yang went to the Leap Program at Zhi Hui's high school in September of his graduation year from Bay Street Community School. I have had my hopes for the success of Yang Yang and other newcomer students, as Yang Yang has shown his academic and social improvement at school. Yet, thinking of Zhi Gao's case, I am also worried as Yang Yang struggles to make his way in his new homeland.

Note

1. Yang Yang's story was used as the data source for the following article: Xu, S. J., Connelly, F. M., He, M. F., & Phillion, J. (2007). Immigrant students' experience of schooling: A narrative inquiry theoretical framework. *Journal of Curriculum Studies*, 39 (4): 399–422.

CHAPTER 7

Life in Transition: Newcomer Boy Jia Ming

生活在变迁: 上海男孩嘉明

PRELUDE

Jia Ming 嘉明, a boy from Shanghai, China, arrived at the Newcomer Support Class of Bay Street Community School in June of my second year at Bay Street Community School. From my observation, it seemed that the naughtiness among the boys of the Newcomer Support Class was "contagious" and would affect new boys. Therefore, I had paid close attention to Jia Ming, who appeared to be a quiet well-mannered boy in my first impression, and I hoped he would not be influenced.

Jia Ming 嘉明, who had been a Grade 7 student in a Shanghai K-8 school, asked me in his first week at Bay Street Community School why these newcomer students' English seemed to be worse than his, although many of them had been in Canada for over one year. I interviewed Jia Ming at the end of the first month of his arrival before the summer vacation and followed him in the LEAP program in September. He was placed in the LEAP II program while many other newcomer boys and girls who had been in Canada longer were placed in LEAP I.

I first met Jia Ming's mom, Shirley Zhang 张莉, at Curriculum Night in the middle of September after Jia Ming attended LEAP II although we had talked over the phone for a few times before then. Jia Ming's parents were among the few families who agreed to participate in my study before they met me. I toured Jia Ming's mom around the school and introduced her to teachers and parents. Jia Ming's mom met Hui Lan 惠兰 at the Curriculum Night. I was happy to see that Jia Ming 嘉明 and Yong Chang 永昌 had become good school friends. Jia Ming's mom talked with LEAP program teacher, Ms. Campbell, Mandarin teacher, Ms. Tan 谭老师, and music teacher, Mr. Wiseman. She asked detailed questions regarding Jia Ming's study in their classes. Jia Ming's mom was actively involved in Jia Ming's schooling at Bay Street Community School; she attended Parent School Council meetings and school events, and talked with Jia Ming's teacher even though the teacher did not schedule her for a parent–teacher interview.

Almost every Chinese knows the story about *Meng Zi's mom who moved her home three times* 孟母三迁 in order to find a neighborhood that favored learning. Meng Zi (Mencius) 孟子 (*fourth century BC*), follower of Confucius, became a great scholar who ranks next to Confucius in Chinese history. Like Meng Zi's mom, Chinese parents located their homes at places that can favor their children's learning. Just as the family first found a temporary home in a basement near Bay Street Community School, so Jia Ming's parents moved to an apartment building near the downtown high school where Jia Ming was to attend Grade 9. I visited Jia Ming's family at their new home in the summer of his second year in Canada before he went to high school. I met Jia Ming's father and toured Jia Ming and his mother around the downtown neighborhood and took them to the nearby bookstore and library.

Jia Ming's parents were independent immigrants according to the assessment of Citizenship and Immigration Canada. They were ranked high in terms of education and professional skills and hence were needed in Canada. Their independent/professional immigrant status, however, did not make them much different from other newcomers. They lived in a downtown house basement near the school. In spite of their education and professional skills, Jia Ming's parents arrived only to find no professional employment. They turned to re-education while doing labor jobs. In many respects, their journey paralleled those who arrived "by boat" as refugees or illegal immigrants. They pushed Jia Ming toward academic success in school. Regardless of challenges and hardships, Jia Ming's family has held on to their hopes and dreams in their difficult journey in a new land.

Episode One: Jia Ming's Life in Shanghai and Toronto

Jia Ming had been in Canada for one month, which was my second year in the school, when I interviewed him in the school library. I explained that it was a casual talk and that I was interested in his Shanghai schooling as I knew that there were big differences between urban and rural schools in China and education quality varied from region to region.

Scene I: Life in Shanghai

June 25, the 2nd Year, Interview with Jia Ming, BSCS Library
Jia Ming was the only Shanghai boy in his class, where most came from Fujian rural areas and some from Guangdong. He told me he was 13 and an only child. His family, he said, included his parents, himself, his maternal grandma, grandpa, two uncles, and two sisters. This meant Jia Ming's two maternal uncles each had a daughter, as children in China often refer to cousins as brothers or sisters. Jia Ming told me his paternal grandparents lived in another province. From birth to age seven, Jia Ming was looked after by his maternal grandparents while his parents worked. He grew up with his *elder sister*, an uncle's daughter, who lived next door to his maternal grandma's home. He said he went to daycare when he was two or three years old.

Jia Ming's parents bought a three-bedroom apartment and moved out of the grandparents' home when Jia Ming started Grade 1 at age seven. This move was so that Jia Ming could attend a top K-8 Shanghai school. He remembered the new home as being nicely furnished and decorated, with few trees outside. He said he liked his grandparents' home more as it was an old style two-story house with many trees. He missed his grandparents.

Scene II: Schooling in Shanghai

June 25, the 2nd Year, Interview with Jia Ming, BSCS Library
Jia Ming started English in Grade 1, using an Oxford English textbook. Children were asked to read texts. Memorization and grammar were emphasized. His school was paired with a sister school in Australia, and he had several Australian teachers who taught Oral English once or twice a month. Jia Ming's regular English language teacher taught English with Chinese as the medium of instruction, especially when she explained grammar points. When I asked Jia Ming if the children liked learning English, he said "so-so".

Jia Ming did not think he was a top student in his school, saying that many students were excellent. His teachers were kind to him, "like parents." He liked his Chinese language teacher who gave him one-on-one feedback. He liked Chinese writing and his teacher often asked him to read his compositions. He thought he was good at math, but his math teacher was strict and never laughed with the students like his Canadian teacher does. Students must sit quietly and, if they misbehaved, would have to leave the classroom.

In the Chinese school system, each class has a coordinating teacher who teaches one major subject and is responsible for all matters associated with the class. Jia Ming told me his coordinating teacher was a young English language teacher. From Grades 1 to 8 at Jia Ming's school, different teachers taught different subjects. Hence, he might meet seven or eight teachers each da y. Jia Ming said:

> I like the Canadian way better as I feel comfortable with one teacher who knows the kids and has a consistent teaching plan; I do not have to adjust to various teaching styles of different teachers. I like the Canadian way of learning, too. I do not have to worry about exams as I did in China. All I need to do is to understand what I have learned every day. I can always ask the teacher for help.

Jia Ming told me about Shanghai Open School days and parent–teacher meetings:

> There are Open School days when parents come to school to watch the students' shows. Also, students make desserts and fruit salad for parents to enjoy.... There are two parent-teacher meetings a year. Parents gather in one big room according to grade, and then go to their children's classes to talk to the coordinating teacher.

Scene III: The Journey to Canada

June 25, the 2nd Year, Interview with Jia Ming, BSCS Library
I asked Jia Ming what he visualized about Canada before he came. He told me about his feeling of moving to a new country and the family's journey to Canada.

> I found it hard to believe. I had been focusing on my studies all the time. All of a sudden, my dad and mom told me that we were going to Canada. So, I felt uncertain in my heart as I did not feel like leaving my classmates. My uncle in Toronto told me that there were not many people here in Canada. I had a dream

one night and saw a heavy snow and no one on the street. But when I got here, I found there were many people in Toronto. The streets in the Chinatown neighbourhood are as busy as the streets of Nanjing Road and Huaihai Road in Shanghai.

It was a long flight. I got airsick when the plane took off and landed. We stopped in Vancouver. The plane was late. So all I remember about the trip is that I was worried that we would miss the flight to Toronto. My mom is the principal applicant. She speaks English well. She worked in business and foreign trade in Shanghai, so we did not have a problem during the trip. My father could not speak English. My mother took care of everything on our way to Toronto. My maternal uncle waited for us at the Toronto airport for many hours as the plane was late. He came to Toronto alone first. His wife and daughter joined him later.

Jia Ming did not feel foreign on his arrival. He said, "Wherever you go, you hear people talking Chinese." But he found Chinatown a little foreign.

You see many foreigners visiting Chinatown. They like Chinese food. So you can always see a lot of foreigners come to Chinatown to have Chinese food. At the same time, I feel at home in Chinatown as there are so many Chinese. I can also see a lot of foreigners. In China, I didn't see so many foreigners. I feel quite at home when I see Chinese characters in Chinatown. It is really nice to see Chinese words in a foreign land.

Scene III: Life in Transition

June 25, the 2nd Year, Interview with Jia Ming, BSCS Library
Jia Ming's parents found Bay Street Community School by phoning the Toronto District School Board to find out which school Jia Ming should attend. His mom took him to register at the Main Office. Jia Ming told me how he felt when he first came to Bay Street Community School, but he talked more about his Shanghai school.

First, I was very excited, for I would meet new students. Second, I missed my school in Shanghai. I missed the facilities there. There was not a big lawn, but we had a very professionally made playground and two gyms and a science building. Our school is one of the best in China. We won a lot of awards which were displayed in a special award room. The awards were in sports and arts. Our school was number-one in handball. The school has always won the championship since 1990. We also won awards in literacy contests. Each time only one composition was selected to represent the whole school to compete for the national award...

I would feel a little disappointed if mine was not selected, but we felt happy for the classmate (whose work was selected). We were taught to care about one another and love one another. We saw it as a collective honour for all of us in the school. We were taught to work harder to achieve the common goal. We had contests between classes in each grade; for example, the best student, the best class and the most awards. We had to work harder together to win the class award. We were disappointed if our class didn't win. When we came back to our classroom, we would say to each other that we must work harder and win the award next semester. We would reflect what we had not done well and what we could do better next time.

When I asked if he had any difficulties at Bay Street Community school, Jia Ming said:

I haven't got used to the teaching style yet. I have some difficulty in English. I am getting along well with my classmates. In China, too, we helped each other. If one was not doing well, the coordinating teacher would send student representatives to visit the student at home, talking to and encouraging the student, and see what we could do to help.

Jia Ming said he still missed his classmates in Shanghai. He kept in touch with friends via e-mail or by phone. He said he left the Shanghai school two weeks before he came to Toronto. His teachers were surprised and asked him to write when he got to Toronto. Jia Ming missed another two weeks of schooling before he was registered at Bay Street Community School. So I asked him how he felt about the gap.

I felt lonely in those two weeks. I missed my classmates. The week before I came, my teacher asked me to go to a farewell party. That day our teacher allowed us to play our favourite game. My classmates wrote cards and gave me gifts. Our teacher bought food and drinks from our class budget, which came from us, not the school. We each donated one or two yuan from our lunch fee and then we would have over 80 yuan each semester as we had over 40 students in class. I always had lunch at school. The food was good. There usually was one stir-fried dish with rice every day, but it varied from day to day. However, I preferred Western food, such as beef on a sizzling plate, Macdonald's, Kentucky fried chicken and pizza. I had it once a week on the weekend.

EPISODE ONE: JIA MING'S LIFE IN SHANGHAI AND TORONTO

"How about now?" I asked.

> Now I feel fed up when I see them, but I haven't had the beef on a sizzling plate since I came. I would like to have a bite of authentic roast beef. When we go on field trips, I bring hamburger... I like walking on the big lawn here to breathe the fresh air. In China, we didn't have a lot of large lawns and the air pollution was bad.

I asked him what he liked and what he usually did after school:

> I like sports. I liked reading sports magazines in China. Here in Canada, I haven't found anything, yet. When I get home, I have to memorise English vocabulary. My mom has asked me to memorise a certain number of English words before supper and to watch only English TV programs. I like pop music. I like Zhou Jie Lun 周杰伦, a Taiwanese singer... In Shanghai, kids like loose jeans, and prefer Nike and Adidas. Here? I do not feel like catching up with the Jones as life is so casual here in Toronto. ... I haven't made new friends yet. I only know students from my class. Out of school? I know a high school student. He is the son of my uncle's friend.

Jia Ming was surprised at the behavior of the newcomer boys in his Toronto class; he thought they were rude and misbehaved.

> I do not like it when students run around in class here. In China, students had to sit quietly by the desk and listen attentively. Some students might talk too loudly or make trouble in class by making fun and making others laugh in class, but no one would hit others. There were student representatives to take charge of small groups in each class. Naughty students would be taken to the office and would stand in the office until 5 or 6 p.m. and do self-reflection. If one student really misbehaved, for example, by taking someone else's pencil box or by hitting others, the teacher would spank him with a ruler. It usually was the coordinating teacher who would take care of the matter and would ask the parents to come to school. Chinese students do not like their parents to come to school, for whenever parents came to school, it was because you got into trouble. So you got into real trouble when you went home.

Jia Ming didn't hang around with the other newcomer boys after school.

> Many students of the class go swimming or play video games in video game parlours in the basement of the Chinese shopping mall. I do not like going to the video game rooms. I don't think those are nice places.

> In Shanghai, after school and at home we spoke Shanghai dialect. In class we spoke Pu-Tong-Hua. In Toronto? At home, I speak Shanghai dialect. Sometimes I speak English with my mom. At first my mom and dad were worried about my English. They heard people say a child would speak English very well in one or two years. Then my mom started worrying about my Chinese. She asked me to read and write Chinese every day. I have to read and write a lot. We brought textbooks from China.

Scene IV: Changes in Life after Immigration

June 25, the 2nd Year, Interview with Jia Ming, BSCS Library
Jia Ming told me about changes in his life after coming to Canada.

> My life is different now. In China, I went to bed around 9 p.m. Here I go to bed at 11:30 p.m. or 12 p.m. My uncle said people here stay up late and it would be considered abnormal if one went to bed at 9 p.m.
>
> I help my mom with the laundry. Her back hurts. So I put the laundry in the sun after she washes it by hand. I do more than I did in China, for my mom is so busy. She has to do housework, study and look for jobs. I have become more caring to my parents and more respectful. My mom said I have become more mature and understanding since I came to Canada. I have learned to take care of others.

However, Jia Ming's daily study routine was not changed much. He went to school in the morning and afternoon and had lunch and supper at home.

> My uncle bought a book of daily English. My mom said I had to memorise a certain number of words so that I would understand what people said. My goal is to communicate with my classmates and English speakers in English and to try to understand everything they say on TV.

Jia Ming wants to go to a first-rate Canadian or American university. He is interested in foreign trade and business. Although his family now lived in a basement shared with his maternal uncle's family, he imagined his future home would be a three-story house with big lawns and two garages. He wanted his new home to be near a good high school in Toronto. He asked about good high schools. I promised I would ask my friends.

Episode Two: Phoning Jia Ming's Home – Mom's Worries

I asked my friend Yin, who moved several times for the sake of their son's education. When the boy entered high school, they moved close to one of Toronto's best high schools. Yin told me recently her boy received offers from seven universities. When I called Jia Ming to tell him what I had found out, his mother answered and said she recognized me. The mother had signed the consent forms that I asked Jia Ming to bring home. We had a long conversation.

Scene I: Mom's Worries about Jia Ming's Education

July 6, the 2nd Year, Phone Conversation with Jia Ming's Mom
Jia Ming's mom worried about her son and reflected on the school system.

> I am not worried about Jia Ming's math, but I am worried about his English. Schooling here is different from that in China. Jia Ming was in a top school at Shanghai. It had good teachers, facilities and teaching and students were streamed from kindergarten to elementary and secondary schools. Jia Ming was in the same school from kindergarten through elementary and middle school. Only good students can stay in the school. Others are streamed out. In Toronto, he is placed in Grade 7 and will be in Grade 8 next year. Students here do not learn as much as students in China. We brought Chinese textbooks on different subjects to Toronto and my husband and I ask Jia Ming to study them at home to make sure he remembers what he learned in China.

"Yes," I said, "the teaching style here is different from that in China. Here, teachers focus more on the process of learning. They try to facilitate children's original thinking, imagination and creativity." Jia Ming's mom continued:

> I hope that Jia Ming will carry on the good things he developed in China and learn the good things in the Canadian school in terms of creativity and original thinking. In China they spoon-feed children. Students learn by memorization and clearly follow the teacher. I hope Jia Ming will make changes in this aspect. I read about education here in the West and I know that high school kids have to make their own choice in selecting classes and academic interest. Jia Ming needs to learn to do this.
>
> Teachers here are responsible and hard working. Chinese teachers are usually too strict. Some teachers are not very responsible due to the social changes in the

recent years in China. At Jia Ming's Shanghai school, parents can make a complaint about a teacher. Unqualified teachers can be fired now with new measures taken to improve education.

Scene II: Mom's Worries about Peer Influence

July 6, the 2nd Year, Phone Conversation with Jia Ming's Mom
Jia Ming's mom knew that many Chinese students at Bay Street Community School are from the rural areas of Fujian. She said:

> Families from rural areas usually lack awareness of the importance of education and the role parents take in their children's education. At Jia Ming's age, friends are important and they influence each other. Jia Ming has a solid foundation from his elementary education in China. What worries me is that, at his age, he might pick up bad habits from other boys.

She said that she had not come to Jia Ming's new school because she knew strangers were not welcome at school. There had been a recent highly publicized child kidnapping in another school, and all schools were extra careful about strangers. But I encouraged her to come to school, telling her that many parents volunteered at the school. She would be especially welcome because of her good English, which would allow her to do translations. She said she would try next semester. She helped Jia Ming with math and English at home, so she said she could help other Chinese students at the school.

Scene III: Meeting Jia Ming's Mom

From Fall of the 2nd Year to Spring, Bay Street Community School
Jia Ming's mom followed up on the suggestion that she visit the school. I met her for the first time when she attended Curriculum Night in September when Jia Ming started LEAP II at Bay Street Community School. After that we met frequently as she regularly attended School Council meetings and other school activities. I informed her of important school events and introduced her to Ms. Steadman, the principal, so she could volunteer to help with school flyer translations.

We met for an interview at 4 p.m. on a Wednesday afternoon in mid-March of their second year in Canada, my third year at Bay Street Community School. She was taking ESL at the LINK program in the school basement in the morning, and I was with the Newcomer Support Class until 3:30 p.m. We talked for two hours at a local public library. Our conversation focused on Jia Ming's education and its relationship to her family goals.

Jia Ming's mom looked young and pretty in a light blue jacket. She said she was studying English and not working. I was reminded of the first time that I saw Tommy's mother at the Parent Centre when she was not working and looked young and fresh. When I bumped into her a year later on the subway on her way home from a clothes factory, Tommy's mom looked tired and the harsh workload showed on her face.

Jia Ming's mom said she was a housewife in Toronto although she had been a department manager in a big factory in Shanghai. Still, she was optimistic about her life. A common Toronto saying is that immigrant taxi drivers are often better educated than their customers. The implications of this saying applied to Jia Ming's mom who was the principal family applicant to Canada because of her professional status. But she could not find professional work in Canada. Her family lived with her brother in a basement close to Bay Street Community School. She said they had a close relationship. She made supper for both families and waited until her brother and sister-in-law came home, so that the entire family ate together. Jia Ming's father worked as a laborer in Scarborough. He used the subway to get to work. They chose Jia Ming's high school in downtown Toronto because it was close to the Bloor–Danforth Subway line.

Overall, Jia Ming's mom expressed more concern for Jia Ming's education than she did for her own work situation. The following episodes reveal her notion of schooling and learning, her efforts and hope for Jia Ming's education, as well as her values, social responsibilities, and sense of belonging.

Episode Three: Mom's Expectations and Efforts in Jia Ming's Education

By the time of the interview with Jia Ming's mom, Li (Shirley) Zhang张莉, I had been in the school for two years and had followed Jia Ming since his arrival. *Shirley* was the English name she used when working in foreign trade in Shanghai and it was the name she used in the school. She went to university in 1980 and I went to university in 1982, so we were close in age and shared much in our educational experiences and values. This no doubt contributed to our good rapport and our long and rich conversation. By the time of the interview, we had known each other for nearly a year. The interview took on the character of a friendly conversation, and a discussion over Jia Ming's schooling and education.

Scene I: Learning and Playing

March 11, the 3rd Year, Interview with Jia Ming's Mom, Toronto Public Library
Shirley was worried that Jia Ming would not catch up with regular students.

> To Jia Ming, playing is more important than his studies. On Sunday mornings he says, "Mama, I have finished reading two texts." So he sounds like he has finished his studies and wants to play for the rest of the day. When he comes home, he says he got a perfect mark in math. I say, "This is not something you should feel proud of because you learned it in earlier grades in China. This was only a review. You got a perfect mark from old math! How much would you get if you were in the regular class? In this way, you can find how much you lag behind." Jia Ming always tells me how fast he does his schoolwork and homework.

Like many Chinese parents, Shirley urged Jia Ming to study harder and not become conceited. She said she did not praise Jia Ming. This is typically Chinese. Unlike Canadian teachers and parents who encourage children more often, Chinese parents and teachers tend to criticize their children, and praise them only rarely. Shirley worried that newcomer students were not evaluated by the same standards as those for students in regular classes. She said that the LEAP teacher recommended that Jia Ming take Level 3 ESL in high school. (There are five ESL levels.). She wondered what good it was if Jia Ming only did well in a lower level. She hoped that Jia Ming could be pushed to study harder now so that he would begin his high school in a regular class. She was a little concerned about Jia Ming going to a downtown high school. She said:

> I heard that schools in north Toronto are better, but I have to think of the family. I cannot move further north. We need to be near the subway. If we moved to North York, it would be difficult for his father. We do not have a car. I wonder if Jia Ming can be transferred to another high school after 2 years. I said to Jia Ming, "Students from a not-so-good high school can also excel and

get into a good university. A student from a good high school may not get into university. It all depends on you."

I tried to ease her fears by telling her that I had observed Jia Ming in the Newcomer Support Class and now in the LEAP program. He was doing well and had not picked up disruptive behaviors. But Shirley was still concerned, saying:

> I am not pleased with him. I am worried. At first he didn't like to watch the TV comedy Friends with me. He liked cartoons. I encouraged him, "Oh, your listening is better than mine. So I can ask you for help if I can't understand." I find this year his English is better. When we first arrived, my English was better than his. Now when we watch Friends together, he understands and laughs, but I can't because I do not understand. He says, "Oh, Mama, now I don't need to translate into Chinese in my mind so as to laugh. Now I can laugh by just listening to the English conversations." I say, "Ah, it shows your progress in English."

Scene II: Parental Involvement and Expectation in Children's Education

March 11, the 3rd Year, Interviewing Jia Ming's Mom, Toronto Public Library
I told Shirley I noticed that Jia Ming talked with his LEAP II classmates in English. On his arrival, he had better English than other Newcomer Support Class children. That was why he was transferred to the LEAP program and soon moved to LEAP II. However, she worried and told me what she said to Jia Ming.

> If you work harder, you can go to a regular high school class. Students from China have limited vocabulary. To live here, your vocabulary is not good enough. You should memorize more vocabulary; and, you should listen more and read more. But you idle away most of your time... (Sigh) playing around rather than studying.

She went on:

> He doesn't like reading. The teacher assigns book reports. At first, he borrowed thick books. Now he reads thinner and thinner books, simpler and simpler.

> I read a book about robots with him. Then I read his book report and I was not pleased. "You do not understand the questions when you answer them. You do not understand what is said in the book. What you wrote is a mess." But he is not strict with himself and he would say, "Mm, I don't understand it... that's ok." I want him to learn to use the big dictionary for his assignments. But he feels there are too many words in it and he uses the digital dictionary, instead. I told him "The digital dictionary translation is not good." Worse, he answers the assigned questions without looking up many words. He told me, "Our teacher said we don't need to look up every word." Actually he is looking for an excuse for his laziness. When I ask him how much he gets, he says 7 out of 10. Then I ask him, "How did you miss the other 3? Can you write the report in more details so as to get 8? If you get 8, you can ask the teacher how to get the other 2 points."

I laughed in my heart: This is typical of Chinese parents' expectations of their children. I remembered Hui Lan made similar comments to her eldest son Yong Chang; and Hui Lan said her husband asked Yong Chang why he was not number one when he was ranked number two in his class. For Shirley and Jia Ming, there were clashes between the mom's and the son's ways of learning. Shirley focuses on what needs to be improved while Jia Ming is getting used to the Canadian way, in which teachers tend to focus more on what the students have achieved.

Scene III: Computers and Learning

March 11, the 3rd Year, Interviewing Jia Ming's Mom, Toronto Public Library
Shirley continued to talk about her efforts to keep Jia Ming academically involved:

> I said to Jia Ming, "Shall we go to the museum?" "Not interested." Then I said, "U of T has free movies. Shall we go to see a movie together?" He said, "Um, I am not interested." Instead, he went to a community centre with his classmates to play video games. I bought a computer but he only downloaded games. I said, "Jia Ming, I have installed WORD, EXCEL. These programs will be useful for your high school. You can learn the software together with me." Eh! He is not interested. I asked him to use the computer for two hours a day. "The first hour must be used for studying. Then the second hour you can e-mail your friends." At first, he listened. But sometimes I find him playing games when I get home.

I told Shirley that Mandarin teacher, Ms. Tan 谭老师, assigned a project on the ancient Chinese history of Emperor Han Wu 汉武帝. I suggested that Jia Ming could download information from the Internet. She replied:

> Jia Ming likes history. In China, I bought him books like "Shui Hu 水浒" and "Legends of Three kingdoms 三国演义". He read them every day and he would tell me the stories, but I was not interested. Now I think I should have pretended interest because his Chinese is getting worse.

Scene IV: Language Issues

March 11, the 3rd Year, Interviewing Jia Ming's Mom, Toronto Public Library
Shirley helped Jia Ming in both English and Chinese by asking him to do vocabulary dictation on weekends. She was concerned with his spoken English.

> I find he only listens to English. He doesn't speak much. So I said, "Jia Ming, would you speak English with Mama at home? I am learning English at an ESL class. Most of the students are Chinese. We often speak Chinese in class. So we are not learning colloquial English as you are at school. If you speak English at home, Mama can learn from you. In this way we can help each other in English listening and speaking." But he is not willing to speak English at home. Then, I help him in dictation. I find he seldom writes anything. I am afraid that he may be able to listen to English, but may not know how to write English.

I said, "It might be good that he doesn't like speaking English at home. Some studies show that many children only speak English at home and are reluctant to speak Chinese with their parents." Shirley was surprised, as she would rather Jia Ming speak English only. She said that she did not notice him doing any English writing at home.

> I'd rather he only speak English at home because I don't think he will forget Chinese. Our family environment wouldn't let him. What I am afraid is that he may forget how to write some Chinese words. I asked him to do a vocabulary dictation. He asked me to tell him how to write the Chinese word and he wrote down its English equivalent. I said, "I read aloud the English word, and you write it down in both English and Chinese." He made a lot of mistakes in both English and Chinese. I told him, "You may understand what you hear, but you can't spell the words. Mama brought many books for you, but you read Secret

Tips for game wizards." He tries them on the computer and says, "I got it. I got it." I said, "Eh, you only got to know how to play games."

Scene V: Mom's Involvement in Son's Education

March 11, the 3rd Year, Interviewing Jia Ming's Mom, Toronto Public Library
The mom's concerns extended to Jia Ming's overall education. She went on:

> I told him, "If you keep on like this, you may not get into university. Why should you come to Canada then?" During my ESL classes in the school basement, I sometimes heard school announcements. Later when I asked Jia Ming what was said, he said, "I didn't pay attention." I was upset: "How come you didn't pay attention to the announcements?!" I know his personality. He lacks concentration. When he was little, I enrolled him in calligraphy. Parents were asked to take the lessons together with their child so that they could tutor at home. Jia Ming did not remember key points. I said, "Look, Mama was listening more attentively than you. Mama used to be a child and a grade school student, too. I couldn't be listening attentively all the time in class, either. But immediately after class, I borrowed a classmate's notes. You can't be absent-minded when the teacher is talking something important. You need to pay attention."
>
> In China, two major classes, such as language and math, are scheduled in the morning with physical education in between. When I asked him why he did not concentrate on the two major subjects, Jia Ming said that in the first class he thought excitedly about phys-ed and in the third class after phys-ed, he was still excited and also exhausted. So he did not concentrate on either major class. I said to him "Look, the purpose of phys-ed class in between is to enable you to better learn the major subjects, but you reversed the order of what is important."

Scene VI: Mom's View of the Teacher's Role on Jia Ming's Learning

March 11, the 3rd Year, Interviewing Jia Ming's Mom, Toronto Public Library
I asked Shirley how Jia Ming had done in his school in China. The mom said:

> It depended on his teacher and teaching methods. When he was in the second semester of Grade 1, his teacher said, "You've got to help this child. He always stays around 80. This is not good." Two weeks before his exams, I made him

study hard. He got 98. His teacher said his score was higher than her expectation. Jia Ming kept his marks over 90 until Grade 3. He started having problems in math. Jia Ming did not like his Grade 3 math teacher. He mimicked for me how slowly and repeatedly the teacher gave instructions. In the second semester of Grade 4, they had a new math teacher. She spoke fast and Jia Ming liked her. When Jia Ming graduated from Grade School, he was ranked fifth in his class and his class ranked No.1 in the school. So, he was one of the top 5 students of the school (in Shanghai).

In grade school, he had a very good coordinating teacher. She was young and strict. She expected the class to win awards. However, in Grade 6, the new coordinating teacher was absent minded and finally quit teaching. So for the whole year, Jia Ming did not study well and was just slightly above average. His learning always depended on the teacher. He didn't find learning hard. At parent-teacher meetings, some parents said their child did homework until 10 or 11 p.m. But Jia Ming finished his work fast, often before supper.

Scene VII: Learning and Testing – Efficiency and Accuracy

March 11, the 3rd Year, Interviewing Jia Ming's Mom, Toronto Public Library

Shirley continued talking about Jia Ming's learning at his Shanghai school. She said she was not pleased that Jia Ming always did his work fast, as his accuracy was not as good as his efficiency. Schools in China tend to be test-oriented and the accuracy needed for high scores is often considered most important. Shirley said:

> Once his English language teacher asked me to meet her to discuss Jia Ming's English test. Jia Ming only got 91. "Look," the teacher said, showing me his test paper. "He was careless here. There he forgot to put 's' after the verb. These are simple grammar points. If he reviewed his answers carefully, he should notice them himself." He wanted to be the first to hand in his test papers. I requested that he should not try to be the first, but he wouldn't listen. Sometimes I took a leave from work to go to his school during an exam to make sure he wouldn't hand in his test paper too soon. I watched him through the window. He was looking here and there. I would make gestures, to get him to concentrate and review his answers. Even so, his English language teacher showed me his answer sheets for multiple-choice questions: He had filled out many nonsense circles to kill time during the exam when he thought he was finished. I was so angry with him! "How could you waste your time like this?"

Scene VIII: Differences in Educational Expectations and Approaches between Chinese Parents and Canadian Teachers

March 11, the 3rd Year, Interviewing Jia Ming's Mom, Toronto Public Library

I asked Jia Ming's mom about Jia Ming's work in the LEAP class. She said:

> I am not satisfied. I cannot push him as hard as I could in China. There they had homework and I could make sure he did it. Here, he is not pressured. When he reads, he chooses thin books. I don't know whether it is because his English is low, or because he doesn't want to read.

I said, "Jia Ming is a good student. His teacher doesn't think she should push him hard as she believes that it is more important to cultivate children's self-motivation and interest in learning. However, I understand Jia Ming might do much better with a little more push." The mom emphatically agreed: "Yes, he can do much better! He has a lot of potential. He has extra time to play around. Too much! In China, he had not a single minute to play around from Monday to Friday."

I asked if she thought it was good for Jia Ming to study all the time. She said,

> That's why we immigrated to Canada, just for the sake of our child. We hope Jia Ming will have more freedom and space for his self-development. I really do not like the way of teaching in China. Even when we were at university, we had no choice. Now students still do not have much choice in China. You have to think about your future job. You have to think if what you learn will guarantee a job. Also, sometimes you have to choose a subject area outside your interest to get into university.

We talked about differences she noticed between Jia Ming's school in Shanghai and the one in Toronto, and different values surfaced. She said:

> Overall, the school here is very good. The schools focus on different things. In China, the school focuses on scores and the overall development of morality, intelligence and health. However, it is said that the purpose of education is to make every flower bloom and every bird sing. I believe in this very much. If one is not a lark, one may be just a sparrow; even if one can only sing like a cicada, it is still very good. You should not force a cicada to sing like a lark. In China, we tend to impose "the best model" on every child. No matter whether you are a

lark, or a sparrow or a cicada, you have to sing in the same voice like a lark. I think it is unfair to some children. It is a misery for them. I don't like that. I think every bird should be able to sing the way as who she or he is.

From this perspective, I do not want to push Jia Ming too hard. I am observing what really interests him. I wouldn't force him to do something he doesn't like; as I did. I didn't like electronics. However, since I had decided to learn it, I did my best out of my sense of responsibility, not out of my interest. When I changed my job to work in the Department of Foreign Affairs and Trading, I was pleased and enjoyed what I was doing.

I read from a book that the greatest happiness in one's life is to do something one really likes while making money out of it. A famous man said, "Do what you like most and also make money out of it. This is the best life." So I have been observing Jia Ming to see what he really likes.

Jia Ming likes sports. I analyzed with him, "Look, you like sports. But sports are not your strength. You are an Asian boy. You cannot be as strong as others here." Also, he has asthma. It is okay for him to keep sports as his hobby, but not his profession. I said, "Other kids of 15 or 16 years old will gradually make up their minds about their future. When you get to university, you will need to choose your subject area and develop yourself in that area." He said, "Mama, I like business." He might think my job in business was easy as it seemed that we just made phone calls and sent faxes. I told him a story to show it was not. "Our company needed a product urgently. So the producer raised the price by 30 percent. I was sent to deal with it. How could Mama buy the last 100 items and also reduce the price? It required negotiation skills, wisdom and courage. It is not as what you thought: Mama's job is easy."

Once when checking the stock market, I said, "Jia Ming, do you think I should sell my shares now?" He seemed to think it over seriously and said, "I think you can wait for another couple of days." I said, "Why do you think I can wait?" He said, "It seems that the stock is going to keep on rising." In two days it went down. I said, "Look, Jia Ming, this shows we do not have enough professional knowledge on the stock market."

Her beliefs about education and her concern for Jia Ming set up tensions for Shirley. She recognized this and said:

I sound reasonable when I talk with you. But when I see him, I become upset. Maybe I have been strict with myself and so I think, "Why doesn't he study as hard as I did?" I sometimes feel that I am dishonest if I praise him, for I really want to scold him. How can I praise him? Sometimes after I encourage him, he turns on the TV when I hope he will open his book.

Shirley felt that their changed circumstances complicated matters.

When we were in China, we three lived by ourselves. We had a rule that we would not watch TV except for the news at 7 p.m. from Monday to Friday. Then we read and Jia Ming did homework. When he finished, he could read whatever he liked. He liked history, and read books like "Legends of Three Kingdoms". He learned history and also improved his language. However, in Toronto, we do not have a good learning environment. We share a basement apartment with a relative. The TV is in the living room, where Jia Ming does homework. He stretches his neck trying to watch TV. I get upset and say, "Why can't you concentrate on your homework?"

His room is too small, only big enough for a small bed. The learning environment is very important, but self discipline is more important. One of our neighbours in Shanghai was addicted to playing Ma-Jiang. However, their daughter was an excellent student. She studied hard and was self-motivated and strong-minded. She made sure she was always the best of her class. I didn't understand this because I had to push Jia Ming to study and model for him by not watching TV myself.

"Maybe it is not good for kids to be too competitive." I said.

Yes, I know it is not good for a child to be overly competitive and to be narrow-minded. But Jia Ming is too non-competitive. If you do not have any sense of competition, it can also be bad and you may not progress.

Episode Four: A Dragon in Shanghai but a Fish Out of Water in Toronto

Scene I: Jia Ming's Mom's Education and Career in Shanghai

March 11, the 3rd Year, Interviewing Jia Ming's Mom, Toronto Public Library
Shirley told me of how she ended up in electronics even though she disliked it.

I entered university in 1980 not long after the end of Cultural Revolution. My homeroom teacher, said, "Those who go to Arts are people who cannot learn math and science. There was a popular saying: "If you can do well in math, physics and chemistry, you are not afraid to walk the world 学好数理化, 走遍天下都不怕". Of course, my father helped me make the decision. He said, "You should learn electronics because China is behind there. You will be useful." Electronics was my least interest. But my generation are devoted to work and to responsibility. You do your best and do not complain even when you do not like your work.

Shirley said after graduation she joined an electronics factory in Shanghai where she did technical work for 12 years. Five years before she came to Canada, her work shifted because her English was good. First she did translation and later was assigned to the Department of Foreign Affairs and Foreign Trade in the factory where she held business talks and did negotiations and contracts with foreign businessmen. She said that though she had no business experience, she learned and worked hard. When she left, her boss said, "Whenever you want to come back, talk with me."

Scene II: From a Shanghai Career Woman to a Toronto Stay-at-home Mom

March 11, the 3rd Year, Interviewing Jia Ming's Mom, Toronto Public Library
We talked about the difficulties newcomers have in finding the right job in Canada. For example, Shirley became a stay-at-home mother and her husband a factory laborer. She said:

> What can we do? We look at newspaper job ads. I think one has to be educated here in Canada to get involved in business. The policies and rules in North America are different from those in China. I am interested in public administration but cannot find a position. I send many resumes, but seldom have a reply. It might be because of the language barrier that makes me unable to present myself well. When I was in China, I had high responsibilities, and I would say I had good communication skills and good relationships with clients. But this doesn't help in Canada.

Like many Chinese newcomers, Shirley felt a loss of her social value and a lack of sense of belonging in Canada. She said, "Now I feel like I am idling away time every day. I feel like a housewife." She laughed.

She found that community services for newcomers were not especially helpful.

> Most newcomers know enough English to fill out forms. This help was nice, but not enough. Helping newcomers fill out forms cannot help them to find a job.
>
> In Canada, many jobs need references. We have the skills they need, but they do not know us. There is a lack of communication; there are barriers in between. They only trust their own people. They trust the people introduced by their own employees. It is difficult for a newcomer to get acquainted with people who can help us find jobs. We do not have the social network. For us, looking for a job is like buying a lottery ticket.

I asked her about her family's long-term plans. She said, "We prefer to stay in Canada. When Jia Ming goes to university, we will have been here five years. Our connections in China will be lost." She said that she and her husband did not regret their immigration even though they had both given up good positions for a poorer work situation in Canada.

Scene III: Self-value and Sense of Belonging

March 11, the 3rd Year, Interviewing Jia Ming's Mom, Toronto Public Library Shirley said she felt the loss of her social value; however, what she said revealed that she appeared to hold on to a sense of social value by seeing her difficulties as limitations in the social system in Canada and she was seeking for a sense of belonging in the new land. I commented, "Your qualifications should enable you to find a nice job. It is a pity for Canada not to make good use of people like yourself." She replied:

> Yes, many immigrants with Ph.D.s wash dishes or drive taxis. It is a waste in this country. Since we choose to come here, we of course love this country. Look, Canada cannot compete in technology with the US even though they are both in North America. But they still keep skilful newcomers out of the workforce with restrictions and regulations. In fact, some work is very basic. Many Asian people can do those jobs but are not given a chance.

I said, "If you are given a chance, you will do a good job." She said,

> Really, we will, because we will value the job very much. We won't be so picky and we will work harder, but there is a lack of communication between the job market and job needs. Many people looking for jobs are educated and skilled, while many places looking for employees do not hire who they need. There is a gap.

Government organizations are so slow. On this point I miss China. Governments in Beijing and Shanghai react faster. Of course, it is not so all over China. But it is too slow here. They discuss a thing for two years with no result. You just have to wait patiently. This is their system. Of course it is a very well-developed system. Overall, it is a fairer system. For example, people can voice their opinions about whether the price should be raised or not. Ordinary people can have their voice heard. In China, no one will inform you when the price is to be raised. One day you find the labels were changed and the prices raised. Eh… I am worried too much about the country. I am out of China, but I am still concerned about it. I really hate corruption, but I still love China.

Scene IV: Values and Traditions to Let Go or Hold On To

March 11, the 3rd Year, Interviewing Jia Ming's Mom, Toronto Public Library
Our conversation continued. Shirley's thoughts returned to Shanghai when she talked about traditions and changing values in China since the Cultural Revolution.

During the Cultural Revolution, I think, people were pure and simple-minded. Cadres worked harder than ordinary people. I miss that time. People lived a poor material life, but were rich in spirit. Society was simple. That was good. The world was fairer then. Nowadays people are snobbish and complicated.

I think our traditional values are good. It is said that we should have new ideas but old morality. Old morality can't be criticized and discarded. When the old morality was scorned and discarded, people lost the basic sense of being human. In our factory, I found many new graduates were selfish. It is all right if you are not satisfied with your job, but you must do your work well. You can't be careless. It is said that we should do things according to our conscience. I think the elderly workers were like me. We thought alike. When we distributed the bonus money from the factory, the new graduates would argue. They made others unhappy. However, no matter how unhappy the older employees were, they still worked diligently and carefully without making mistakes. Those new graduates would say, "Um! Let it be. I don't care." We are middle-aged now. They are young. If the moral standard goes down like this and if China is built by such young people, it is terrible.

Scene V: Respect the Elderly and Care for the Young

March 11, the 3rd Year, Interviewing Jia Ming's Mom, Toronto Public Library
When I asked Shirley about her education of Jia Ming, apart from school, she said:

> I hope he will respect the elderly and care for the young 敬老爱幼, like I do. My father, who worked in the School Board, supported our immigration and thinks it is good for Jia Ming's education. My mom is more traditional. She would prefer her children to stay close, as she is getting older.
>
> I love my parents and they love me. Now they transfer their love and caring to Jia Ming. So, how we treat our parents has an influence on his behavior. We model for him. For example, I tell him, "Grandpa and Grandma are getting older. We should take care of them. When it is Chinese New Year or holidays, we should send money to them no matter how hard our life. It is not a lot of money. It is a gesture to show them that we care about them and want them to be happy."
>
> When we were in Shanghai, I always asked Jia Ming to give the money to the grandparents for us. I would say, "Jia Ming, let's go and give money to Grandpa and Grandma." Or, "Grandpa is sick. We've got to go and see him." Filial piety is not just on one's lips; it has to be in action. I hope the way I care about my parents will set an example for Jia Ming.

It was overcast with light drizzles when we left the library. Shirley waited with me until my bus came. As we waited, she repeated many of her concerns and said how things were much more difficult in Canada than she imagined. Their life was not advancing as they had imagined it might.

Episode Five: Efforts, Sacrifices, Dissonance, and Hopes

Jia Ming graduated from Bay Street Community School in June of his second year in Canada. I took pictures for him and other Chinese newcomer students in the LEAP programs and in the Newcomer Support Class. The children dressed up and Jia Ming looked like a young man. During the summer, Shirley e-mailed me to say they had moved to a neighborhood close to the Collegiate (academic high school) where Jia Ming would attend Grade 9. She invited me to visit their new home. I was to be their first guest.

Scene I: *Different Accounts of Discrimination at School*

August 17, the 3rd Year, Home Visit and Interview, Jia Ming's New Home
I looked for Shirley's building. With many high-rises, the neighborhood looked like a residential area in newly developed places in China. I found the building and buzzed the code. Jia Ming opened the door. The one-bedroom apartment had a small bed in the living room and a small sofa and desk with chair on one side close to the bed by a big window. At the end of the bed against the wall was a TV. To the left, was a small kitchen with an open space extending into a dining room/living room complex. The apartment looked more spacious than it actually was.

I asked Jia Ming what he was doing. He said he was reading *New Concept English*, a set of British textbooks that have been popular among Chinese learners of English since the 1980s. I learned *New Concept English*, from Book 2 to Book 4 as a university student in Suzhou. Jia Ming said his mother asked him to copy one text every day, so he was copying the text before I arrived. I suggested that he listen to the tape before copying, because this would help his listening comprehension. I explained the text and showed him how to pay attention to the idioms, colloquial expressions, and sentence patterns to learn how to use the language as well as understand the text.

I asked Jia Ming what he was doing during the summer. He said, "I have been to summer school because Ms. Campbell said my English wasn't good enough. After we moved, I went back to Bay Street Community School to play football and basketball with my friends." He told me his friends were Yong Chang 永昌, Kwan, and Xin Yin 欣颖 from the LEAP II class. They took language with Ms. Campbell, but science, math, music, and art with other teachers. He also made friends with students in regular classes in Rooms 46 and 47. I asked him if he experienced any discrimination in those classes. He said he didn't. Jia Ming told me:

> At the beginning we LEAP students were quiet, especially in Mr. Schwartz's Room 46 math class. But we did well in math, and better than other students. The students admired our math talent and became friends with us. We talked and joked together.

It seemed that language played a crucial role here. The reason I asked about discrimination was that it was raised by other newcomer students in

Ms. Corter's Room 48 class when they talked about having integrated sessions in regular classes. Xiu Hua 秀华, a newcomer girl from Fujian, had told me a story about this situation. When the newcomer students were in Room 46, regular students would derogatorily call them "ESL students", commenting that they could neither speak nor understand English. She also told me about discrimination in other situations, such as lunchtime in the cafeteria. Eventually Xiu Hua and several other newcomer girls brought their lunches to a classmate's home close to the school. Jia Ming commented on this, saying:

> It is mostly because they couldn't speak English. We Chinese students from Ms. Campbell's class were all good at math. The foreign students from Room 46 were really impressed.

> At the regular class in Room 46, the newcomer students from Room 48 always sat together with us LEAP students from Room 49. They wouldn't sit with the regular class students in Room 46. When Mr. Schwartz (teacher of Room 46) asked them a question, they always asked LEAP students to translate. Also, they went to Mr. Schwartz's math class only twice a week while we went every day.

Scene II: A Father's Sacrifices and Hopes

August 17, the 3rd Year, Home Visit and Interview, Jia Ming's New Home As we talked, Jia Ming's father, Mr. Lin, arrived home carrying three grocery bags in each hand. This was the first time we had met. He said workers in his workplace were on strike and were not allowed to go into the factory. They were required to sit outside or walk around. Today there was an agreement, so the workers could go home. During the strike, he said, workers were given half pay by the union, so they had a dilemma: They had to support the union, but were afraid of losing their jobs if they did. Jia Ming's father said that it was hard as a newcomer: He did not know the rules and his rights, and had to do what he was told to do. His wages were the family's only financial source. As the father spoke about Jia Ming, he echoed Shirley's views.

> We came here for Jia Ming's sake. We wanted him to have a better education and get into a better university. But if he came later by himself, we wouldn't

know how he was doing. Therefore, we preferred to come now with Jia Ming although we gave up our life and careers in China.

I asked him if he regretted immigration. The father said, "Not as long as it is good for Jia Ming. We hope our sacrifices make it the best for Jia Ming's future. We hope he studies hard and goes to university."

Mr. Lin said his wife had told him to boil dumplings for lunch. She made them yesterday and wanted me to have home-made Shanghai dumplings. Mr. Lin took them out of the freezer and went to the kitchen. There were no walls blocking the view between the small kitchen and the living room. While he cooked dumplings, we talked. In China, Shanghai men have a reputation for being gentle husbands and caring fathers. Jia Ming's father seemed to fit this description. He spoke gently.

> I sacrificed everything for Jia Ming's sake. I worked in a big company in Shanghai that produced a good brand of TV. My wife and I both had well established careers in Shanghai. We owned a three-bedroom apartment and our life was comfortable. But we wanted to come to Canada with Jia Ming to make sure he followed the right track in his life. There were many newspaper reports of Chinese students coming to North America alone and not studying hard. Some got disoriented and lost. Some committed crimes. We take it as our priority to help Jia Ming adjust to society and life here. When he gets into university, we will feel more secure and confident. We want to watch over him to make sure he stays on the right track. So we've been very careful about what kind of friends Jia Ming makes. At the same time, we encourage him to make friends. He likes sports, so we encourage him to play with his friends.

The telephone rang. Jia Ming answered. He gave the phone to me, saying his mom wanted to speak to me. Shirley apologized for not being home and said that she had to stay with her friend longer than she thought. She asked me to urge Jia Ming to study harder. She said, "One word by you is worth 10 words by me." Wen Feng's, Yang Yang's, and Zhi Gao's moms said the same when asking me to talk with their boys.

Mr. Lin asked Jia Ming to bring me a bowl of dumplings made of sticky rice powder. The father brought another bowl for Jia Ming. I thanked him and asked him to eat with us. He said the pot was small and he could only made enough for two, so he would wait until his wife got home. He urged us to eat first and went to another room to let me talk with Jia Ming.

Scene III: *Jia Ming's Reflections on His First Year in Canada*

August 17, the 3rd Year, Home Visit and Interview, Jia Ming's New Home
I first interviewed Jia Ming at the school library one month after his arrival in Canada when he was placed in Mr. Anderson's Newcomer Support Class. At that time, he talked mostly about his school life in Shanghai. Now, one year later, Jia Ming spoke confidently and excitedly about his Toronto school life, his LEAP class friends, and their teachers.

> I feel that I have made great progress in the past one year in all aspects of my English. When I was in Mr. Anderson's class, I had just arrived in Canada. I was not confident in English, so I dared not talk much English in class. Next semester I was transferred to Ms. Campbell's LEAP class. At first, I felt the same and dared not speak English. Most of the time, I couldn't understand the teacher. Gradually, I made progress. Students in Ms. Campbell's class always spoke English, like Xin Yin欣颖, *Yong Chang*永昌, *and Yuan Ping*袁平. *Gradually I could understand what the teacher said. I became more active and also made a lot of friends.*

I nodded and remembered how interactive the LEAP II class was. I asked Jia Ming how he liked the teaching methods. He said,

> In Mr. Anderson's class, we didn't learn English. Everyone spoke Chinese. Most students couldn't speak English. In Ms. Campbell's class, if I wanted to borrow something from Xin Ying or Yong Chang, we always spoke English. So I found I made great progress in her class. Mr. Anderson was easy with the students while Ms. Campbell was strict. Some students said Ms. Campbell was one of the strictest teachers in the school. I like her. She often joked with us and chatted with us. When she lost her temper, mostly it was because students didn't do their schoolwork or homework, or were repeatedly late. Then Ms. Campbell would scold the student very harshly.

I laughed and remembered how the naughty boys were trained and disciplined by Ms. Campbell to walk quietly in the hallway when they went to the library. I noticed that Ms. Campbell had different approaches to working with different students. She often joked with her LEAP II students who were more self-motivated in learning, but put on a face that was tight enough to keep the loud boys quiet in the LEAP I class. The boys who were transferred to LEAP from the Newcomer Support Class were trained strictly by Ms. Campbell to learn how to behave themselves in class and on field trips.

When asked, Jia Ming told me how he liked other classes.

> At the beginning, I was not quite comfortable in other classes. In our own class, when the teacher asked a question, we answered without raising our hands and our teacher often joked with us. In the other class, the teacher looked serious and students would be serious and wouldn't feel free to talk. I liked summer school math. The teacher first gave us simple math and then more difficult questions. When we were doing the difficult ones, the teacher said I was the only student who could work out the answers. So she gave me a math book and asked me to do more.

I asked Jia Ming if he found any difference between what he learned in Toronto from what he learned in Shanghai. He said what he learned in Canada was more practical and related to real life. He gave an example of coin tossing in his Toronto math class.

> For example, toss the coin. We each tossed a coin many times and counted the number of times it landed on "heads" or "tails". It is for us to learn the ratio and the percentage. We were asked to toss the coin by ourselves, and to write down the frequency. Each one of us got a different answer.

> I feel more relaxed here than in China. In China, we had to sit still and keep quiet. Here you can answer the teachers' questions without raising your hand. You can also joke with the teacher and play games. This is impossible in China.

Jia Ming told me most of his friends were from Room 49, the LEAP program.

> The friendship is very profound, important and special for me, because we share the same experience and we usually help each other when we are in difficulties. We cherish our friendship very much; for example, my friendship with Kwan, the Vietnamese boy. At the beginning, we didn't talk much when we first arrived and were both placed in Room 48, the Newcomer Support Class. Then, in the new semester we both were transferred to LEAP, Room 49. We both felt challenged at the beginning, as we couldn't understand what the teacher was saying. So we were quiet in class. The teacher often paired two of us to do homework or to do projects together because we were at the same level. From that time until graduation, we always worked together. I am better at math, so I helped Kwan with his math, and Kwan is better at art so he helped me with my art. We also went out together playing ball. When I was in China, I had friends, but I took it more or less for granted and I didn't think of friendship as something very special. Here it is different.

I asked Jia Ming if he kept in touch with teachers and friends in China.

> We just bought a computer. I got on the Internet. As soon as I got into their chat room, they said, "Wow! Where did you emerge from? Haven't heard from you for a long while. We haven't talked for a long time. We really miss you!"

Jia Ming said he chatted with his Shanghai friends by typing half Chinese and half English.

Shirley came back. Mr. Lin went to the kitchen to boil more dumplings. We talked about Jia Ming. Shirley said she always pointed out Jia Ming's weaknesses:

> Yesterday, Jia Ming protested that I always focused on his weaknesses and ignored what he had achieved. I said, "I want you to do better. Others out of politeness may not point out your weaknesses. But I am your mom. I have to let you know the truth so that you can realize what you need to improve, rather than being too proud of yourself and self conceited."

I said, "Children need to be encouraged. He might just give up if you tend to ignore his achievements." Shirley said she was concerned that Jia Ming was so young that he might not realize his own weaknesses and he might become too self-conceited if she always emphasized the positive side.

Scene IV: Dissonance and Hope in the New Homeland

August 17, the 3rd Year, Home Visit and Interview, Jia Ming's New Home
We watched the Olympic games together and talked about the biased report made by the CBC during the Olympic Games. Jia Ming's mom said that China got 10 golden awards and other medals, but only once did she hear the Chinese anthem. She felt kind of sad that "in multicultural Canada, the CBC only reported American athletes, Canadian athletes, or Australian athletes, only White athletes, not Chinese, other Asians, or Africans".

I understood how she felt. We talked about how Chinese immigrants like Canada with their hope for the best for their children. They do labor work with their professional skills, with a belief that their children will have a better education and a better future here in Canada. But at the same time, they still feel strong connections with China and hold on to Chinese cultural values. Just like early European immigrants who brought to Canada and the United States their customs and habits that have since become the mainstream American and Canadian cultures, new immigrants, too, bring with them their cultural connections and values. We did not understand why CBC, the national channel, would simply ignore the big population of immigrants of Chinese origin when they reported the Olympic games. We thought that public appreciation of immigrants' home country and of their home culture could help them maintain their self-esteem and re-establish their life in the new country and also find a sense of belonging in the new inclusive homeland.

I said goodbye to Jia Ming's father and took Shirley and Jia Ming to the Reference Library as it was only a 10-minute walk from their home. They both were amazed by the size of the library and by the number of people in the library. We went to the Language Centre on the fifth floor where people could learn English. I explained, "People can borrow books and videos or cassette tapes and listen and watch them here. Sometimes they need to make a reservation by making a phone call." Interestingly, Jia Ming did not show much interest in this section. He asked the librarian where he could find a Japanese textbook to learn Japanese. His mother said, "He wants to learn Japanese because he loves Japanese cartoon movies and he sings Japanese songs." Jia Ming said he was also interested in the language itself.

I was amused because the mom hoped that Jia Ming would improve his English and also learn French, but Jia Ming seemed to be more enthusiastic about Japanese. We spent a long time at the multiple language shelves. Jia Ming's mom learned some basic Japanese in Shanghai. She helped Jia Ming search for textbooks, but they did not find what they wanted. Language books in Canada start from simple conversations, not the alphabet. Jia Ming wanted to start from the alphabet and learn Japanese phonetics. That is normally how a language is learned in China. From the textbook search, we could see the different approaches and concepts about language learning in China and Canada.

I said, "In China, we learn Chinese by starting with pin-yin but you wouldn't be able to find such a Chinese textbook that starts from the very beginning here." Shirley said she did not realize how difficult Chinese was until her friend who taught Chinese in Japan gave her examples to show how difficult Chinese was.

> I did not realize the Chinese language had grammar, such as a past tense, a present perfect tense like English until my friend gave one word as an example that actually meant past or present tense in English. I never thought of grammar when I was speaking Chinese, so I didn't realize there were different Chinese tenses.

I said:

> Yes. We Chinese did not learn Chinese starting from grammar and tenses. We learned by speaking it, so children pick up the language from adults before they read. But when we start learning English or another foreign language, we start from grammar and vocabulary. It makes language learning tedious.

Shirley said, "Now I realize why language learning here always starts from simple conversations. That is how people usually learn the language."

Jia Ming did not find the Japanese textbook he wanted. I suggested he check out some English books to read. I asked him if he was interested in *Harry Potter*. He said he watched the movies but he had not read the books yet. I suggested he borrow the *Harry Potter* books. "The point is to be interested in English reading." I said. But the system showed that all *Harry Potter* books in Toronto libraries were checked out. I said that he could reserve one and then the library would call him when the book was available. Obviously Jia Ming often visited libraries. Without referring to his card, he typed in his library card number and PIN and searched the catalogue, controlling the mouse skillfully. He must have used the computer a great deal when he visited the libraries.

We walked down Yonge Street. It was a beautiful day. Both sides of the street were full of strolling people of different ethnic backgrounds. Before I took them to Indigo, the big bookstore, we dropped by Dollarama, the one-dollar store where most items show "Made in China" labels. I said, "You can get pens, pencils and notebooks in Dollarama." Jia Ming's mom, thinking of the cost of time, materials, and the Chinese workers, was surprised that every item in the store was only one dollar. She felt sorry for the Chinese workers. I was not too surprised by the low prices. Even in

Toronto, with laws to protect the basic rights of workers, there are problems. Xiu Hua秀华, a newcomer girl from Fujian, told me she helped her mom in a clothes factory and was paid 15 cents per item. In the summer she worked for two weeks. She finished almost 10,000 items, and was paid $347.

We went into the Manulife Centre. I showed them around different stores. Jia Ming's mom said that if I did not take them, they might never enter these buildings because they were not sure what this building was and whether they could go inside. They lost their sense of direction inside the Manulife Centre. When we came out on Bloor Street, I pointed towards the east and said they would find their home by walking that way. I felt the same when I first arrived. For months, I did not walk as far as the bookstore Chapters and did not know how close Bay and Yonge Streets were to my university. It took time to get familiar with a new environment and get used to it. We said goodbye and said we would stay in touch.

Interlude

A Positive Light on the Way

Jia Ming went to Grade 9 at the downtown high school and Shirley started taking courses in public administration at a community college. We stayed in touch over the phone. Jia Ming told me there were many Chinese students in his new school, some from Bay Street Community School. Shirley had wanted Jia Ming to study harder to get into a regular class. She became worried when Jia Ming got 55 in his English in the regular class after his transfer from LEAP. They had to decide if Jia Ming should stay in the regular class or go back to the ESL class. Jia Ming wanted to stay in the regular class, for he liked his math teacher who often gave him challenging math work. Shirley told me the principal suggested that Jia Ming should drop one of his optional courses, French or Computer studies. Jia Ming loved them both, but he said he would drop Computer Studies as he wanted to learn French.

One year later, in November of his second year in the high school, Jia Ming told me he felt he had caught up in his studies and is confident about himself in Grade 10. When asked, he told me he no longer thought of changing schools, for he had made new friends and enjoyed his life at the high school. He said he would stay at the same high school until he got into university. Shirley has found a temporary job at a downtown office.

Regardless of some current frustrations, Jia Ming's family persists with their hopes, efforts, and determination. I feel happy for the family as life is moving along in a positive direction.

点评:

SHI JING'S REFLECTION

Jia Ming's parents are typical of Chinese families who make their children's education the family priority. To them, home is where the best school is. Chinese parents and grandparents make strong efforts and great sacrifices to provide the best education and thus a better future for their children.

Jia Ming's maternal grandparents played an important role in his childcare and early education. The grandparents' home was the boy's first home, one that he loved and treasured in his memory. From Grade 1 in Shanghai to high school in Toronto, Jia Ming has moved from one home to another. Each time the home was relocated according to where Jia Ming attended school and what worked best for his education and future. Jia Ming's parents and grandparents believed that Jia Ming would get a better university education in Canada or the United States and hence have a better future. With this belief, Jia Ming's parents, with no regrets, gave up their established careers and comfortable home in Shanghai. His grandparents supported their daughter's immigration to Canada even though, during their old age, Chinese parents would prefer their children to be close by.

The generational narratives of Jia Ming's family tell the differences between Chinese schools and Canadian schools in terms of parental involvement, the teacher's role, homework, notions of learning and playing, and educational approaches and expectations. The differences, frustrating as some may seem to be, reveal aspects and necessities of mutual appreciation and reciprocal learning between Chinese parents and Canadian teachers, and between Chinese schools and Canadian schools.

Newcomer families work hard and hope for the best for their children in Canada. Many, like Jia Ming's parents, though educated with professional skills, cannot find appropriate work. Dissonances are created. This dissonance that newcomer families experience reveals a longing for a sense of belonging in their new homeland. At the same time, they keep strong connections with China, their motherland, and hold on dearly to many Chinese cultural, educational, and family values. It is these Chinese values that, to a great extent, help newcomers like Jia Ming's parents maintain a sense of social worth in diminished social circumstances. These values are a source of strength as they work hard and move forward with determination, perseverance, and few regrets. The journey to home in Canada, where they believe their children will have a better education and a better future, is a difficult one.

CHAPTER 8

Intersecting Newcomer Families' Narratives on Landscapes in Transition

LANDSCAPES IN TRANSITION

How best to interpret, portray, and narrate the stories in Chapters 3 through 7, stories that take twists and turns across time, place, and social relationships? As I have discussed in Chapter 1, at one point, I was perplexed by the fluidity of the lives that I intended to study in a settling school due to the fluidity of immigration and settlement patterns. More importantly, changes in China, changes in Canada, and changes in the world interact with and influence one another, which in turn have most impact on those who live in this changing world. I have been seeking a way to capture the fluidity of people's lives, as well as the fluidity of my inquiry into their lived experiences that involve so many complex situations, dimensions, and domains. In Chapters 3 through 7, the stories are told and recorded in such a way that they have their own shapes and boundaries, partially set by me of course, but mostly driven here and there by following the life paths of the participants.

To achieve a narrative grip on these stories, I have adapted Connelly and Clandinin's (1995) notion of *landscapes of experience*. "Landscape" refers to the expression of experience physically, temporally, and socially. Expanded from Connelly and Clandinin's (1995) work, *landscapes in transition* is a concept intended to capture the experiential richness and the fluidity of the changing world in which newcomers live. It is a term that imagines multidimensional, multifaceted, inclusive, and fluid interpretations of experience. Furthermore, the multiple dimensions of landscape make it possible for landscapes to interact and overlap with one another, across physical, conceptual, cultural, social, and/or disciplinary boundaries. The term captures the dimensions in which people move physically and conceptually, personally, and socially. I use this concept as a frame for interpreting the family stories of Chapters 3 through 7, which travel across time, cultures, and continents.

The landscape notion is used by writers in a variety of areas seeking a metaphorical expression of complex experiential phenomena (e.g. Ames 2004; Bender 1995; Greene 1978; Hall and Ames 1999; He 2003; Martin 1994; B. Mitchell 2005; W. Mitchell, 1994; Phillion 2002; Xu and Stevens 2005). For my work, landscapes in transition portrays the Chinese way of seeing the world and reflects the way the Chinese sense and perceive reality. For instance, in the perceptive eye of the Chinese painter, Tao Chi 石涛 (1641–1707), mountains flow like rivers. For him, the proper way of looking at mountains is to see them as ocean waves frozen in time; similarly, rocks are seen not as static objects but as dynamic processes with their own particular configuration of energy–matter (Tu 1985). Moreover, most traditional Chinese paintings were drawn on hand scrolls. To be appreciated, they are opened and viewed slowly from right to left. The hand-scroll is considered to be a "special mobile form for artistic appreciation" (Zhuang and Nie 2000). When enjoying a hand-scroll painting depicting a landscape, the viewer seems to ride on a vehicle or a boat: he or she sees ever-changing scenes as the vehicle or boat moves. When doing a long hand-scroll painting, a Chinese artist does not have a fixed point of vision. This is described as "moving perspective" or "multi-point perspective" (Zhuang and Nie 2000). From such points of vision, nothing is perceived as permanently fixed. As Tu (1985) points out, the worldview that sees human beings as an integral part of a continuous process of cosmic transformation, in its continuity, wholeness and dynamics, enables the Chinese to perceive the self not as an isolated individual, but as the center of relationships, a concept, a landscape vision, which forms the Confucian perception of learning.

My family narratives have this quality of landscapes in transition viewed as the hand-scroll is unrolled. My participants in this perception, and worldview, are at the center of a set of holistic relationships. This is the idea that has guided my interpretive thought and writing as I come to grips with the Chinese newcomers' search for home.

I believe this Eastern conception, married with the narrative idea of landscapes in transition, resonates with Dewey's educational thinking which denies any disconnection between mind and body, and between the personal individual and social individual. For Dewey (1922/1964), there are no fixed ends, no fixed self-enclosed finalities, which exist for all normal changes in nature. "Ends are ends-in-view and, in a strict sense, an end-in-view is a means in present action; present action is not a means to a remote end" (Dewey 1922/1964, p.72). "Ends are, in fact, literally endless, forever coming into existence as new activities occasion new consequences" (Dewey 1922/1964, p. 76). It is the dynamic character of becoming rather than the static perfection of being that is the defining quality of the world of experience (Grange, 2004). My vision in this study of five immigrant Chinese families is that these families, and families like them, are the bridges, or at least a bridge, uniting East and West culturally, physically, and spiritually.

With such an end-in-view, "a device of intelligence in guiding action, instrumental to freeing and harmonizing troubled and divided tendencies" (Dewey 1922/1964, p.76), at the intersection of dialogues between the East and the West, I position my work in Confucian *continuity of being* and Deweyian's *continuity of knowing* with a three-dimensional narrative inquiry framework. I perceive landscapes as being in transition and in constant change temporally, socially, spatially, and conceptually. They are shaped and reshaped by the interactions of everyone and everything in and on the landscapes, including people, places, languages, cultures, concepts, ideologies, systems, policies, practices, space, and boundaries; and vice versa. In summary, landscapes in transition manifests and embraces space, connotations, dimensions, and domains thereby, permitting me to understand and interpret newcomer families' narratives of cross-cultural schooling experience and their search for home, a search for multicultural harmony in diversity.

No Longer Others' Stories: Why We Should Care?

Featuring five newcomer Chinese families in Canada, Chapters 3 to 7 profile the cultural and cross-cultural experience of schooling from the perspectives of grandparents, parents, and children. Typically Chinese as they appear to be, these family narratives are no longer the stories of individuals who can be labeled as "others". These personal narratives of Chinese families' cross-cultural experiences of schooling, different as they are, construct a shared educational narrative that has personal and social significance, focally for the Chinese communities, locally for Canadian and American societies of increasing diversity, and globally for the increasingly interdependent world community. They are part of us, not "other" to us.

Changing Face and Changing Landscape

Changing immigration patterns and sources in Canada have significantly increased the proportion of visible minorities in the Canadian population — from 6 percent of the Canadian population in 1986 to 11 percent in 1996, to 13 percent in 2001. Roughly one out of every five people in Canada is expected to be a member of a visible minority by 2017 (Statistics Canada 2005). Visible minorities are defined by the Employment Equity Act (1995) as Canadians who state that they are not White and not Caucasian, and are not aboriginal in their descent. Under this definition, regulations specify the following groups as visible minorities: Chinese, South Asians, Blacks, Arabs, West Asians, Filipinos, Southeast Asians, Latin Americans, Japanese, Koreans, and other visible minority groups, such as Pacific Islanders. According to Canada's 2001 Census, 58 percent of immigrants to Canada between 1991 and 2001 came from Asia and the Middle East (Statistics Canada 2001 Census). The facts and figures publicized by Citizenship and Immigration Canada (CIC 2005) indicate that since 1998, the influx of Chinese immigrants to Canada has put the People's Republic of China as the first of the top 10 source countries of immigrants. The CIC 2014 facts and figures report that China has remained one of the top three source countries for immigrants to Canada in spite of slight drop of Chinese immigrants since 2010. The Chinese, along with South Asian and Black communities, have become one of the largest visible minority groups, in Toronto, Vancouver, and Montreal where most settle.

Diversity is not simply changing the face of Canada's largest cities; it is changing Canadian values. With the adoption of Canada's multiculturalism policy (Government of Canada 1971) more than three decades ago and the implementation of the Multiculturalism Act (Minister of State (Multiculturalism) 1988a, b), Canada has adopted a unique national project, designed to enhance the understanding of, and respect for, diversity to build a cohesive society that makes it possible for all Canadians to realize their full potential (Minister of Public Works and Government Services Canada 2005a). One of the roles of CIC is to promote

Canadian citizenship and to support the successful integration of newcomers by "delivering the highest quality immigration, refugee protection and citizenship programs inspired by integrity, efficiency and responsiveness to community needs" (CIC, Canada 2005). Seventy-three percent of Canadians believe that immigrants are having a good influence on the way things are going in Canada (Ipsos-Reid 2004). According to the Ethnic Diversity Survey (Minister of Public Works and Government Services Canada 2005b), 79 percent of immigrants who arrived in Canada between 1991 and 2001 said they had a strong sense of belonging to Canada. Specific educational policies and practices have been developed and implemented to support English language learners in K-12 Canadian schools. In Ontario, for example, the Ministry of Education has developed a series of curriculum documents to help both in-service and pre-service teachers with guidelines and workable approaches and strategies to work with students who do not speak English as their first language. "Supporting English language learners: A practical guide for Ontario educators Grades 1 to 8" (Ontario Government 2008) and "Many roots, Many voices: Supporting English language learners in every classroom. A practical guide for Ontario Educators" (Ontario 2005) are good examples from the curriculum series.

Emerging Issues in New Situations

While government institutions and numerous organizations provide a variety of services and supporting programs to meet the changing needs of a multicultural population, improving and promoting Canada's multicultural reality is a continuing challenge. My study with Chinese newcomer families reveals that many well-intended programs and services do not work as well as expected. Program effects often do not match program hopes. This finding suggests that mainstream organizations at policymaking levels may not adequately represent visible minority perspectives. Part of the difficulty, as experienced by my participants, is that programs are developed and implemented without detailed insight into the lives of newcomer families on landscapes in transition. One of the purposes of my work is to provide a lens to explore these lives in a way that may be useful to program development and implementation.

Perhaps the main things this lens reveals are family struggles in the search for home on the physical, cultural, and educational landscapes in transition. The family, with its holistic emphasis on an idea of home is the primary support unit for new immigrants. But immigration and settlement patterns have reshaped and reconstituted notions of "family" and of "home". The diversity of Canadian families is magnified in the changing landscape of Canada (B. Mitchell 2005). Single-parent family situations, legislation on same-sex marriage, "astronaut families" in which a wage earner (usually the husband) works in a different country, and involuntarily separated families among immigrants, give rise to new social and educational concerns and to a potentially confusing sense of family and home for newcomer Chinese on one hand and the mainstream society on the other (see B. Mitchell 2005; P., Li 1998). Furthermore, my Chinese family stories, especially those of Zhi Gao and Yang Yang, show that newcomer families face new challenges in childcare and child discipline. Parents find shifting, unstable, even threatening boundaries when they find some of their habitual ways of parenting turn out to be inappropriate or even illegal in Canada. Puzzles and questions have constantly emerged throughout my work with Chinese newcomer families: What negotiation and communication can we make between the so-called Chinese way and Canadian way of child discipline and childcare in dealing with emerging parenting issues in new situations? How can these concerns be reflected in programs for newcomers? The landscape in transition can be confusing and disconcerting for newcomers in their search for home.

Another tension typical among Chinese families, revealed in Hui Lan's family story and in Jia Ming's story, is that Chinese families, labeled among the "Asian model minorities" in Canada and the United States (see Lee 1996; C. Park et al. 2003; Suzuki 1989), are known for parents' high expectations and aspirations for their children's academic success (see Louie 2004, 2001; Zhou and Kim 2006). However, these educational goals are related to Chinese cultural beliefs, shaped by a Confucian tradition. Zhou and Kim (2006) point out that, in addition to this cultural narrative, immigration selectivity and supportive ethnic social structures are additional factors in the Asian academic success story in Canada and the United States. The family narratives in my study not only resonate strongly with the cultural narrative, but also point to the underlying daily effort and sacrifice of Chinese parents, grandparents, and sometimes other family members, directed at supporting children's academic success. This effort and sacrifice is mostly unknown and invisible to teachers and others in mainstream society. While Chinese families' successful adaptation is highlighted in mainstream discourse, the variations, and special needs of Chinese families, especially those who have children at risk, tend to be unseen (see Lee 1996; Louie 2004; Suzuki 1989; Yeh 2002). When noticed, newcomer families' special efforts tend to be perceived as an expected response to immigration. There is a common attitude that newcomers are expected to adapt to the new society. But, as my family narratives overwhelmingly portray, newcomer families bring into their children's education, and into education generally, special knowledge that needs to be recognized. Newcomers need help, but they also have something to offer. Newcomer families should be recognized as contributors to the making of Canadian society that is constantly reshaped and reconstituted by newcomers' cultural interactions with, and adaptation to, the existing society. People who are considered as mainstream or who have adapted to the mainstream need to see themselves as part of the adaptation process in the changing landscape. This reciprocity can help contribute to a society that is multicultural and inclusive for all. The generational narratives in my study provide a detailed account of newcomer families' lived experience in their search for home on landscapes in transition. Their stories reveal both hidden needs, such as in Zhi Gao's case, and special contributions to a multicultural society.

Family Narratives versus Public Discourse

As noted in the previous section, a public narrative, constructed from government policies, official reports, and large-scale surveys, tells a somewhat Pollyannaish tale of recent immigrants' successful adaptation and sense of belonging to their new country. Using a narrative approach and the idea of landscapes in transition, I am able to understand Chinese newcomer families' personal narratives in a three-dimensional narrative inquiry space by exploring and observing closely how they experience home in Canada. I focus on how their lived experience in China and their cross-cultural lived experience in Canada have shaped and reshaped their notion of home as well as their notion of learning and schooling in cultural tensions and harmonies. The newcomer families' narratives in my study reflect cultural aspects in that Chinese families' notion of home and sense of family are closely related to their notion of learning and schooling in Confucian thought. For Chinese families, education includes both school education and family education. Chinese parents and grandparents like Hui Lan, Jia Ming's parents, Julian's grandma, Grandpa Jiang, and Freeman make special efforts to support their children/grandchildren to pursue academic success, and to adapt to the mainstream culture, which, they believe, is crucial to the children's and hence the family's future. In the meantime, at home, Chinese parents and grandparents emphasize the importance of educating children as to how to be human in traditional Chinese values, in the hope that they will bring up their children to be not only a good son or daughter of the family, but also good citizens of the society in a Chinese holistic worldview. In the cases of Zhi Gao and Yang Yang, both mothers tried their best to keep the boys focused on their schooling and emphasized the importance of their boys *growing up to be a good man even if they may not succeed in school* "不成才要成人". These values are beautifully and profoundly elaborated in Hayhoe's (2006) portraits of eleven influential Chinese educators.

It is apparent that language and culture play an important role in newcomers' adaptation, sense of belonging, and/or dissonance in the new land. However, the inclusiveness of the host society is an important factor that may decide whether a newcomer feels at home as they journey in the new land. For instance, in spite of government efforts to diversify mainstream broadcasting, claiming that "multicultural diversity is increasingly reflected by the content and on-screen presence of television hosts and lead actors" (Minister of Public Works and Government Services, Canada, 2005a, p. 13), newcomers may experience a sense of marginalization in the media. The story of watching the Olympic Games, as told in Chapters 4 and 7, where participants felt the Chinese were poorly represented, is illustrative. Visible on streets, in offices and schools, the "visible" Chinese minorities feel invisible in the public media. There is a domino effect of media portrayals, or lack thereof. Media portrayals of racial and minority groups affect how these groups are perceived and accepted in society. These perceptions are felt by newcomers and in turn influence how they forge their sense of belonging to the society. The portrayals, perceptions, and experience of the perception create a complex value matrix that has the potential to impact children's education. Later in the chapter, I discuss the lack of cultural role models in the public discourse of the mainstream society for children from families of visible minorities, especially newcomers, and the importance of role modeling in children and youth's education.

Reciprocal Learning Needs

Multiculturalism is an official Canadian policy and has been part of public discourse in Canada across many domains. In reality, attitudes are always under development. Dozens of years after the adoption of multiculturalism policy (Government of Canada 1971), one can still hear statements such as: "You came to our country. It is you who should learn and adapt, not me"; "We have been brought up this way. If you don't like it, you should go back to your own country." These expressions hold a view of immigration and multiculturalism that implies that it is the newcomers who should adapt and integrate. While there is some truth in this attitude, there is a greater truth in an inevitable process of mutual adaptation, and reciprocal learning.

The generational narratives in my study bring attention to the reciprocal educational needs of both newcomers and mainstream people. Immigrant adaptation is not a matter of replacing the old with the new, of exchanging one language for another, one value system for another. It is a process of merging historically founded cultural and personal narratives of experience. These narratives can never be replaced, but only altered and re-shaped, with much being retained and taking on new shape. Though not as obvious, the same is true for the recipient society and its cultures, which are also being influenced, modified, and re-shaped in this process. While a newcomer's learning may be most obvious and most easily identified, the recipient learnings, perhaps less obvious, are, in the long run, equally important.

By using narrative methodology and a narrative notion of landscape, I am able to simultaneously study the cultural tensions and communications in the processes of cultural adaptation while, at the same time, appreciating the knowledge and values brought to Canada and the United States by newcomers. In the following sections, I bring forward the knowledge and values revealed in these family narratives that are resources for multicultural and interdisciplinary curriculum studies and teacher education. I hope they will provide insights for education that works best for our children, education that allows our children and youth grow up favorably in culturally, ethnically, and linguistically diverse communities.

Through the Lens of Generational Narratives

Notion of Home and Notion of Learning

In Chinese, home (家jia) is family (家jia) and family is home. Children's education is always the priority of a Chinese family as children are the future and hope of the family. Thus, to most Chinese families, home is where the best school is, and many families move their homes to where the neighborhood favors learning most. These parents follow the example of

孟子 Meng Zi's mother (Meng Zi, or Mencius, Confucian scholar of the fourth Century BC), one of the exemplary parent role models in Chinese cultural narratives that have been transmitted from generation to generation for over 2000 years. Millions of newcomer Chinese families seek home in Canada because they believe that their children can have better education and hence a better future in Canada. But is Canada truly "home" for newcomer families? Why do many Chinese families make Canada their home but still hold on dearly to Chinese traditional values and keep strong ties with China? In the following section, I relate Chinese families' personal narratives to Chinese cultural narratives to illustrate the point about Chinese families' notion of home and the connection between their notion of home and their notion of learning.

Essential Roles of Grandparents[1]

In my family I have observed how my parents and their generation acted as the major caregivers for their grandchildren and now how my brother and sister help take care of his and her grandchildren. This is a common practice, a circle of life, generation after generation, lived by many Chinese families in or out of China. My research with Chinese immigrant families in Toronto also show such a circle of life (Xu 2011b). Among Chinese immigrant families, grandparents are the major caregivers who bring school-aged children to and from school. Chinese grandparents are seen at the Parent Centre, in the hallway, and in Bay Street Community School's front yard, and at school concerts or Curriculum Nights. They take a crucial, sometimes central, role in childcare and children's education.

Julian's grandma and her husband took early retirement and joined their daughter's family in Toronto. She was a senior teacher at a high-rank elementary school in downtown Guangzhou, one the most prosperous regions in China. In spite of the fact that she loved taking care of Julian and his little brother and tutoring them to learn Chinese and math after school, her lived experience in Toronto showed that she lost her sense of home when the traditional family structure and values, as well as the interdependent family relationship, were challenged by new situations on landscapes in transition. In a sense, it is their Chinese family values that caused their cultural dissonance and family tensions, and resulted in these grandparents' lack of sense of home on the landscapes in transition. On the other hand, Chinese family values help explain why these grandparents stay in Canada to help their daughter and/or son, sharing family difficulties and responsibilities despite their dissonance and disillusion. They take it as the priority in their life to care for their grandsons and help with their education.

As expressed in Grandpa Jiang's story, Chinese grandparents find joy and see continuity in their life in the upbringing of their grandchildren. Wherever they are, Chinese grandparents serve as bridges across the boundaries of age, generation, culture, and country. Grandparents, as shown in stories of Julian's grandma, Grandpa Jiang, and Freeman and his wife, contribute greatly to young children's bilingual/bicultural and/or multilingual/multicultural education in Canada. Freeman and his wife illustrate how Chinese grandparents play an important role in their grandchildren's education. Freeman's grandsons, Stephen and Donald, spent most of their pre-school years and after-school time at their grandparents' home. It was the grandparents who took the parenting role and responsibility of taking care of the boys during and after school time, including after-school programs such as homework club and violin lessons. Freeman often shared with me his joy and pride in his grandsons' academic progress at school, and also in Stephen's violin awards. He took me to an exhibition where Donald, his daughter's son, received the national award for his innovative use of recycled bottles to build an amphibious helicopter. This project was inspired by Freeman who had worked in an airplane manufacturing corporation before his retirement. Like Freeman and his wife, the two boys manage four languages and immerse themselves in several cultures at their grandparents' home, their own homes, schools, local Chinese/Cantonese communities, the Burmese community and mainstream society. Chinese grandparents, such as Julian's grandma, and Freeman, are not only culture brokers and bridges for grandchildren on cross-cultural landscapes in transition, but also role models for the young generations as to how to be human in Confucian values. They believe the sacrifices they make are worthwhile because, as seen in Grandpa Jiang's story, Chinese grandparents believe they are making a contribution to family harmony, and hence to the harmony and growth of society.

Chinese grandparents and parents' dedication to the family and their sacrifices for the next generations are rooted in Chinese cultural traditions that emphasize family ties. From the Confucian perspective, selflessness as a primary virtue is more self-realization than self-sacrifice. Grandpa Jiang's personal narrative shows how Chinese people maintain supportive family connections which benefit family members in difficult times. This value and its practice are rooted in the Confucian tradition in which personal order and social order are mutually entailing (Hall and Ames 1999). As Fei (1947/1992) illustrates, Chinese society is "egocentric" in that each person is at the center of his or her own network. To Confucius, as his follower Mengzi (Mencius) summarized in his works on Confucian thought, self, family, and the nation/society are interrelated; hence, one's learning/self-cultivation (修身 *xiu-shen*) contributes to the prosperity of the family (齐家 *qi-jia*) and thus to the harmony of the nation/society (治国平天下 *zhi guo ping tian xia*. In Chinese, speaking of "nation" is to speak of "nation family"(国家 *guo-jia*); to speak of "everyone," is to speak of "big family" (大家 *da-jia*); to speak of Confucianism or Taoism is to speak of "the family of Confucian scholars" (儒家 *ru-jia*) or "the family of Taoist scholars" (道家 *dao-jia*) (see Hall and Ames 1999). Thus, it may be said that Chinese grandparents' sense of home, as revealed in Julian's grandma, Grandpa Jiang, and Freeman's family stories, is expressed in their help and sacrifice for their children and grandchildren. To help the grandchildren is to search for self-value, and to support the family and the society, the *nation family*. As Hall and Ames (1999, pp. 33–34) point out,

> The centrality of this idea of family as the grounding metaphor pervasive in Chinese culture arises from two Confucian insights. First, the family is that institution in which people give most wholly and unreservedly of themselves… Second, the continuity between humanity and the world—between culture and nature—leads to the singular importance of the family metaphor in the definition of relational order within Chinese cosmology.… In the Chinese language, "the world" is *shijie* 世界, literally "the succeeding generational boundaries" which conjoin one's own generation to those who have come before, and to the generation that will follow this one; the pursuit of wisdom is literally, "to know the way (*zhidao* 知道)." This pursuit has, from classical times, centered on finding a way to stabilize, discipline, and shape productively and elegantly the unstoppable stream of change in which the human experience is played out.

Many Chinese grandparents live out this philosophical thought in their daily life; Grandpa Jiang summarized everything concisely when he said, "so, it is worth it." Also, following the path of Confucian tradition, an answer may reveal itself to the puzzles about Danny's great grandma who appeared to be mistreated by her granddaughter in-law, but chose to stay with her grandson's family even though she had better personal choices (see Chapter 2). It is a special happiness for a Chinese grandparent to see his or her great grandchild and live in a *family of four generations* 四世同堂. The granny seemed to treasure this special happiness even though hers was somewhat sour and bitter, with younger generations having grown up in a ruptured cultural landscape where Confucius was denounced and Confucianism was scorned during the twentieth Century, especially during the 10 years of the Cultural Revolution (1966–1976). More edges are added to the family tensions and challenges on a new cultural landscape when the young generation adopts what they perceive to be the Western way of living, as revealed in stories of Julian's grandma.

Role modeling in Chinese Parenting

Role modeling is an important Chinese cultural practice that can be traced to the Confucian way of learning. Confucius wrote extensively about the Sage Kings, the ancient exemplary cultural models. Confucius (孔夫子 Kong Fu Zi, or 孔子 Kong Zi), along with 孟子 Meng Zi (Mencius), 老子 Lao Zi and many cultural and historical figures in Chinese history, have been Chinese cultural models. Chinese parents and grandparents often teach their children/grandchildren by referring to these cultural role models; as well, parents and grandparents use these models for their own behavior, thereby teaching children and grandchildren how to be human in Chinese traditional values. For example, Hui Lan modeled for her sons in her daily life. She urged her husband to send money to his mother out of their tight budget. She and her husband lived out the traditional family values by being supportive of the large family circle.

However, the landscape of China has been in rapid and constant change. Traditional, reciprocal, interdependent family relationships are being challenged during the process of modernization in China, as well as by the younger generations' adoption of Western values. Regardless, Hui Lan wanted her sons to learn to be human according to traditional Chinese values. Furthermore, she made special efforts to learn English herself and to help her sons succeed in school with the family dream that they will go to university in Canada and the United States and integrate successfully into mainstream life. At the same time, she ensures that her boys are aware of being Chinese and of their duty to serve the Chinese community. Hence, she urged them not only to learn English well, but also to learn Chinese well. She herself would not give up learning English despite the difficulties as she believes that, if she keeps learning, "there is no reason for the boys not to study hard or to give up learning" (see Chapter 3). The same is true with Shirley, Jia Ming's mom. She explicitly modeled for Jia Ming the Chinese family motto: 敬老爱幼 *Respect the elders and care for the young*, an important Chinese traditional virtue, valued from generation to generation.

Stories about Zhi Gao and Yang Yang, on the other hand, reveal that issues and problems emerge when children lack role models in their upbringing. In Zhi Gao's case, the boy appeared to have had no male role models in his early life in China. While his mother managed to make a living for the two of them in China, there were no grandparents to share the parenting role and family responsibility. His lack of sense of home in his stepfather's house in Toronto culminated in school, home, and social tensions in his life in transition. It seemed that his search for home was temporarily and partially realized, in a sense, at Bay Street Community School where his teachers worked hard to help and care for him, and where he developed a special friendship with other newcomer students in similar circumstances of lives in transition. Still, he walked "the edge of a cliff" at elementary school. He often said he wanted to quit school, but he always returned. However, when he moved, without his friends, to high school, he appeared to lose all sense of belonging. He was lost on a new school landscape, and eventually "fell off the cliff". My conversations with Zhi Gao suggest that, to a certain extent, his difficulties at school could be traced to his lack of role models that, in traditional Chinese families, help create a vision of the future, and model effective behavior in striving to achieve the vision.

For Zhi Gao, the sense of belonging, the sense of being "at home" and in the home, was closely related to his apparent search for belonging and being "at home" in school. The search for home, especially for the Chinese, is a search for belonging in a wider, expanding set of relationships, in connection with home, school, community, the Chinese way of life. When this sense of belonging in relationship is missing, school success may be one of the casualties. Also, as one of the teachers pointed out, some boys were at risk of falling into the hands of gangs when they mistook gang members who appeared to be strong and powerful, for male role models.

Throughout my study with Chinese families and my personal and professional cross-cultural journey, I observed that it was a challenge for visible minority groups to find appropriate role models for their children when cultural role models are not well represented in the mainstream society. I believe that the Chinese idea of role modeling in education helps explain the strong attachment I experienced with Chinese families in my study. Several mothers, especially Hui Lan, Jia Ming's mom, Zhi Gao's mom, and Yang Yang's mom, often called me to discuss their boys' education, and often asked me to talk to their boys. Because I was a professor before I came to Canada and I was a doctoral student during the time when I did my fieldwork at the school, I was the most educated Chinese person at the school in terms of formal education. I could have been thought of as "an egg head", a person of little possible practical understanding or sense of the realities of immigrant educational life in a Western critical eye, yet it was the opposite among the Chinese families. The fact that I was a doctoral student appeared to offer space and hope for my participant Chinese families to imagine the tomorrow they want for their children. Parents and grandparents referred to me as "that university student 大学生" when they talked about me in the Parent Centre. When universities and colleges in China were returned to normal upon the end of the Cultural Revolution, the title "university student 大学生" connoted a special social status. It is the family dream of many newcomer families that their child/children will go to a Canadian or an American university. This family dream is, for many, the main motivation for immigrating to Canada. Education has always been the priority of Chinese families, and higher education is the goal of the educational pursuit. Even Zhi Gao changed his defiant attitude and listened to me respectfully and cooperatively when he learned, from the research consent form, that I was a doctoral student. He told his mom about me in a way that expressed his admiration for higher education: "She is a woman, but she is a doctoral student!" Hui Lan and Shirley stopped calling me by my given name and insisted on calling me "许老师 Xu Lao Shi" (Teacher Xu) when they learned that I was a university teacher in China even though I told them that I preferred to be called Shi Jing. They also asked their children to call me 老师 *Lao Shi* (Teacher) although earlier Hui Lan had asked her little boys to greet me as *Auntie*. My interactions with Chinese families reveal that Chinese parents and children perceived me in various roles: a doctoral student and a researcher from University of Toronto; a cultural broker between parents and teachers, and between home and school; a teacher who speaks both languages and knows both worlds; and a role model from whom they can envision their children's future. Ms. Corter, the Newcomer Support Class teacher, said to me several times that she wished she had more people like Mr. Feng and myself who could visit her class to serve as role models for the Chinese newcomer students.

Homework in Chinese Learning

In the family narratives in my study, homework stands out as one of the major concerns. The cultural root of homework can be traced back as early as 2,000 years ago in Confucian learning. Although Confucianism was denounced for many decades in the past century, Confucian educational thought and values have become part of Chinese social practice and daily life in various forms with or without the "Confucian" label. Homework is such an example. Chinese families put special emphasis on their children's homework, and the major complaint Chinese families have about schools in Canada and the United States is the lack of homework (see Dyson 2001; J. Li 2001; G, 2002).

Unsatisfied with Canadian elementary school practices, especially in terms of homework, Chinese families tend to take more or less the same compensatory approaches. Julian's grandma was unhappy thinking that Julian played all day long at school without any homework. She tutored Julian half an hour every day after school in his math and Chinese. Hui Lan gave additional homework to her boys every day after school and during holidays, and sent her boys to out-of-school programs to learn math and English at the local community centres. Freeman took Stephen to the Homework Club offered by the school and a community centre. Shirley closely monitored Jia Ming's homework and assigned him additional homework to make sure, she said, that he concentrated on his studies, rather than "wasting" time watching TV or playing computer games. For Zhi Gao's mom and Yang Yang's mom, homework seemed to be a special way to monitor and discipline their boys. When they met with the teacher, they would ask that their boys be given more homework. I participated in many parent–teacher interviews, and homework always stood out as the major issue of concern for Chinese parents and grandparents. The importance of homework transcended specific learnings and played a part in representing and ensuring that overall Chinese values were being taught. Moreover, homework provided a vehicle for parents, wary of possible bad influences in their children's social life, to monitor and direct them in Chinese living.

As with other aspects of the search for home, Chinese parents' sometimes seemingly obsessive pursuit of homework is associated with

Confucian educational notions. Chinese families may not necessarily be self-aware of this cultural narrative root, because of the denunciation of Confucius in the twentieth century. However, Confucian thought is so deeply rooted in Chinese society that Confucian values and tradition have become part of social and personal daily practice in education and life. Quotations from 论语 *Lun Yu*[2] (the Analects), a collection of Confucius' conversations with his disciples, on educational thought and the way of learning and being, have been so frequently cited, modified and applied by Chinese teachers and parents that they have become colloquial idioms in daily language and an important part of practice in Chinese teaching and living. For example, 学而时习之 (The Analects: 1.1. *Frequently review and practice what has been learned*); 温故而知新 (The Analects: 2.11 *Review the old as a means of learning/realizing the new*); 学而不厌, 诲人不倦 (The Analects: 7.2 *Continue studying without feeling bored, and teach others without becoming tired.*); 三人行,必有我师 (The Analects, 7.22: *While walking together with two other people, I am bound to find one person who can be my teacher*); 性相近,习相远 (The Analects, 17.2: *By nature, people are much alike, but learning and practice set them apart.*) 学而优则仕 (The Analects, 19.13: *Learn with the pursuit of excellence and thus become an official scholar*).

To a great extent, it is most Chinese families' ideal that their children "learn with pursuit of excellence and thus become an official scholar 学而优则仕" by going to the best school and hence the best university. Ironically, this Confucian ideal was mostly criticized and denounced during the Cultural Revolution as scholars were criticized for being too far away from the common people, workers and peasants, at the bottom of the Chinese society. The fact that the denounced ideal was quickly and firmly restored in Chinese families' minds reveals how deeply the Confucian values are embedded in Chinese society and in Chinese people's daily life. On the other hand, in China, it is a common parent complaint that children are overloaded with too much homework. It is commonly believed that homework as part of teaching practice has been utilized in extreme ways in China in a test-driven educational system. Chinese newcomer parents like Jia Ming's mom wanted their children to be educated in Canada instead because she felt the Chinese system was too rigid. Nevertheless, she and many other Chinese parents and grandparents become worried when they feel that their children seem to play all day without homework in Canadian schools.

The narrative of the cultural root of homework helps to explain why Chinese families persisted in their pursuit of their children's academic excellence with a special attention to homework no matter how reassuringly Canadian teachers tell them not to worry. In the matter of homework, a dissonance, even a clash, is evident between the narratives of Chinese families and those of Canadian teachers.

It is apparent that Chinese families' notion of home is closely related to their notion of learning, which is deeply rooted in Confucian thought. In search of home in Canada on landscapes in transition, Chinese families engage in integrating and harmonizing Chinese learning with Western knowledge and with the Western way of learning by negotiating, communicating, and interacting with Canadian teachers and families of other ethnic groups. Home is constantly being reconstituted on landscapes in transition. Home is where the best school is. Home is where Chinese learning is integrated and harmonized with Western learning for the prosperity of the family and the harmony of the society in a changing landscape of increasing diversity.

To Be Human in Confucian Values[3]

Some of my participants, such as Zhi Gao's mom and Yang Yang's mom, did not finish grade school and were marginally literate in Chinese and less in English, while some had university degrees. Yet, while pursuing their children's excellence in learning, the Chinese families in my study, whatever background they are from, all emphasized the importance of being human (Xu 2011b). To be human is to be a good person with Confucian values; this belief stresses the importance of a person's moral nature. "To be humane is to be man 仁者人也", Confucius said, in 中庸 *Zhong Yong* (*The Centre of Harmony* or *The Doctrine of The Mean*), one of the four books of Confucianism. To Confucius, humanity, being humane, is the fundamental quality of people, and without this quality a person is not a real human being.

> It means to love other people; to help others to stand up when one wants to stand up oneself, and help others to understand things when one wants to understand things oneself; and not to impose on others what one does not desire oneself 己欲立而立人, 己欲达而达人. 己所不欲勿施于人.

Hence, as Hayhoe (2006) observes in her portraits of Chinese educators, Chinese parents, including those with very limited education and means, share common concerns with their children's education, both in school and at home.

To Help Others

"To help others" is the basic moral quality of being human among the Chinese. Freeman, who had volunteered at the school's Parent Centre for a dozen years, continued helping Carmen and the Chinese families at the Parent Centre even though his family no longer had a child attending Bay Street Community School. Hui Lan, who volunteered at the Parent Centre, helped Xiao Feng's family when the boy's mom was hurt in a car accident. Hui Lan looked after the boy when his mom returned to China twice for several months. As Hui Lan put it, "We are friends. We just help when friends are in need."

Grandpa Jiang, however, was concerned over the fact that "nowadays in China many people do not want to help others". Grandpa Jiang found it wrong to discard the old way in which people had followed the Confucian principles of how to be human and how to live together with others. He thought that, "It is good to do something for others." He helped his younger sister and brother to establish their life and urged his daughter to send money to his aged big sister-in-law and another brother-in-law who used to help him when he was in need. He gave money to aged women in the village where the villagers treated him kindly during the Cultural Revolution. He built a tomb for his big brother and sister-in-law, something that nowadays in China sons may not do for their parents.

Return to Others in Abundance

Grandpa Jiang's story also reveals another important human quality cherished in Chinese tradition: Return to others in abundance for a bit of help you received (滴水之恩当涌泉相报 *Return with a bubbling spring for a drop of water that you received when you were in need*). Grandpa Jiang's big sister-in-law came to his family as a bride-to-be for his big brother, but the family had the girl more for the purpose of doing housework and looking after Grandpa Jiang when he was a baby boy. Grandpa Jiang left his hometown many years ago, but he never forgot what his big sister-in-law had done for him and his younger brothers, and he paid back in multiples to the big sister-in-law who turned into an aged lady with no source of income. He also returned his gratitude to his wife's brother whose help to Grandpa Jiang and his family during the Cultural Revolution had made it possible for the family to survive the difficult times.

Hui Lan and her husband also demonstrated this special virtue when her husband's former boss was ill. Although her husband's wage was the only source of family income and despite the pressure from his mother requesting money, Hui Lan's husband, with her understanding and support, declined a better-paid job to continue to work for the ill man, saying that his boss gave him the job when he was most in need. "Now the boss is sick and in need, it is not nice to leave him. I must stay when my boss is in need."

Share With Others and Care for Others

Julian's grandma said, "In China, we always share with others whenever we eat something, or at least we ask if others would like to have some before we eat alone. It would be rude if a person started eating without asking others." Freeman and his wife Mrs. Wong, Julian's grandma, Hui Lan and other parents would ask about me and worry when I did not visit the Parent Centre for a few days. They would phone me to find out if everything was all right especially during difficult moments, such as the SARS crisis, and during a time when there were a series of robberies in the downtown neighborhood. When the family shared a basement apartment in a downtown house with her brother's family, Jia Ming's mom made dinner for the whole family every day and waited until everyone got home to have dinner together no matter how late it was.

Regardless of the consequences of denouncing Confucius in the twentieth century, and regardless of the impact of a market economy that has changed the landscape in China economically, socially, culturally, morally, and politically, Confucian values continue to have an impact in Chinese society. Care about others is a quality promoted and cultivated in school curriculum and in teaching practice. Jia Ming said, "In China, we helped each other. If one was not doing well, the coordinating teacher would send student representatives to visit the student at home and to talk to and encourage the student and see what we could do to help." It is common for Chinese students to visit one another at home and help those who have difficulties in their studies or who are in need. It is also a common practice in China for teachers to visit a student's home to communicate with the parents and to understand the student better. This support helps students to develop a sense of belonging to school and a sense of home within one's class. The coordinating teacher (homeroom teacher) often encourages students to see their class as a family and asks them to help and care about one another like brothers and sisters.

A few times I helped the teachers at Bay Street Community School sort out puzzling situations. A boy or a girl would tell the teacher that his or her sister was coming to pick her or him up, but the child did not know the sister's name when the teacher asked. It turned out that the sister was a neighbor's daughter who attended senior grade at the school and helped the family by picking up the child. It is customary among the Chinese to call neighbors, parents' friends, or colleagues by family relationship terms such as grandpa, grandma, uncle, aunt, brother, or sister. This tradition is still in practice among the Chinese communities, especially in rural communities or small towns in China where everyone knows everyone else, often for generations.

Think of Others

"Do not impose on others what one does not desire oneself 己所不欲勿施于人" (The Analects: 15: 24) is a fundamental principle for Chinese people. In the words of Hui Lan, who applied this moral principle to her daily life, "You must do to others what you expect others do to you." This principle helped her to deal with family tensions, both in China and in Canada. This Confucian principle matches the Christian "Golden Rule", which may explain why Hui Lan, a Buddhist, is no longer concerned about Yong Chang participating in activities at the Christian Learning Centre; moreover, she also sends Yong Sheng and Yong Ming to attend programs offered at the center. Being a mother of three sons, Hui Lan can think of her mother-in-law and understand, from the perspectives of the mother-in-law, her request for help even when her husband, the son, found the request unreasonable. She wanted her husband to set a good example for their sons to follow: to respect the elderly and care about the young. She took over the house-keeping job at the Parent Centre so that Carmen could have more time to teach. She helped her husband's friend when the friend's family was in need. She did not press to meet with Yong Chang's high-school teacher although she was concerned about how her son was doing at high school. She was cautious about interrupting the school's regular routines or habitual way of doing things.

Julian's grandma appeared to be exhausted from doing multiple jobs, but she would rather her daughter take a rest during her off-work days. She said she wanted her daughter to rest as she looked thin and she was not happy that her daughter "worked like a farm animal" in a clothes factory. She was not pleased with her son-in-law as he appeared to be too self-centered and not to care about others. He would not let his wife take ESL classes, nor did he let Allen, Julian's little brother, take painting lessons. While Julian's grandma worked for the family and thought on behalf of the family to see what would work best for everyone, she was not happy that her son-in-law seemed to care more for money than for people.

Jia Ming's mom's story shows that she was a dedicated worker in her workplace in Shanghai, and she thought of other colleagues during a conflict of interest when she put the factory interest first. She was concerned about the current social phenomenon in China where young people have become more self-centered and care less about others. She worried at the loss of the collective in the expression of self-interest. Jia Ming, modeling himself after his mother, learned to think of others, and said, "I have become more caring to my parents and more respectful. My mom said I have become more mature and understanding after I came to Canada. I have learned to take care of others."

"Think of others" is the family golden motto at Freeman's home. His wife, Mrs. Wong, told me that she and Freeman had never argued during their long life together. "You do not feel so upset if you can think of others from their perspectives." Mrs. Wong said. Her sons, daughters, and their spouses would follow her example and lead a harmonious family life. She has treated her daughter-in-law like a daughter and her daughter-in-law respects her like her mother. Her big extended family was a family of four generations with a 90-year-old granny, the great grandma. At the time when I did my fieldwork at the school, both Freeman and his wife were older than 70 years, but every Sunday Freeman would accompany his wife to visit the great grandmother. This large extended family wonderfully illustrates a harmonious Chinese family of four generations that respects the old and cares for the young. This example is a dream of elderly Chinese, which can come true when all family members think of others. Here is a family, who were once newcomers, who have searched for and found home.

According to Confucian values, to adhere to moral principles is everyone's first and utmost important consideration. For Confucius, humanity is the supreme principle for which one should give up everything else, including one's life if necessary. Confucius said, "A humane man never gives up humanity to save his life, but he may sacrifice his life to realize humanity 志士仁人, 无求生以害仁,有杀生以成仁" (The Analects, 15.9). In connection with humanity, Confucius promoted other virtues, such as righteousness, propriety, wisdom, trustworthiness, loyalty, reciprocity, filial piety, and brotherly love.

BRIDGING THE EAST AND WEST DICHOTOMY: CONFUCIAN CONTINUITY OF BEING AND DEWEYIAN CONTINUITY OF KNOWING

Confucian Notion of Being[4]

The Chinese family narratives highlight the idea that the focus of Confucian learning is to learn to be human. To learn to become a true person in the Confucian sense is to be honest with oneself and loyal to others (Xu 2011b). This entails a ceaseless process through which humanity in its all-embracing fullness is concretely realized (Tu 1985). In the concentric circles that define the self in terms of family, community, country, and the world, the self is not the generic self as an isolated entity; rather, self is an open system and the center of relationships in which personal identity is realized first and foremost through the cultivation of those roles and relationships that locate one within the family, the community, the country, and the world (Hall and Ames 1999). To a certain extent, Chinese names manifest concisely such relationships, with the family name being the first name and one's own name being the last name; in a traditional Chinese name, one's middle name is the generation name. This is in contrast to a Western name in which one's own name goes first and one's family name is last. I followed the Chinese newcomer students' habitual way of putting his or her family name first when referring to a person by his or her full name, but only used their given names in narrating major characters' stories to avoid confusion. The underlying principles of Chinese names and Western names, as I observe in my cross-cultural journey, speaks to the phenomenon that people in the West emphasize individuality, and hence, individual rights and identity issues are often the major concerns; in contrast, people in the East worry more about their social values and are loaded with social responsibilities and family obligations, as articulated in the story of Shirley, Jia Ming's mom. Shirley, like many other Chinese professional immigrants, was troubled when her social values did not seem to be attained in the new homeland. The phenomenon of many Chinese immigrant professionals who have established their lives in Canada choosing to return to China in recent years might be attributed to the Confucian notion of *being* in which one's self-realization can be fully accomplished only through one's social contribution and belonging. In the Chinese tradition, self-realization involves the establishment of an ever-expanding circle of human-relatedness through the structures of the self, the family, the country and the world, where the country and the world are conceived as an enlarged family that emerges out of the process of self-cultivation, and the self is embedded in communal roles and relations (Hall and Ames 1999; Tu 1985, 2002). Therefore, "self-cultivation", the essential part of Confucian learning, is not only learning for oneself, but is also a societal and communal act.

The Self in Chinese Society versus the Self in Western Society

I had been puzzled about the fragmentation in the seemingly well-structured Canadian educational system; I wondered why such a well-staffed and equipped system with excellent personnel and rich educational resources could not prevent newcomer boys like Zhi Gao from falling out of the school system. Fei Xiaotong (1947/1992, p.21), a Chinese sociologist trained in the West before the mid-twentieth century, observed "the substantial differences between an egocentric Chinese society and an individualistic Western society" (Hamilton and Wang 1992). He used two metaphors to forcefully illustrate the differences: Western society is represented by straws collected to form a haystack, and Chinese society is represented by the ripples flowing out from the splash of a rock thrown into water. I find his metaphorical comparisons of the Chinese society and the West helped me understand some of the puzzling phenomena in my study. Fei (1947/1992) observes that,

> Western societies are somewhat like the way we collect rice straw to use to cook our food. After the harvest, the rice straw is bound into small bundles; several bundles are bound into larger bundles; ... Each piece of straw belongs in a small bundle, which in turn belongs in a larger bundle, which in turn makes up a stack. The separate straws, the separate bundles, and finally the separate stacks all fit together to make up the whole haystack. In this way, the separately bound bundles can be stacked in an orderly way (Fei 1947/1992, p.61).

According to Fei's (1947/1992, pp. 61–62) argument, in the West individuals produce their society by applying an "organizational mode of association".

> In Western society, these separate units are organizations… Each organization has its own boundaries, which clearly define those people who are members and those who are not.

Fei's (1947/1992) metaphor of haystacks depicts the structure of the Western society in which people create groups with clear boundaries. Membership in these groups is unambiguous, and the rights and duties of members are clearly defined (Hamilton and Wang 1992). Fei illustrates that, in an organization with distinct boundaries and particular requirements for membership qualifications, people show their respect to individual rights and follow regulations defined by the law. Fei's metaphor helps me to understand and articulate the visible and invisible boundaries over which newcomer children and their families in my study often stumbled.

Fei (1947/1992, pp.62–63) compared the structure of the Western society with that of Chinese society:

> In Chinese society, the most important relationship – kinship – is similar to the concentric circles formed when a stone is thrown into a lake. Everyone stands at the center of the circles produced by his or her own social influence. Everyone's circles are interrelated. One touches different circles at different times and places.

He further compared some interesting aspects of the differences of the notion of family between the Chinese and the West.

> Families in the West are organizations with distinct boundaries. If a Western friend writes to you saying that he will "bring his family" to visit you, you know very well who will be coming with him. In China, however, this sentence is very ambiguous. … In Chinese, the word *jia* (family) is used in many ways. *Jialide* (the one at home) can mean one's wife… *Zijiaren* (my own people) may include anyone whom you want to drag into your own circle, and you use it to indicate your intimacy with them. The scope of *zijiaren* can be expanded or contracted according to the specific time and place. It can be used in a very general way, even to mean that everyone under the sun is a *jia* (one family). (Fei 1947/1992, p.62)

As Chinese family narratives reveal, confusion and misunderstanding arise between home and school when teachers and parents do not share the same cultural and societal narratives. Drama of the sort expressed in Hui Lan and Yang Yang's stories was thus created in the lives of newcomer families.

The Need for Reciprocal Learning between the East and the West

Every December since 2010, the Program for International Student Assessment (PISA) tests have been the headlines of all media coverages. Top test scores from Shanghai in 2009 assessment reported in December 2010 stunned educators in the west (Dillon 2010; Fallows 2010; OECD 2014), which have resulted as a wake-up call that "a Sputnik moment is back", along with heated discussions and debates (also see ABC news by Pham 2010; Bruce 2010). The 2013 results, from tests taken in 2012, continued to show that the highest performers were in Asian countries. It showed the United Kingdom and the United States failed to make progress on previous tests and there was more attention for Shanghai's top results (OECD 2014). There have been doubts and follow-up analysis trying to prove that the reports on Shanghai students' performances, as well as Chinese education, were flawed (e.g. ABC news by Pham, December 2010). *Washington Post*, in December 2013, asked if Shanghai had cheated in PISA. In December 2016, East Asian students, again, are reported to perform the best with Singapore having the highest scores in all three subjects. "Singapore top in global education rankings and UK lags behind in global school rankings" was the headline of BBC news (Coughlan 2016). *Los Angeles Times* asked the question, "Does America have a math problem" when reporting that "American teens' math scores fall on an international test" that "was taken by more than a million 15-year-olds in 72 countries, including 5700 in the US" (Resmovits 2016).

Whether it is a "flawed" PISA report or "another Sputnik moment", East Asian students, including those from Shanghai, Macao, Hong Kong, and Taiwan China, continue to perform at the top of the international test and have attracted serious attention among Western media, educators, and policymakers. In addition to onsite visits, there have been studies on the East Asian countries in terms of their school education. For example, in May 2016 World Bank released its study that "shows Shanghai's #1 global ranking in reading, math, and science rests on strong education system with great teachers" (World Bank 2016). According to the World Bank 2016 report, Shanghai students' stellar performance on international tests of student learning is linked to a strong education system with efficient public financing, rigorous pre-service teacher training, and ongoing professional development as well as a system-wide policy to pull up the performance of weaker schools through the "entrusted school" management model in which high performing schools provide management and professional support to low-performing schools (World Bank 2016).

Among the heated debates and discussions, I notice that there have been strong emphases on economy and educational systems with little attention to the historical, social, and cultural narratives of education lived by students and their families. Deng and Gopinathan (2016) explain Singapore's education success by examining the development of Singapore education system from a historical perspective, instead of a simple comparison of PISA test scores. I hope my study of Chinese immigrant families' cross-cultural schooling experience can help provide insights into Chinese and Asian education that go beyond the comparative educational phenomenon manifested in the performances of the PISA international tests.

Drawn on intersecting newcomer families' cross-cultural schooling narratives on landscapes in transition, the central point to my ambitions and hopes for the global world is concerning the reciprocal learning in education between the East and the West by "harmonizing Chinese Learning and Western Knowledge" (Xu 2011b). In the following few pages I return to the central idea driving my ambitions and hopes for such global education.

Just as Confucius takes self-cultivation as being of utmost importance, Dewey holds the view that education is life and life is growth. Education is a process of living and not a preparation for future living (Dewey 1897). In the following quotation, Dewey's idea resonates with what Confucius says about reviewing what has been learned as a means of learning something new:

> We may reject knowledge of the past as the end of education and thereby only emphasize its importance as a means. When we do that we have a problem that is new in the story of education: How shall the young become acquainted with the past in such a way that the acquaintance is a potent agent in appreciation of the living present?"(Dewey 1938, p.23)

The educational lives of newcomer children and their families discussed in this book demonstrate the potential and power of reciprocal learning. Beyond the empirical evidence demonstrated by these family narratives, the philosophical notions at the heart of Eastern and Western societies that lead to moral educational judgement of the two systems come into focus. The ideas of individualism and communitarianism and the philosophical notions of *Confucian continuity of being* and Deweyian *continuity of knowing* provide the philosophical/cultural structure for the metaphorical bridge created and crossed by newcomer families as they undergo their narrative journey. On this matter I have drawn heavily on a book by Hall and Ames (1999) with the philosophically eye-catching title, *The Democracy of the Dead*, in which the "dead" were Confucius and John Dewey. Though not school educators, Hall and Ames's ambitions and hopes have provided me with insights and inspirations. They write:

> *We Westerners, and we Chinese, have a choice. We can continue along the present line of mutual recrimination and moral preachment, or we can take up the task of building a world community that presumes parity for both Asians and Westerners... In many ways our entire essay may be understood as an attempt to encourage both Chinese and Westerners to include one another in the term "we." (p.239)*

Finding a Way for Reciprocal Learning

Hall and Ames draw on two profoundly important philosophic systems in a search for language and ideas that might lead to conceptual bridges connecting the East and the West. Confucian philosophy of communitarianism and Deweyian experientially based pragmatism provide the philosophic frames for thinking about Eastern and Western philosophy and productive points of contact among them. Educationally the study of newcomer families and the education of their children presented in this book provide living empirical illustrations of these productive points of contact. Moreover, Hall and Ames' choice of Dewey to represent Western philosophy is especially useful in thinking about newcomer families because John Dewey was a preeminent educational thinker as well as a philosopher more generally. Dewey spent time in China. There is reason to believe that his experiential pragmatic philosophy was influenced by Confucian Chinese thought. (See for example Jessica Ching-Sze Wang's

2008 *John Dewey in China: To Teach and to Learn* (Wang, 2008)). His work remains known in Chinese educational circles (see, for example, Huajun Zhang 2013 *John Dewey, Liang Shuming, and China's Education Reform: Cultivating Individuality*).

The conceptual point of contact between Confucius and Dewey as representatives of Eastern and Western philosophic ways of thinking comes in recognizing the common perspectives in each view. The common contrast is between Eastern communitarianism where the individual is viewed as shaped by society and Western individualism where society is viewed as shaped by individuals. But Confucian communitarian thought is heavily invested in the individual while Deweyian pragmatic thought is heavily invested in the social and communal. Tu (1985) points out that what it means to be human in the Confucian notion of being is to be part of an ever-expanding circle of social influence. Personhood he points out is at the metaphoric center of expanding ripples of influence. A saying such as "Be true to yourself" means being true to your family, your community and to all relevant social configurations that give meaning to your life. Fei (1947), in a discussion of the concept of the self in Chinese thought, used an organizational model to contrast Eastern and Western ideas of the self by describing the Western idea as a haystack made up of bundles or sheaves of discrete units. The Western haystack separates out into discrete building blocks of sheaves whereas the Eastern haystack it is a massive interconnected unit with no discernible building block units. In modern agricultural terms, it is the difference between a haystack made from loose hay and a haystack built of baled hay. In each of these metaphorical renditions of the self in the Confucian notion of being the emphasis is on social relations but the individual is developmentally foundational.

In important ways Dewey's thinking begins in a different place but ends up in what I later call a commonplace with Confucian thought. Dewey's basic description of being human is to describe the transition from what is fundamentally, genetically, individual and biological, the babblings of a newborn child (Dewey 1887). Dewey's philosophy is grounded in learning and educational growth and he goes on to describe how the child's babbling is reflected back to him or her by parents and caregivers in the form of language. For Dewey, this social/communal process begins at birth and continues through life. Thus, for Dewey, there is no such entity as an individual independent of the communal network in which the individual participates. Dewey's well-known works on such matters as democracy and education (Dewey 1916) have a strong communal base.

In this way, there is a sense of harmony between Confucian ways of being and Dewey's ways of knowing. Both Confucius and Dewey account for social/communal relations and the individual, but the emphasis in each differs. Bridging the gap between the East and the West and achieving reciprocal learning among the cultures depends on unpacking the similarities and differences in such a way that acknowledging similarities does not invalidate cultural differences while acknowledging differences does not repudiate commonality.

Curriculum, Commonplaces, and Harmonizing Newcomers' Educational Practices

The heart of this book and its search for reciprocal learning is practical education as experienced by newcomer families. Reciprocal learning occurs in curriculum and teaching encounters in the educational lives of participant families. Joseph Schwab's writings on the philosophical nature of curriculum as practical (Westbury and Wilkof 1982) connects the practice of education to the philosophical matters brought forward in our discussion of Confucius and Dewey. Just as Hall and Ames's philosophy, and this book, are aimed at finding a productive way of crossing Eastern and Western cultures, Schwab was concerned with the passionate and divisive literature of education which argumentatively moved among different starting points. Using the Aristotelian notion of the topics (Aristotle 1984), Schwab argued that, somewhat like Fei's Haystack, the literature of curriculum is a whole in which different authors focused on different starting points. Schwab called the starting points "commonplaces" and he named four; i.e., teacher, learner, subject matter, and milieu (Schwab 1962). He showed that while the literature of practical school curriculum was sharply divided between those who argued for individual development and those who argued for social/cultural development, authors of one persuasion necessarily took into account the starting points of those with competing starting points. Schwab's point was that the argumentative split between the individual and the milieu in curriculum thought was somewhat like that between Eastern communitarianism and Western pragmatism, a matter of perspective and that each inevitably took the other into account. A writer arguing strongly, for example, for the development of a strong competitive United States of America needed to take into account individual children being taught across the nation. Likewise, someone arguing for individual development of the self inevitably cast the argument in terms of social value.

This way of thinking about the practical lives of newcomer families is important because it demonstrates the interconnected nature of an abstract philosophical world of ideas and the practical teaching and learning lives of those involved in education. It shows how discussions of Confucian communitarianism and Western Deweyian pragmatic experiential thought demonstrate a potential for reciprocity at theoretical and practical levels. The reciprocity seen in the grand scale of Confucian and Deweyian ideas coincides with the practical educational Schwab theory. Both help make sense of concrete newcomer educational experience in the daily educational lives of newcomer families. The participant narratives brought forward in this book represent heartfelt daily life experience of culturally uprooted newcomers. At the same time these narratives represent reciprocity between the grand traditions of Eastern communitarianism and Western pragmatic experiential thought.

I, We, and Reciprocal Learning

Communitarianism is a term that captures the common, social, sense of the self shared between Eastern and Western thought. Hall and Ames remark that "conversations between China and the West are likely to lead to a mutual extension of *'we consciousness'* only to the extent that the communitarian interests of both sides are foregrounded." (p. 239). Hall and Ames do not elaborate on the idea of we-consciousness and, in fact, use the term only once in their book. However, from a Western vantage point the idea of we-consciousness is powerful because of the Western language of individualism and the emphasis on rights, responsibilities, and self-development. For purposes of cultivating a global democratic community including one another in the term "we" instead of making distinctions in "other terms" is important.

Accordingly, in the next chapter, I will explore curricular issues of Chinese families' personal and social narratives, with such "we consciousness". I will discuss the social significance of my work not only for the sake of the education of Chinese children and families, but also for families in diverse ethnic groups. Rather than arguing for self-cultivation as a Confucian way of knowing in contrast with the Western way of knowing routed in Europe, we can seek for the way of knowing with our "we-consciousness" in a world of increasing diversity. Such "we-consciousness" is extended and expanded not only in Confucian thought but also in Dewey's communitarian pragmatism and in diverse cultural traditions. By bridging the East and West dichotomy and harmonizing Eastern learning with Western knowledge, we can find a way that is not defined or categorized in any Eastern or Western terms but the *way* or the *divine order* as it is, in the *continuity of knowledge* and in the *continuity of being*, which leads to the harmony of societies and diversity in the harmony of the global world community.

Notes

1. Part of the discussion in this section on the roles of grandparents on pp. 215–218 has been used and summarized in the following book chapter: Xu, S. J. (2011). Bridging the East and West dichotomy: Harmonizing Eastern learning with Western knowledge. In Janette. Ryan (Ed.). *Understanding China's education reform: Creating cross cultural knowledge, pedagogies and dialogue* (Ch 11, pp. 224–242). London, UK: Routledge.
2. Citations from Lun Yun (The Analects) are translations modified from the following references:
   论语=Analects of Confucius 中文译注 蔡希勤; 英文翻译 赖波, 夏玉和。北京: 华语 教学出版社, 1994.
   中华文化信息网 http://www.ccnt.com/wisdom/rujia/lunyu/lunyu7.htm Confucius. (1998). *The Analects of Confucius: A philosophical translation* by Roger T. Ames and Henry Rosemont, Jr. New Work: Ballantine Books.
3. Part of the discussion on "To be human in Confucian values" in this section has been summarized in the following book chapter: Xu, S. J. (2011). Bridging the East and West dichotomy: Harmonizing Eastern learning with Western knowledge. In Janette. Ryan (Ed.). *Understanding China's education reform: Creating cross cultural knowledge, pedagogies and dialogue* (Ch 11, pp. 224–242). London, UK: Routledge.
4. My discussion of the concepts of "Confucian notion of being" and "Deweian continuity of knowing" was summarized and further illustrated in the following book chapter: Xu, S. J. (2011). Bridging the East and West dichotomy: Harmonizing Eastern learning with Western knowledge. In Janette. Ryan (Ed.). *Understanding China's education reform: Creating cross cultural knowledge, pedagogies and dialogue* (Ch 11, pp. 224–242). London, UK: Routledge.

CHAPTER 9

Sketching Unseen Lives of Immigrant Children between Home and School

EXPLORING CURRICULAR ISSUES FROM PERSONAL AND SOCIAL NARRATIVE PERSPECTIVES

Learning with Reflection

Confucius said, "Learning without reflection leads to nothing; reflection without learning leads to indolence. 学而不思则罔, 思而不学则怠." (The Analects 2.15)

Through Chapter 3 to Chapter 7, the five major participant family narratives provide a detailed account of immigrant children's cross-cultural experience of schooling on landscapes in transition. Observing and reflecting on Chinese families' lived experience in my three-year fieldwork and two-year follow-up at Bay Street Community School, I find what puzzled me most is the unseen lives newcomer students live between home and school. In this chapter, I reflect on the issues that emerge from these unseen lives. My purpose is to provide insight useful in improving newcomer Chinese students' schooling experience, and to consider how these insights may also be useful for the education of children of other cultural groups.

Narratives of Newcomer Student Experience

Dewey believes that examining experience is the key to education. In narrative inquiry, as Connelly and Clandinin (1988) illustrate, curricular issues are explored from the perspective of personal and social narrative history (p. 109). Hence, we need to broaden our idea of education beyond that of schooling. Education, in this view, is a narrative of experience that grows and strengthens a person's capabilities to cope with life (Connelly and Clandinin 1988, p. 27). While some such experience occurs in school, important educational experiences also occur outside school. In my study, I find that immigrant children's school experience is mostly unknown to parents while the children's out-of-school experience is mostly unknown to teachers. As explained in Chapter 8, the idea of landscapes in transition in the context of a narrative inquiry approach provides a way for me to examine and understand Chinese families' lived experience across a broad historical and intercultural landscape of experience. This notion permitted me to study my participants' lives in such a way that life in and out of school is illuminated. Hopefully, this work will make the school less opaque to parents; and will make home and community life less opaque to teachers.

Curriculum as Experience in Situations

Following Schwab's concept of curriculum as practical (1971a, 1971b, 1971c, 1973, 1983) and Dewey's notion of experience and education (1932/1990, 1938), Connelly and Clandinin (1988) understand curriculum as something experienced in situations. This concept deviates from the more widely understood view of curriculum as subject matter, courses of study, and syllabus. Experientially, a common subject matter curriculum has different meanings for people of different backgrounds. For Chinese families, with rapid social change in China and with immigrant families' life in transition in Canada, parents experience curriculum differently than do their children, both in school and in out of school situations. In Dewey's (1938) notion of learning through direct experience, *continuity* and *interaction* are the two key principles that decide the quality of experience.

> Different situations succeed one another. But because of the principle of continuity something is carried over from the earlier to the later ones. As an individual passes from one situation to another, his world, his environment, expands or contracts. He does not find himself living in another world but in

a different part or aspect of one and the same world. What he has learned in the way of knowledge and skill in one situation becomes an instrument of understanding and dealing effectively with the situations which follow. (Dewey 1938, p. 44)

But I find that immigrant children are often thrown into "a divided world", "a world whose parts and aspects are not hung together" (Dewey 1938, p. 44). I believe this discontinuity and fragmentation accounts for most of the difficulties and struggles that immigrant children experience in school and at home.

Commonplaces in Joseph Schwab's (1971) Concept of Curriculum

Schwab (1971b) writes that, "Theories of curriculum and of teaching and learning cannot, alone, tell us what and how to teach, because questions of what and how to teach arise in concrete situations loaded with concrete particulars of time, place, person, and circumstance" (p. 322). To translate the practical into curriculum, Schwab (1973) emphasizes that four commonplaces of curriculum thought must be taken into account: learner, milieu, subject matter, and teacher.

In the following section, I use Schwab's commonplaces to sketch and discuss the unseen lives immigrant children live in different curriculum situations – lives that are either unseen by the teacher or unseen by the parent when *continuity* and *interaction* are missing from their cross-cultural lived experience. Using the four commonplaces helps organize the meaning of these family narratives by weaving narrative threads together with a focus on each of the commonplaces and by discussing how each is related to the others. As Connelly and Clandinin (1988) point out,

> The commonplaces are as empty of meaning as possible. Meaning is filled in as texts are read. The assumption is that a comprehensive curriculum argument is one that has something to say about the learner, the teacher, the subject matter, and the milieu. What the author has to say about those matters is the way in which the commonplaces are "filled with meaning." (p. 85)

Connelly and Clandinin (1988) further explain that milieu refers to everyone else and everything else in a curriculum situation where any one of the commonplaces is of interest. By the same token, milieu can refer to the community of the school, and the school, in turn, can be the milieu for a classroom. This concept of "a pagoda of milieus"(Connelly and Clandinin 1988, p. 86) helps illustrate the complexity and multiplicity of immigrant children's experience of schooling on landscapes in transition by making it possible to understand student experience in a diversity of aspects specified by the commonplaces and their interrelationships.

Sketching Immigrant Children's Unseen Lives in Curricular Terms

The Subject Matter

Subject matter has always been the major concern for most Chinese families in their children's education. Chinese family narratives show that Chinese families see language and math as the most important subjects. While children learn English and math in a Canadian way at school, they are often tutored and pushed at home in more traditional Chinese approaches by their parents. Language seems to play the most important role in the quality of newcomer students' experience of schooling. Multiple language situations add to difficulties for newcomer students who learn English in multilingual settings rather than in a second language acquisition environment. Boys like Yong Chang and Jia Ming live in different curriculum situations when they have to adapt to the Canadian way of learning at school and also to their mothers' traditional approaches at home.

More than Two Languages

With bilingualism and multiculturalism at the core of Canadian values, newcomer students experience bilingualism and multiculturalism somewhat differently when traveling between home and school. They find themselves in multilingual educational learning environments. *Multilingualism,* in a sense, describes their educational situations better than does the term *bilingualism.*

Chinese newcomer students, especially those from Guangdong and Fujian, deal with multiple languages in their daily life. In a certain sense, many Chinese immigrants with formal education in China are bilingual – in one's home dialect and in Pu-Tong-Hua 普通话 (the official standardized Chinese language, also known as Mandarin outside of Mainland China). Pu-Tong-Hua (Mandarin) is a synthesized language based mainly on northern Han dialects of China. Han dialects share the same written form known as Chinese (*Han Yu* 汉语, literally *the Hans' speech*), while southern dialects such as those in Guangdong (Canton), Fujian, Shanghai, and Zhejiang vary greatly in pronunciation, syntax, and vocabulary. Cantonese is a prime example and is normally considered a different language outside of Mainland China.

In Toronto, for example, it is common to think that there are two Chinese languages, Cantonese and Mandarin. Cantonese and Mandarin are so different that in an English setting it is often the case that speakers of the two languages/dialects will communicate in English when one or the other is not fluent in Pu-Tong-Hua.

In China students learn to speak and write the Chinese language as Pu-Tong-Hua 普通话 at school while most of them speak a hometown dialect. Most Chinese people do not speak Pu-Tong-Hua with those who speak the same dialects. For example, at the Parent Centre, Tommy's mom told me she did not learn to speak Pu-Tong-Hua until after she left her hometown and came to Toronto where she learned it by singing Chinese songs. At the Newcomer Support Class, Fujianese students speak Fujian dialects among themselves and the Cantonese students speak Cantonese among themselves. This can lead to misunderstandings and tensions as students misunderstand one another or feel excluded. Liang Liang, the only boy from northern China at the beginning of my fieldwork, was singled out and made fun of by southern boys. At the Parent Centre, some Mandarin-speaking parents and grandparents did not return to the center after a first visit, because the majority of Chinese grandparents and parents in the center spoke Cantonese. Most Cantonese grandparents came from rural areas of Guangdong. They had little formal schooling and could not speak Pu-Tong-Hua (Mandarin), so they could not communicate with parents and grandparents from other parts of China. Freeman and Hui Lan served as translators and mediators between Cantonese- and Mandarin-speaking groups at the Parent Centre. Julian's grandma often translated for me when I joined the Cantonese grandmas' conversations.

As Jia Ming's story shows, in China he almost exclusively spoke the Shanghai dialect at home and at school with his classmates. In Toronto, Jia Ming speaks the Shanghai dialect at home, Pu-Tong-Hua with other Chinese people, and English with non-Chinese people. After moving into the LEAP program, Jia Ming also began learning French as the second official language in Canada although his interest seemed to be more in Japanese. His mom, Shirley, attended Cantonese class in addition to English class in the LINK program since, she said, people who speak both English and Cantonese have better job opportunities in Toronto. Just as Hui Lan's second son Yong Sheng chose to learn Mandarin since he already spoke Cantonese at home, Yang Yang, who speaks Fujianese and Pu-Tong-Hua, took Cantonese instead of Mandarin at the International Language Program (Heritage Language Maintenance Program) of Bay Street Community School. As his mom told me, though he struggled learning English, Yang Yang became fluent in Cantonese.

English as a Second Language versus English as a Foreign Language
English is taught as a second language to newcomer students at school in approaches guided by second language acquisition theories. In China, most students start learning English as a foreign language in middle school, and some, especially those in cities, such as Jia Ming, begin in earlier grades. As Jia Ming's story tells, Chinese students learn English with more traditional approaches that focus on grammar and vocabulary. The input and output of the language are mostly in the form of repetitive exercises and homework. Shirley brought English textbooks from China and urged Jia Ming to use these materials to study English. She tended to use a traditional approach featuring memorization, dictation, and drill. Traditional approaches had proved to be helpful for Shirley to learn English in China, and so she used these approaches to help Jia Ming to improve his English in Canada. In the same manner, Hui Lan, who did not speak English, asked her boys to copy English texts every day as homework. Copying texts to help memorize vocabulary and to make sense of the written form of the language is an effective method in Chinese language learning. This approach is also related to the Confucian cultural narrative of learning discussed in Chapter 8. Chinese parents believe that practice is effective in learning.

At parent–teacher interviews, teachers often encouraged anxious Chinese mothers by telling them not to worry, for, they would say, studies show that it takes five to seven years or more to acquire a second language. Chinese mothers became even more anxious with this information, for they wanted their children to overcome the language barrier efficiently and in a timely manner to catch up with regular class students. They believed their children needed to work at a quickened pace to catch up with native-born children. Hearing that their children would learn more slowly than they expected, and that this was expected by their teachers, was of considerable concern. They were aware of the gap between their children and regular class students. They were uncomfortable when informed that their children were "doing fine" at school, because they sensed that their expectations for their children and the teachers' expectations were quite different.

The Confucian educational values described in Chapter 8, combined with what parents view as a language deficit in Canada, lead to a narrative of curricular conflict with the school system. For example, in Hui Lan's story, Yong Chang's high-school teachers did not seem to understand, or even approve of, her academic demands of Yong Chang. Shirley would come to parent–teacher interviews to meet with Jia Ming's teacher even though she was not scheduled for a meeting since his teacher considered he was doing well. In many ways, the teachers and Chinese parents did not share the same educational ends-in-view. For Chinese parents like Hui Lan and Shirley, they not only want their boys to catch up but also to excel in a regular class in order to go to university. They were not satisfied if their boys were doing well in programs with ESL standards, which, they knew, were lower than those for native English speakers. Hui Lan wanted Yong Chang to go to a medical school to become a doctor while Shirley hoped that Jia Ming would go to a top Canadian or American university. Both mothers pushed their boys to study hard and not to be satisfied until they could excel in a regular class. Chinese students like Yong Chang and Jia Ming have lived in different curriculum situations in tension between parents and teachers who hold different ends-in-view created by their different cultural narratives and lived experiences.

In addition, many newcomer students, such as Zhi Gao, and Yang Yang, live in their home language community in Toronto, which resembles more or less the foreign language learning environment of their home country. In an important sense, these students learn English as a foreign language even though they are in Canada since they rarely use English and have little exposure to English out of the classroom. Zhi Gao and Yang Yang, like many other boys, spent most of their after-school time playing video games. When they watch TV, they only watch Chinese movies or DVDs and, as illustrated by the case of Zhi Gao, they tend to read Chinese cartoon books when reading for pleasure. Although they do have homework, it is often not given in written forms. More often homework may consist of half-an-hour of reading English or watching English TV programs. Parents like Zhi Gao's mom and Yang Yang's mom, who do not speak English, find it hard to monitor the boys' studies. They have been accustomed to large amounts of written homework in China that they could see and check. Reading for half an hour and watching TV is something hard for them to check especially as many newcomer parents work late hours and many newcomer students have long hours of after-school time with no or little adult supervision. Zhi Gao's mom and Yang Yang's mom, who had not attended middle school in China, depended completely on the school for their boys' learning. They repeatedly asked the teacher to give their boys more homework, for they believed that if their boy was kept busy with homework, he would be learning and would be kept away from video games.

How can we help newcomer students overcome language barriers in a more sufficient and efficient way? Cummins (1981a, 1981b, 1984a, 1989) shows that it takes one or two years for a child to acquire context-embedded second language fluency, and five to seven years or more to acquire context-reduced fluency. Studies also show that native speakers are not sitting there waiting for non-native speakers to catch up (Cummins 1989, Collier 1995). As Baker (2001, p. 258) summarizes, the goal of proficiency equal to a native speaker is always a moving target for the language learner. The fact that many newcomer students have little or no exposure to English out of the classroom and have little internal motivation and external pressure to learn English makes it almost impossible for them to catch up with their native English-speaking peers. It is almost inevitable that boys like Zhi Gao drop out of high school where subject matter requires more advanced language proficiency and higher cognitive skills as well as overall intellectual competence.

My study shows that Chinese immigrant students, though given little profile in educational planning, have important curricular needs to close the language gap. My study also shows that the school system needs to learn to work productively with Chinese families who have strong desire to monitor and foster their children's education, so as to close this gap. As Cummins (1989, p. 29) points out, educators need to be aware of the fact that English language learners may require more than five years to catch up with their native-English-speaking peers in English academic skills, but at the same time the programs for students of ESL background must "be tuned to students' level of English in order to provide them with the comprehensive input necessary to sustain academic growth" (Krashen 1981; Wong Fillmore 1983).

Bilingualism and Multiculturalism as Experienced
Many studies have shown how a child's first language competence affects his/her performance in a second language. In his cognitive studies of bilingualism, Cummins (1981b, 1996) uses the iceberg analogy to

represent his common underlying proficiency model of bilingualism and points out that the two separate languages do not function separately. Both languages operate through the same central processing system. Hence, the ability immigrant children develop in their home language (L1) can transfer to English (L2) (Cummins 1984b). This finding is the basis for additive bilingualism education programs designed to help a child achieve superior performance by allowing the child to operate in his or her more developed home language (see Cummins 1981a, 1981b, 1984a, 1984b, 1989, 1996, 2000; Cummins and Corson 1997; Collier 1995; Soto, 1997; Wong-Fillmore 1991a, 1991b, 1992).

Positive transfer from L1 to L2 is well manifested in Jia Ming's learning. Jia Ming was good at Chinese in his Shanghai school and his Chinese writing was often chosen by his language teacher as an example read to the class. In addition to his overall cognitive development, what he achieved through L1, such as self-discipline, good learning habits, good learning strategies, communicative skills, and high-order thinking, transferred to learning ESL as well as to learning math and other subjects in English. Jia Ming was transferred to the LEAP program after one month at the Newcomer Support Class and was soon upgraded to LEAP II. He drew favorable attention from all his math teachers in Canada – from his Grade 7/8 regular class teacher and summer school teacher to both his Grades 9 and 10 math teachers. This success, in turn, contributed to his self-confidence and self-esteem when tackling his difficulties in English language. In addition, the positive transfer in learning led to his positive overall schooling experience. Instead of feeling discriminated against by regular class students, as some Newcomer Support Class students did, Jia Ming felt at home. Speaking of this, he said that in the beginning regular class students did not speak to him. But they were soon impressed by his and his LEAP classmates' math performance in class and became friendly with them.

However, Zhi Gao and Yang Yang's stories are quite different. Zhi Gao's education in China was fragmented. He grew up without a male role model, was transferred back and forth between rural and urban schools in Guangdong, and experienced difficulties in his schooling. His Canadian difficulties in English learning and his misbehavior, to a great extent, are a narrative carry-over of his China experience. His cross-cultural journey amplified the negative transfer to its maximum. Yang Yang's story has similar features: He had only managed to finish Grade 3 in China, but he was put in a Grade 5

English curriculum situation in Canada because this placement was age-appropriate. He had not fully developed his first language and had hardly made sense of schooling and learning in L1. He was soon identified as a student of special needs in a L2 curriculum situation of Grade 5 level in his first Toronto school. Zhi Gao and Yang Yang's stories are not unique. Research shows that academic success in a second language requires the first language to be developed to a high cognitive level. English language learners perform better in their second language curriculum when their first language and culture is enhanced and maintained (Cummins 1983, 1993; Cummins and Danesi 1990; Collier 1995).

My work also reveals some important nuances relating to this general finding in regard to minority children's learning. To begin with, Chinese students tend to be viewed as successful and without special educational problems. This view is often supported by findings from quantitative studies. A Toronto District School Board report (Brown 2006) is one example that tends to strengthen this view. My study shows that there is a "hidden minority", an invisible minority of Chinese students, like Yang Yang and Zhi Gao, whose family narrative profiles deviate from the somewhat romanticized Chinese family profiles in the myth of "Asian model minorities". Furthermore, my work shows how variable home background in the country of origin can be, and suggests the importance of assessing, in detail, newcomer students' educational background. Finally, my study shows how irrationally random a well-intended and well-supported educational system can be. Yang Yang's Grade 5 placement in his first Toronto school, after a Grade 3 accomplishment in China, is difficult to understand. Decades ago Cummins (1984b, 1986) had drawn attention to the importance of discovering the minority children's prior learning experiences and out-of-school situations so as to understand and enrich the children's present learning in school. Yang Yang and Zhi Gao's stories demonstrate what is still missing in our current educational policy and practice.

Another complicating and long-time challenging factor I wish to discuss in this section on the experience of bilingualism and multiculturalism is the loss of home language, referred to as subtractive bilingualism by Lambert in1974 (see Baker 2001). Again, this issue has been an important concern for bilingualism and multiculturalism educators and researchers (see Wong Fillmore 1991a, 1991b, 2000). Among the newcomer students in my study, even academically successful students like Jia Ming tend to lose their home language. Jia Ming and his mom point out that he is losing his Chinese because he seldom writes Chinese and does not study Chinese at a more advanced level. For students like Zhi Gao and Yang Yang, the loss of L1 exacerbates the damage to their educational development.

With the heritage language maintenance program (now called International Languages in Toronto), some students of ESL family backgrounds are able to continue to learn their first language. However, their first language can never be as fully developed as that of their peers in their home country because Canadian immigrant children learn the major subjects in English and accumulate their new knowledge in English. The Mandarin teacher at Bay Street Community School, a recent immigrant from Mainland China, saw what was missing in the prescribed curriculum of the Heritage Language Maintenance program for newcomer students. She expanded the prescribed curriculum by asking students to write a Chinese composition every week, learn classic Chinese, write Chinese poems, and learn Chinese history. She tried to modify the prescribed curriculum, which she saw as too easy for many students, in order to help newcomer students maintain and develop a high level of Chinese language proficiency. The prescribed curriculum tended to be geared to students of Chinese origin who have little or limited Chinese. However, even if she had had full control over the curriculum, her job would have been hugely complicated by the fact that students were grouped in the program according to grade rather than language proficiency. In the class for Grades 7/8 students, as I observed, she had to teach students from five language levels: from beginners who just began learning Mandarin as Canadian-born Chinese to advanced learners of the language like Jia Ming who had completed Grade 6 or 7 in China.

Finally, it is important to note some aspects of student language learning related to the official Canadian bilingualism policy. Canada's official languages are English and French, and much thought has been given to teaching French- to English-speaking students. While the French immersion program is geared mostly toward native English speakers, French as one of the two official languages is mandatory in school curriculum for Canadian children, including those from homes where English is not their first language. This policy creates certain curricular ambiguities and creates a general perspective partially at odds with the language learning needs of students from homes where English is not their first language, especially newcomer students such as my participants. At Bay Street Community School, newcomer students usually spent one year in the Newcomer Support Class to learn English as their second language. When they progressed to the LEAP program, the bilingualism policy required that they study French as the second official language; French is usually the newcomer students' third or fourth language. Consequently, many Chinese immigrant children are managing or struggling with three to five languages. Yet, on their horizon is the recognizable view that to succeed in Canada both English and French are required.

Stephen, Freeman's eldest son's boy, began a French immersion program in Grade 6 in a different school. After dropping the boy at the French immersion school, Freeman often stopped by my university office telling me how much the boy enjoyed his French immersion program. Following the example of Freeman's family, Hui Lan had decided to send Yong Sheng and Yong Ming to a French immersion program when the boys went to Grade 4. She wanted her boys to learn an additional language like their big brother Yong Chang who can speak Spanish. The boys continued to learn Cantonese, their home language, at the International Language Program at school, and took Mandarin lessons at Saturday school. Although many of them do not know much about educational research, the Chinese families show their full confidence in bilingualism and multiculturalism education through their lived experience. They are aware of the important role language plays, and they take action to help their children become not only bilingual but also multilingual in Toronto where people live daily lives of multilingual and multicultural diversity. Hence, the multilingual education situations and needs of newcomer/immigrant families call for new considerations of educational research, policy and practice in language education.

Math in Traditional Approach vs. Math in Communicative Approach
As was the case for language education, newcomer Chinese children experience a shift in mathematics teaching and learning from a traditional Chinese approach to a more open and interactive communicative approach in Toronto schools. Here in Canada, they experience the two different approaches in different curriculum situations in school and at home.

Mr. Feng's math tutorials were very welcome at the school as he not only helped newcomer students catch up with their math in Chinese, but he also served as a role model and provided affective support to the newcomer students as a Chinese teacher. Chinese newcomer students moved back and forth between different curriculum situations in their math learning. Mr. Feng's math lessons were teacher-centered and focused on the content knowledge, something that students were familiar with from China, while with their Canadian teachers, students learned math in a more communicative approach. There was less pressure on students in the communicative approach, and as Jia Ming's story shows, students seemed to prefer this method. Jia Ming used the example of coin tossing to illustrate how he learned the concept of ratio and the infinitive in a self-motivating, fun and interesting way. In a traditional approach, he said, students were taught to aim for a fixed and accurate answer, using math worksheets.

That is what Hui Lan continues to do to assist her boys to learn in the traditional Chinese way that she believes was effective for her when she was a school student. She made large numbers of math worksheets for Yong Sheng and Yong Ming, the two little brothers, to practice at home. The boys studied her math lessons and remembered the rules by drill and memorization in their mother's "home schooling". Yong Ming, as a kindergarten child, had little written schoolwork, and Yong Sheng's math schoolwork appeared to be easier in terms of its content knowledge when compared to his mom's math homework and the Chinese math book of the same grade level.

Like many Chinese children of his age, Yong Sheng is skilled at mental computation. He appeared to be better than his Canadian-born peers in math. Yet, Yong Sheng only got Bs in his report cards, to my surprise. His home and school math differed in focus and in method of teaching/learning. School math was more practical and relevant to everyday life. For instance, the students were shown different ways to tell the time with graphs, diagrams, charts, pictures, and texts. Rather than focusing on reaching an absolute correct answer, students were encouraged to use their imagination and find answers by trying alternative ways. The home math focused more on abstract content knowledge of math with accuracy and efficiency emphasized. There appear to be benefits in both methods. As Jia Ming's mom said, she wanted Jia Ming to benefit from both. She liked the fact that Jia Ming had laid a solid foundation of knowledge in his elementary education in China, but appreciated that Jia Ming was developing more original and creative thinking in Canadian schools. She imagined an intellectual home for learning at the intersection of Chinese and Canadian ways.

The different approaches in China and in Canada reveal different notions of learning and schooling. In many Chinese parents and grandparents' eyes, it is a waste of time for their children to play at school with little or no homework. They do not see play as part of a child's learning and intellectual development. Chinese people believe in the adage "no pains and no gains". Learning is thought in terms of hard work. By contrast, in the eyes of Canadian teachers, who are educated in the concept of "play and learning" (Cook 1996, 2000; Oliver and Klugman 2003; Samuelsson and Johansson 2006; Sutton-Smith 1979; Smith 1984), play is always an important part of a child's learning. In an expression of Dewey's philosophy, the "whole child" tends to be emphasized. Self-discipline in learning is more important than pushing a child to learn with homework and authoritative rules. I often heard Canadian teachers say, "They are children. Of course they should have fun." As I observed in class, Canadian teachers often gave students time to play games and have fun in class at intervals of regular lessons. Chinese newcomer students enjoyed these classes, though they appeared to view them with some shock at the beginning. Parents and grandparents generally considered such activities to be a waste of time.

In summary, children live in different curriculum situations with different notions of learning and schooling and with different ends-in-view. They find themselves at the intersection of different cultural narratives that create unexpected situations and that may lead to dissonance between parent and school, leaving children puzzled in their search for home. Ideally, the curriculum, drawing on traditional approaches, can help students transfer smoothly between different curriculum situations with continuity and interaction. Thus, students may benefit from different curriculum situations and have more positive schooling experience and learning outcomes.

The Learner

As revealed in the previous section, Chinese learners at Bay Street Community School, who came from the same defined cultural group, have diverse experience of their cross-cultural schooling on landscapes in transition. These diverse narratives of experience are as important, perhaps even more important, than recognizing and identifying the children as "Chinese" in the curriculum.

Julian's grandma has tutored Julian in Chinese and math half an hour every day since kindergarten. Julian, however, did not like learning, as the grandma told me. He liked watching TV and playing, so the grandma would bring him and his little brother to the Parent Centre no matter how bad the weather was, so that Julian would interact with people rather than sitting in front of the TV. On the other hand, Allen, Julian's little brother, loved learning. The grandma was pleased and proud to tell me that. She had taken care of Allen since birth.

Hui Lan's three sons all liked reading and studied hard under Hui Lan's careful guidance and strict supervision. The three brothers shared an interest in playing video games, but they followed their mother's restrictions and played within time limits. At a very young age, they each had set up a different life goal: Yong Chang wanted to become a doctor; Yang Sheng, a dentist; and Yong Ming, a policeman.

Among the Grades 7/8 newcomer Chinese students, Yong Chang and Jia Ming appeared to have had a relatively smooth transfer at different curriculum situations between home and school, from Newcomer Support Class to Leap Programs, and from middle school to high school. But the family narratives reveal the tremendous amounts of time and efforts the boys and their families invest for their academic achievements, and for their overall intellectual development, as well as for their understanding of what it means by learning to be human in Chinese traditional cultural values.

Zhi Gao and Yang Yang, in comparison, had more dramatic and different transitions. They came to Canada before Jia Ming and some other newcomer students. Yet they remained in the Newcomer Support Class until they graduated from the elementary school while Jia Ming and many others moved on into the LEAP programs or even to a regular class. Zhi Gao and Yang Yang were both addicted to video games, perhaps as a respite from the difficulties encountered in their learning and in life. This is strongly suggested in Zhi Gao's story of sudden misbehavior at school after a period of progress. The cause was found to be associated with the tensions he had with the Internet Café manager who erased his credits earned from winnings at video games. Zhi Gao, who was struggling in school, seemed to have taken comfort in the credits which were a kind of proof of his success, though in a virtual world.

While Jia Ming and other LEAP program students seemed to enjoy their integrated classes with regular class students, Zhi Gao, Zhi Hui, Xue Hua and other newcomer boys and girls in the newcomer class felt a sense of discrimination in the regular classes. They attended integrated regular class sessions reluctantly. Academically and socially the Chinese students in my study were diverse. To refer to, and treat them, in the curriculum as Chinese without acknowledging their diversity would be inappropriate.

Diversity among the Chinese Learners[1]
The great variations among the Chinese newcomer students' cross-cultural schooling experience show that just as a unitary Asian label does not fit diverse Asian groups in the "Asian model minority myth", the umbrella of *the Chinese* cannot cover the variations among the Chinese groups.

Among the people referred to as the Chinese, there are Mainland Chinese, Hong Kong Chinese, Taiwan Chinese, American Chinese, Canadian Chinese, and many other Chinese groups who share the same overall Chinese cultural heritage, but who do not necessarily share the same historical, political, social, and personal narratives. Their lived experiences vary greatly across historical, political, social, economic, and geographic landscapes. With the Hans as the majority Chinese group, there are altogether 56 ethnic groups in China, each having its own language and cultural tradition. The Hans who make up the majority of the recent Chinese immigrant population, also vary greatly, as has been discussed in the previous section; the Hans include Cantonese, Fujianese, and Chinese people from other parts of Mainland China. There are also great variations among urban families and rural families. McKay and Wong (1996) argue for recognizing the multiple identities of "being Chinese", but refer to Chinese new immigrants in their US study as, "coming out of an aggressive, confident, industrialized, and newly rich East Asia" (p. 587). This description could hardly be further from the narrative histories of Zhi Gao's and Yang Yang's families. The two families grew up in rural areas of Guangdong (Canton) and Fujian provinces respectively in south China, with little formal education and certainly not "industrialized, and newly rich". The tone of the McKay and Wong article is that the group of Chinese new immigrants they studied represents the modern Chinese who are educated and affluent and "arrived already armed with information about the U.S. educational system". Readers with a formalistic habit might easily adopt their description and thereby misunderstand in the most important ways the experience of children such as Zhi Gao and Yang Yang as well as other newcomer families in my study. Zhi Gao and Yang Yang's stories, set against research literature that demonstrates the dangers of homogenizing experience into formal cultural qualities (see also Liu 1999; Louie 2004).

The Learner and Cultural Labels
Ayers (1998) points out that teachers work in institutional settings of hierarchy and power where children are often labeled according to different categories, and "the language of schools is a language of labeling and

reduction" (p. 53). The lived experience of my participants who are categorized by cultural labels supports Ayers's (1998) view that teachers must look beneath and beyond labels, not only those in terms of deficits, but also those in terms of cultures.

The family narratives reveal that the use of cultural labels not only tends to neglect variations within one cultural group, but also may exclude some cultural groups and hence doubly marginalize them. This can have particular consequences when certain groups are of more focal interest and attention in educational policy, practice and research than are others. This phenomenon validates many Asian American scholars' concerns about Chinese and other Asian students who find themselves stuck in between as they are neither born as White nor perceived as people of color (see Lee 1996; Parker et al. 2001, 2003; Louie 2004). The success narrative of Asian Americans doubly marginalizes Chinese along with other Asian groups in educational policy, practice, and research when these groups are "thrown into a social positioning" (Parker 2003, p. 95) as "those already secured within the mainstream" and as "model minorities" (S. Lee 1996). Their needs are not met when their efforts and struggles are invisible to educational policymakers and practitioners.

In addition, Stacey Lee (1996) points out the consequences of racial tensions created among visible minorities when news media routinely comment on the success of Asian immigrants in schools in contrast with the persistently high dropout rates and low test scores of inner-city African Americans, Native Americans, and Mexican Americans. Okhee Lee (1997) also draws attention to the fact that Asian American students' success masks the extensive amount of effort and time required and overshadows the learning needs of many others who have limited English and who lack resources and support at home. In *Becoming Asian American*, Nazli Kibria (2002) critiques the model minority image as socio-historical rather than cultural or ethnically innate. The model minority myth may distress those who find themselves to be the non-model minority as they do not fulfill the myth's expectation. Kibria (2002) points out that students of Asian heritage perceived in such ascribed identities as "Asian Americans" have to struggle to find spaces for their personally constructed selves in marginalization.

As stories about Chinese newcomer boys such as Zhi Gao and Yang Yang tell, great variations within one defined cultural group need to be brought to light and considered in regard to educational policy, practice, and research considerations. Those who are invisible and doubly marginalized need to be seen. Focusing on the details of family narratives and on experience, rather than on cultural form, can contribute to this goal. While culture does play an important and complex role in learning, what matters most is how immigrant children and their families experience their cultural and cross-cultural schooling. It is important to understand culture to make meaning of immigrant children's experience of schooling. But, as the family narratives in this study show, it is simplistic and problematic to discuss educational issues with cultural labels and categorized cultural terms.

The Teacher

What is the teacher to Chinese families? What is the teacher to Canadian teachers? I have wondered what matches and what doesn't between Chinese families and Canadian teachers in their notions of *what it means to be a teacher* when I perceive differences in their expectations and approaches as to what and how to teach children. The meaning of "teacher" is personally, socially, and culturally constructed. My work with Chinese families and with Canadian teachers shows that mismatches in the meaning of "teacher" may lead to miscommunication and misunderstanding between parent and teacher. Chapter 8 provides a cultural narrative context for exploring this aspect of the curriculum.

"Teacher" in Confucian Learning

In Confucian learning, the teacher is highly respected. In the twentieth century when Confucius was denounced, "师道尊严 Respect the teacher's way of knowing" was criticized, and respect for the teacher's authority was challenged. Regardless, the Chinese tradition of respecting the teacher has remained an important value among Chinese people. "Teacher" is not just a job title referring to school practitioners. *Teacher* in Chinese 老师 *Lao Shi*, which literally means *Old Master* (of knowledge), has been a respectful and almost sacred term in China, used to refer to a person one considers more knowledgeable than oneself. Accordingly, in China, teachers are called "Teacher" plus the family name, such as "Teacher Fang (房老师 *Fang Lao Shi*)" instead of Ms., Mr., or Mrs. Fang. For example, Chinese mothers call me "Teacher Xu (许老师 *Xu Lao Shi*)" and we call Julian's grandma "Teacher Fang (房老师 *Fang Lao Shi*)".

Developed from the Confucian notion of respect for teachers, a Chinese saying goes like this: "一日为师终身为父 A teacher one day is like a father the rest of one's life". On one hand, the learner should respect his or her teacher like he or she respects his or her parent; on the other hand, the teacher should teach the learner with care and responsibility, like a parent with his or her own child. This saying is one of the Confucian ideas criticized during the Chinese denunciation of Confucianism as the teacher's authority over students was considered to have been overemphasized for the past centuries and hence should be challenged. But the criticism went to such an extreme that it missed the point Confucius made about the teacher's role and the teacher's responsibility. Confucius said, "I teach everyone without making distinctions according to their social class 有教无类" (The Analects, 15.39), a notion which resonates with the promotion of equality, democracy, and anti-discrimination in modern Western society. "Teachers should teach according to the characteristics of each learner in order to meet the individual needs of each learner 因材施教". This educational approach, developed from Confucian learning as revealed in the Analects, has been a teacher maxim promoted in Chinese teacher education and teaching practice.

Teacher Metaphors in China[2]
Developed from Chinese cultural values, Chinese people "live in" many teacher metaphors. Ferrymen, gardeners, parents, and candles are common teacher metaphors constructed socially and culturally in China. Chinese teachers have traditionally taken a dual role: to transmit knowledge and to cultivate humanity in their mission to educate students to become a knowledgeable, socially conscious human person 教书育人. As "ferrymen 摆渡人", teachers take learners from the unknown to the known, and carry them from one shore of their life to another; as "gardeners 园丁", teachers transform the learners personally and socially and hence have their students become "blossoms of peaches and plums blooming all over the world 桃李满天下" through their life-long dedication to education as a lofty career. Like parents, teachers care about students. Like candles, teachers burn up themselves to light up their students' lives and brighten their future. A poem written by Li Shangyin 李商隐, a poet during the Tang Dynasty hundreds of years ago, is often quoted to portray the image of Chinese teachers' life-long hard work and commitment to education: "春蚕到死丝方尽，蜡炬成灰泪始干: Silk worms would not stop giving silk until they died; candles would not dry up until they completely burnt out." Chinese teachers, especially those of the older generations, lived out these teacher metaphors that are explicitly

stated and culturally acknowledged in China. Chinese teachers, students, and parents hold a common image of what it means to be a teacher socially and culturally constructed in these teacher metaphors. The eleven influential Chinese educators portrayed by Hayhoe (2006) are typical examples of such teachers.

Narrativizing Parent-Teacher Relations in Personal and Social Narratives
Being a Chinese teacher and sharing the same cultural narrative history as to what it means to be a teacher with the Chinese families, I understand why Chinese parents often ask me to talk with their boys and tell me that, "One word said by you is worth 10 words said by me". I also know why Chinese mothers urge Canadian teachers to take more responsibility for their children's learning. I understand why I often receive phone calls from Chinese mothers such as Zhi Gao's mom and Yang Yang's mom when the boys are in difficult situations, and why the Chinese parents ask me to take roles that might lead me to step over boundaries in Canadian contexts. On the other hand, having worked closely with Canadian teachers at school, I can also understand why Chinese parents' requests sometimes appear unreasonable or too demanding from the perspective of Canadian teachers.

From my observation at parent–teacher interviews and my work with the teachers and families, I noticed three major misunderstandings between Chinese parents and Canadian teachers in their communication.

First, Chinese parents almost always urge their child's teacher to give more homework. As discussed in Chapter 8, Chinese parents see homework as an important means of reviewing and practicing what has been learned. Moreover, in a confusing, sometimes apparently inimical landscape, homework is a way parents may monitor, control, and discipline their children. In Canadian teachers' eyes, Chinese parents often appear to demand too much of their children. Canadian teachers believe that play is an important part of a child's learning and growth. "All work and no play makes Jack a dull boy", as an English saying goes.

Second, Chinese parents almost always urge the teacher to be stricter with their child no matter how positive the teacher's comment about the child is. Chinese parents seem never to be satisfied with their child's learning outcomes and often appear too pushy and demanding to Canadian teachers. For example, one of Yong Chang's high school teachers could not understand why the mother urged him to be stricter with Yong Chang as the boy was a good student in every teacher's eye. The teacher eventually said to Hui Lan, "How would you like me to push your son? Make him as good as me?" For Chinese parents, the answer is "yes"; they believe that, "严师出高徒 Strict teachers make good learners" and "山外有山 There are higher mountains beyond this one". Chinese newcomer parents, who project the child's future, know the gap between the child and regular class students, so parents are not satisfied until their child catches up with regular class students. Many parents, such as Hui Lan and Shirley who hold high expectations of their boys, want their boys not merely to catch up but also to excel in a regular class in order to get into a good university. Canadian teachers, on the other hand, tend to focus more on the present moment of a student's life. More importantly, Canadian teachers tend to highlight the positive side of a child and to be encouraging and supportive to a child instead of being critical as they believe that it is more important to strengthen a child's self-esteem and to develop a child's self-motivation and self-discipline in learning. A Canadian teacher would tend to be careful in her choice of words even when she talked about a boy who had badly misbehaved in class. She would tend to tell the details of what happened to the parent without criticizing the child. At parent–teacher interviews, when I was privy to such conversations, I wondered if the parent really understood how his or her son behaved at school and why the teacher reported the incident to him or her. In many cases, the parent would turn to the boy, saying, "Listen to your teacher. Do you hear me? Listen to your teacher!" Many Chinese parents have kept the tradition of respecting the authority of the teacher. "Listen to your teacher" is a request that every Chinese parent might make to his or her child. "Yang Yang, listen to your teacher!" Yang Yang's mom said to the boy when I visited their home. "Zhi Gao listens to you, Teacher." Zhi Gao's mom often said so to me. No matter how much the teacher's authority has been challenged in modern China, and no matter how much voice is emphasized in Canadian education, for many Chinese parents, listening 听话 (literally means *listening to what the teacher or the parent said*), carries a connotation of being obedient, an important quality for them at school and at home. "Not listening" is almost an offense. Yang Yang's mom frequently phoned me and told me that Yang Yang was "not listening" as he continued playing video games and would not do according to what she said. Jia Ming's story and Zhi Gao's story reveal that, when a parent is called to school by the teacher for his or her child's misbehavior in China, the parent disciplines the child harshly at home to make sure the child listens to the teacher. As Jia Ming said, Chinese students do not like parents coming to their schools, for whenever one's parent was called to school, it meant the student was in trouble at school and would "get into real trouble when he gets home" for not listening to his teacher.

Third, out of their respect for the teacher as someone who knows, and who knows best what works for their child, Chinese parents often ask the teacher to tell their child to do this or not to do that. To teachers, such requests, when frequently repeated, tend to sound like demands that the teacher take on added responsibility not normally considered part of the teacher's job.

The different cultural narratives of Chinese parents and Canadian teachers can lead to simple but significant differences in interpretation. When parents ask teachers to discipline their child, and when they tell the teacher that their child listens to them, they do so out of respect for the teacher. To make these requests is to express a Confucian sense of teacher. But teachers infer that the request contains an implied criticism, or that the parent was asking the teacher to take on parental responsibilities. For instance, during a parent–teacher interview, a Chinese mother kept asking me to tell the teacher that she would like the teacher to tell her boy to do this and not to do that. The teacher said to me, "She is the mother of the boy. This is not my business." In another class, a teacher told the mother how good her boy was in class, but the mother complained to the teacher about how the boy misbehaved at home. She told me to ask the teacher to be strict with the boy and discipline him harshly. The teacher looked puzzled and asked me to explain again how good the boy was in her class. But the mother continued urging the teacher to be strict with the boy, discipline him harshly, and tell the boy to behave at home. The teacher eventually looked upset and said, "He is behaving well in my class. If he is misbehaving at home, it is your responsibility to make him behave, not mine."

Having worked closely with Canadian teachers at different grades in the school, I understand that Canadian teachers expect shared responsibility in a child's schooling. Some Chinese parents, however, especially those with little formal schooling in China and with little English, depend heavily on teachers for their children's schooling. Also, with their narratively driven respect for the school and the teacher, Chinese parents tend to trust the school and the teacher as the authority of knowledge and as the ones who know better than they themselves know how to educate their child.

One of the formal, institutionalized ways parents and teachers are expected to share responsibility is through participation in School Councils, a committee set up within guidelines from government and the Board of Education. The School Council, made up of parents, school administrators and teachers, and community representatives, has considerable curricular decision-making authority. However, during my years at Bay Street Community School, it was a struggle to get Chinese parents to attend monthly council meetings, let alone actively participate. It appeared that they did not think they should interfere in the school's business; in addition, they trusted the school and the teachers, as discussed earlier. Even as participatory as Hui Lan is in her boys' education and her volunteer work in the Parent Centre, she believes that every school has its own way of running a school and that she should not interfere. As a parent, she does not want to do anything that might interrupt the school's routines. Furthermore, my field notes show that when Chinese parents did attend meetings, they often showed less interest in discussions that appeared either too political or not sufficiently focused on the particular needs of their children in terms of teaching, learning and achievement.

My reconstruction of parent–teacher relations from a personal and social narrative perspective is aimed at helping communication and understanding between home and school. On the one hand, narrativization may help Canadian teachers understand the narrative roots of some seemingly unreasonable or confusing requests and demands made by Chinese parents. On the other hand, Chinese parents need to learn and understand new curriculum situations. The school may find ways to reach out to those families who tend to rely on teachers for their children's schooling. With the assistance of culture brokers and mediators, the school can help families make sense of Canadian schooling and help them understand new curriculum situations. Cultural brokers can search for ways to capitalize on the interest Chinese parents have in their child's education, and also encourage parents to communicate and interact with the school, the teachers, and parents of diverse ethnic groups as to various ways of parenting and educating children in new situations on landscapes in transition.

The Authority of the Teacher
As discussed earlier, the authority of the teacher has been challenged in modern society, especially in a world that emphasizes democracy, equity, and social justice in schools. Chinese families, however, still respect the authority of the teacher. Part of the Chinese newcomer students' culture shock is to find their Canadian teachers less authoritarian and more

oriented to student initiative than teachers in China. Most of my participant Chinese students like the Canadian teachers' approach. But there are misunderstandings around boundaries. Chinese students sometimes interpret the new situation as one without boundaries where students have freedoms, *freedoms* which are actually not permitted in Canadian schools. For example, some of the boys in my study misbehaved in ways that they would not do if they were in a Chinese class with an authoritative teacher. Also, some boys appeared to consciously take advantage of the fact that their teachers could not understand Chinese and that their parents could not speak English. They took advantage of the different worlds in which they live: parts of which were unseen by their parents and parts unseen by their teachers. It is a situation where both teacher and parent lose authority over the boys at a time when they are most in need of guidance. In addition, the institutional structure and its built-in protocols tend to worsen the situation. For example, when Zhi Gao misbehaved, he was often sent to the Main Office, or to a social worker if his behavior was out of control. Well-intentioned and well-structured as the system is, it creates communication gaps between the teacher and the student. Sending a boy to the Main Office or to a social worker effectively sends a message to the child that the teacher lacks the authority to deal with him. In this child's mind, the teacher loses authority by these actions and, in effect, worsens the classroom situation that gave rise to the incident. Zhi Gao's case reveals that the more outside support was utilized, the more out of control he seemed to become. He became furious with his parents when he learned that the Children's Aid Society was involved during a time when his teachers and parents tried to help him return to his high school. On the other hand, it is too demanding for Canadian homeroom teachers who have to teach almost all subjects and also have to deal with everything that happens in the class. In China, teachers usually only teach one subject to different classes of the same grade. In Chinese schools, a coordinating teacher is assigned to each class, who functions like a homeroom teacher in Canadian schools, but only teaches one major subject. The coordinating teacher takes more responsibilities coordinating all aspects of the students' school life between home and school and between teachers of different subjects and between different classes and grades of the school. While home visits are common and part of the teaching practice in China, Canadian teachers are not supposed to go into students' homes, a job that can be done only by social workers.

In the next section, I discuss how shifting boundaries on landscapes in transition cause institutional fragmentation in the seemingly well-structured school system in Canada, fragmentations that can trap students, and even teachers, in between.

The Milieu

As I have discussed the social milieu in terms of landscapes in transition earlier (see Chapter 8), here I focus my discussion of the milieu in the school system. The school system, with its diversity of programs and difficulties in adequately responding to Chinese family narratives, puzzled me throughout my inquiry.

When I first began my fieldwork at the Parent Centre in the elementary school in downtown Toronto, I marveled at the rich educational resources in Canadian schools. I often said to Carmen that I wished I were a small child again to be able to attend a Canadian school and participate in its Parent Centre, daycare, kindergarten, and grade school, and to enjoy all the interesting curricular and extra-curricular programs. I was fascinated even more when I began participating in school life, attending classes, going on fieldtrips, attending school events, and assisting at School Council meetings. I came to know many excellent hard-working school staff members such as Newcomer Support Class teachers, LEAP program teachers, international language teachers, newcomer settlement worker, guidance teacher, vice principal, principal; and also community workers and volunteers. I heard about the work of social workers and the Children's Aid Society. I had direct and indirect contact with school psychologists, Special Ed program teachers, school board trustees, and community centres and services through my work with the school and with the families. I am fascinated by a school system that is so well structured, supported, and staffed. Therefore, I was puzzled and also frustrated during the time when I worked intensively with the Chinese families helping newcomer boys with their life in transition, especially boys like Zhi Gao. I wondered why so many people's hard work could not prevent boys like Zhi Gao from falling out of the school system and why the mother, with so many services for children and youth, would still call me in despair, seemingly having nowhere else to turn for help.

Defined Terms, Categories, and Boundaries
The first time I heard the LEAP teacher, the settlement worker and International Language Program teachers mention their boss, I thought they each were referring to the principal of the school. I was surprised to

find out that they were each affiliated with different organizations, each with a different boss. For a long while I could not quite understand the school's relations to these different organizations and institutions and how the organizations and the affiliated teachers were related to the school, and in what way they were related to one another.

With my three-year intensive fieldwork at the school, I came to understand that teachers of different programs, the vice principals, principal, the guidance teacher, the settlement worker, the social worker, and supporting staff members all work within the confines of certain boundaries categorized in specifically defined terms. The school system is structured in the ways captured by Fei's (1947/1992) metaphor of haystacks that depicts the structure of the Western society in which people create groups with clear boundaries, each group its own haystack. The benefits of the organizational boundaries, as Fei (1947/1992) points out, are that the rights and duties of members are clearly defined, and hence people show their respect to individual rights and follow defined regulations. My work with the school and with the Chinese families, however, shows the downside of such distinct boundaries. The fact that people from different organizations work within the confines of boundaries with defined terms means that they cannot form a web of relationship to support boys like Zhi Gao. Well-structured and well-staffed as it appears, the system cannot function to its best advantage as fragmentation, in the form of several haystacks each with special borders, is created in-between the boundaries. From my work with teachers at school, I learned that, according to the defined terms of the union, a classroom teacher cannot pay home visits to a student. A social worker is called upon if home visits are needed, but a social worker works according to his or her schedule with a single worker covering several schools. The one who worked with Zhi Gao said he had to cover eight schools. Newcomer settlement workers help to make bridges between home and school, but one settlement worker usually covers two or three schools. Also, the category of newcomer students is defined as those who have been in Canada for less than two years. Accordingly, a settlement worker who had worked with the school and the teacher to help Zhi Gao in the first two years could no longer continue her work with Zhi Gao just at the time when Zhi Gao was most in need. She still helped, but out of empathy, and at the risk of stepping beyond her working boundaries. Her services to Zhi Gao's family were no longer regular. Also, according to the defined terms, only schools that have more than 40 newcomer students are eligible to have a settlement worker sit in an office at the school. Bay Street

Community School almost lost its settlement worker one year by a "deficit" of two newcomer students as there were only 38 newcomer students who fit into the specified category that year.

More importantly, supporting staff such as social workers and settlement workers are bound to work with students in discontinuity as they do not work with the students on a daily basis in their classroom and hence do not know the student's school life, and know even less of the student's home life. The fact that Zhi Gao would talk with me but bang the door on the face of the social worker explains that we need to deal with children and youth educational issues in continuity and interaction of situations. For the same reason, Chinese mothers preferred me to translate for them at school council meetings and parent–teacher interviews rather than the professional interpreters because I knew their children's school life. The interpreters are called upon by the school with little knowledge of the students' lived experience at school and at home.

One-on-One
Individuality in the Western world, manifested in daily work and life, is as pervasive as is family as a metaphor to depict Chinese social relations. From my observation, in Western society things tend to be done mostly on a one-on-one basis. While a one-on-one model may work better to meet individual needs, often outcomes in the school system turn out to be less effective and efficient than expected.

Take Zhi Gao's case for example. With so many possible resources and so many people's hard work, the boy still dropped out shortly after he went to high school. Some resource people said, "We have done what we can. It is his choice." Someone asked, "Don't you think boys like Zhi Gao will fail no matter where they are?" Still others thought that there was a problem at home and the school could do little. There was a sense of inevitability about his situation.

As I saw his story, Zhi Gao's situation was so complicated that no one could solve his problems single-handedly. It seems that boys like Zhi Gao stand at the edge of a cliff off which they would inevitably fall. However, by observing and traveling across his changing landscapes at school, at home and in the community, I believe a more communal approach, in the Chinese holistic sense, holds helpful possibilities.

It is true that the system is well-structured with many well-staffed, resource-filled programs and services. However, in practice, boys who are at risk of falling out of the system, such as Zhi Gao, are often like a ball being passed from one person to another, with each person working within the confines of his or her working boundaries. One-on-one has limitations. Everyone involved with Zhi Gao worked hard, but alone and ultimately in vain. In a ball game, all the players play the game within their zones by following a set of defined rules and regulations. One who steps out of their boundaries is considered as violating the rules. However, when being passed around from one player to another, the ball remains the focal attention of everyone else in the game. The individual players play together in coordination and collaboration with one another as a team with a common goal in mind, and also with overall plans and strategies as to how to win the game as a team. At times when they seem to be losing the game, a team stops and meets with the coach, to discuss together a better plan and better strategies. In school practice, however, the teacher, the administrator, the social worker, the settlement worker, the community worker, and many other people work on a one-on-one basis, instead of forming a collaborative team. There are no overall plans and strategies as to how to deal with one case holistically as a team. It is as if a soccer team were formed by players from different clubs with each person playing the game on his or her own with little teamwork nor overall plans and strategies; hence, there is little chance to win the game. I believe one of the greatest policy needs in the educational system is to find productive ways to make school "home", with a collaborative, holistic plan, in which children at risk have the attention of people with different roles and responsibilities, and hence, are able to find "home", a sense of belonging, in school.

Shifting Boundaries and Invisibility of Visible Minorities
The family narratives show that newcomer students live lives in transition from China to Canada, from middle school to high school, and from childhood to adolescence. These transitional lives are lived in between more than two languages and cultures and in different curricular situations. I have already pointed out that boys like Zhi Gao and Yang Yang live lives that tend to be unseen either by teachers at school or by parents at home. It also appears that they tend to live in a virtual world of computer games perhaps to escape challenges in the real world. School system boundaries tend to foster invisibility and the leading of such virtual lives. This is a consequence of the fragmentations of the system: in a one-on-one sequence of settings the child appears and disappears from different caregivers' purview.

Furthermore, it is more challenging for newcomer visible minority families, from cultures very different from the mainstream, to make sense of boundaries defined in social cultural terms. On landscapes in transition, boundaries are shifting. What used to be visible boundaries for newcomer students and families in their home countries suddenly disappear on the new land. On the other hand, many boundaries visible to the people who have grown up in mainstream society, majority or minority, are invisible to newcomers due to language and cultural barriers.

Visible minority newcomers are the most visible group in mainstream society with differences revealed in their faces, in their languages, in their behaviors and in their life styles. On the other hand, they are invisible to those who are not thrown into the same social positioning and do not share the same lived experience in the defined terms and categories in which visible minority newcomers live. Programs and services for these newcomers are built on what mainstream society can see and, in general, on what newcomers need to fit in and reduce these visibilities. But many of these programs and services have little basis in newcomer families' actual lived experience in between the visible and invisible boundaries. Furthermore, language and culture barriers often prevent newcomers from locating, or even being aware of, appropriate programs and services. One of my most common tasks throughout this study was helping newcomers find out educational options and possibilities in a complex educational system.

Hence, newcomer children/students tend to live a fragmented school life due to their families' immigration and also due to the institutional structure of our schools. Newcomer students and their families are at risk of falling between the fragments of the institutional structure of our schools. This happens in spite of the well-intended efforts in policy and in practice. By narrating the stories of Chinese newcomer families who live lives in transition in between the visible and invisible boundaries, I bring attention to the challenges and difficulties newcomers face with respect to educational policy and practice. It is important to take into account parents' insights in policymaking and practices and utilize parents from diverse ethnic cultural backgrounds as a powerful source of knowledge in educating children and youth (Ayers 1993).

The Role of the School
As a Chinese parent said at a School Council meeting, since students spend more time at school with their teachers and peers than with their parents at home, the school needs to take more responsibility for children's education.

That, he said, is what a school is for. With a similar perception, Yang Yang's parents pulled him out of the downtown school intending to send him to a boarding school. Chinese parents often choose their home based on the quality of the local school. To them, the school plays the most important role in their children's education and hence in their future.

"Bay Street Community Public School: Where You Belong" is the school's mission statement (see Connelly et al. 2004). The fact that Zhi Gao did not quit school during his two years at Bay Street School shows that, at least to a certain extent, he had a sense of belonging to the school when he did not find a sense of home in his stepfather's house. He ran away from school when he was sent to the Main Office for misbehavior, but returned to class in the afternoon. He argued with Zhi Hui and other boys one moment, but became friends and played together in another. He liked his Canadian teachers who were friendly and did not discipline him physically. He trusted his Cantonese teacher who spent much time talking with him in class. He was in the same boat with his classmates, most of whom were struggling with English. They argued and sometimes even fought, but more often played together as friends. As Jia Ming said, Chinese students are taught to be caring and supportive to one another like brothers and sisters of one family. His classmates in China visited one another and helped one another. Teachers would send class representatives to a student's home when that student appeared to have difficulties in his or her studies or did not show up in class.

School and classmates make up the most important part of the lives of Chinese school-aged children and youth. Chinese parents pay careful attention to the kind of school their children attend and they follow up with their classmates to ensure their child has appropriate friends. Teachers pay home visits to keep open lines of communication with parents and also to better understand the family situation.

With shifting boundaries in a changing landscape, we can find alternative ways by learning from different educational practices to enhance home and school communication. With care in curriculum and care from teachers and care among classmates, a sense of home can be developed in class, and hence at school. Students of diverse linguistic and cultural groups can live a life with promise in harmony if they can develop a sense of belonging to school during those critical years of their lives in transition.

Many researchers in the United States and Canada recognize the importance of the role the school plays in the lives of children and youth (e.g., C. Suárez-Orozco and M. Suárez-Orozco 2001, 2003; Gibson 1998; Goodwin 2002); as well they recognize the importance of care in curriculum (Noddings 1992), the cultivation of a web of relationships (Gilligan 1982), and the importance of care and a web of relationships in school and in teacher's professional development (Stevens 2006; Stevens and Xu 2005). Although many studies focus on elements that cause marginalization, there are calls for inquiry into factors related to schools that foster belonging (S. Lee 2002; Louie 2005). My study contributes to this latter purpose. My hope is that my study will contribute to policies and practices aimed at fostering a sense of belonging. I want to find ways to help newcomers in their search for home.

MULTIDIMENSIONAL BRIDGE ACROSS CULTURES ON LANDSCAPES IN TRANSITION

Schwab's commonplaces of curriculum structured my discussion and permitted my discussion to focus on important aspects of schooling. I have sketched the unseen lives of immigrant children between home and school – lives lived in-between shifting visible and invisible boundaries on landscapes in transition. These boundaries prevent rich educational resources from being utilized to the best advantage of newcomer families. One of the purposes of my work is to bring these unseen lives to light for cross-cultural and multicultural curriculum and teacher development in terms of educational policy, practice, and research.

Culture and Experience

In Chapter 8 I brought forward the cultural knowledge and values revealed in Chapter 3 through Chapter 7 to help understand Chinese newcomer families' cross-cultural schooling experience in the three-dimensional narrative inquiry space. My intention is to highlight the contribution Chinese newcomer families can make for communication of values and knowledge across cultures. My work is not a study aimed at defining newcomer identity nor is it a study of newcomer problems and difficulties. Nieto (1999) points out that individual differences and cultural values may influence learning, but social, political, and economic context also affects learning (p. 11). I understand Chinese newcomer families' lived experience in narrative terms of "landscape", rather than in distinctive cultural terms. Cultural differences are often used to account for success or failure of minority groups. There is a danger in doing so. Cultures are often perceived as superior or inferior to one another. The Chinese, commonly labeled as a model minority favoring learning and growth, can become doubly marginalized and hence victimized. I have shown how this occurs as students like Zhi Gao and Yang Yang have tended to be invisible in the discourse on anti-racism and special educational needs, and when they have difficulties, they tend to be seen as personally responsible. Furthermore, the system, with values of democracy, personal freedom, and individuality, emphasizes self-motivation. Individual rights, responsibilities, and initiatives are valued over shared social responsibilities; boundaries are honored over shared obligations across boundaries; self-identity and self-esteem over common, shared goals; and personal responsibility over social responsibility and cultural role models. To complement insights on cultural characteristics presented in the previous chapter, this chapter focuses on experience in understanding the cultural and personal narratives of Chinese newcomer families.

Bridges across Cultural Boundaries

As this study is helpful to identify and share the issues faced by Chinese newcomers, so studies on education for the Blacks, Latinos, and First Nations also provide shared and varied insights for improving newcomer/minority students' cross-cultural schooling experience. For example, just as there is a lack of cultural role models for Chinese newcomer students, studies have found that one of the major factors among Black children's education is lack of cultural role models and positive public images (e.g. Solomon-Henry 2005). Issues with Latino children in their subtractive schooling experience resonate with newcomer students' experience such as Zhi Gao's and Yang Yang's (see Suárez-Orozco and Páez 2002; Valenzuela 1999). The Chinese newcomer students who fall out of the system may follow a similar pathway to Latinos and others. Stacy Lee (1996) takes this thought a step further and alerts us to the danger of creating tensions between visible minority groups when the successes and failures of different groups are emphasized (see also Park et al. 2003).

On the other hand, Chinese newcomer families' narratives provide insights into understanding how much a positive role one's home country's cultural values, family values and educational values can play in helping newcomer children integrate into the host culture. Family narratives such as those of Hui Lan, Jia Ming, and Freeman also serve as examples that offer insights into the education of children and youth of native-born visible minorities.

When arguing for diversity as a deliberative asset and answering the question why multiple social perspectives are a necessary resource, Parker (2003, p. 97) explains that "multiple perspectives contribute to social knowledge. Group difference increases a diverse society's collective knowledge base and enlightens its public decision making. It enlarges each participant's knowledge of people and perspectives beyond one's own social position and experience" (p. 98).

While "celebrate differences" has become a popular slogan in American and Canadian education (Parker 2003), multiculturalism is still, and always will be, a journey and a dialogue (Beairsto and Carrigan 2004, p. 4). My hope for this journey is that people of all cultures can be engaged in dialogue, listening to and learning from one another on matters of social problems, perspectives, and social position.

In a world of increasing diversity, we need to understand the term "culture" with an expanding horizon. As Nieto (2000) points out, culture has many features: dynamic, multifaceted, embedded in context, influenced by social, economic, and political factors, created and socially constructed, learned, and dialectical (p. 49). Hence, the complex and important role culture plays in learning makes it quite challenging and somewhat problematic to discuss issues only between two cultures: home and school – with home representing a defined subordinate culture and school as the dominant culture categorized as "the mainstream". The bridges we make are often bi-directional and sometimes even unidirectional between the dominant culture (the mainstream) and a subordinate culture such as the Blacks, the Latinos, the First Nations, or the Chinese, for example, with little communication and appreciation of knowledge and values across diverse cultural groups. In a sense, different ethnic groups seem to work separately to bridge the cultures of home and school on such bi-directional and unidirectional bridges. Gagné's (2006) project "Closing the gap: Exploring the relationships between immigrant parents and teachers", in which I was partly involved, is leading a way to close the gap not only between home and school, but also to enhance communication across newcomer parents of diverse cultural groups.

On landscapes in transition with increasing diversity in this fluctuating world, we need to understand the complexity of culture through people's multilayered lived experience to build a multidimensional bridge that can let people from ethnically, socially, culturally, and linguistically diverse backgrounds travel across landscapes. With our shared and differed educational ends and means, values and concerns, people from diverse backgrounds can interact with and learn from one another to enhance communication and appreciation of values and knowledge. All cultures are essential components of the repertoire of the world civilization.

In summary, there are reciprocal learning needs for mutual sharing of ideas, knowledge, and values between newcomers and the mainstream society and among people of diverse ethnic and cultural groups. Newcomers and visible minorities need to be acknowledged and appreciated as contributors who bring values and knowledge as well as great opportunities that contribute significantly to the making of a new society, a society that is multicultural for all socially, economically, and culturally. In the processes of cultural adaptation, "the family" is "fluid and constantly being negotiated and reconstituted both spatially and temporally" (Creese et al. 1999, p. 3) on cross-cultural landscapes in transition, not only for newcomer families, but also for the mainstream society.

This shift in thinking will help us to include people of diverse cultures as valuable contributors to bridging values across cultural, ethnic and political borders and boundaries to provide education that works best for children growing up in culturally, ethnically, and linguistically diverse communities. Thinking narratively of the continuity and wholeness of our life experience enables us to extend and expand our mutual *we-ness* in dialogues across civilizations. We can have hope of cultivating "a compassionate world community with mutual respect and understanding" (He and Phillion 2002) in our mutual "we-consciousness" through reciprocal learning.

Notes

1. Some ideas in this section are developed and expanded from Xu et al. 2007 in which some of my research data with Yang Yang was used in the JCS article.
2. More elaborate ideas on teacher metaphors can be found in Xu and Stevens 2004, 2005.

Epilogue

My work has been a fluid and open inquiry. There are no conclusions, but more inquiries as life moves on and hence my inquiry continues with broadened horizons. Chinese families have regarded me as a teacher and a well-educated person throughout my work with them at Bay Street Community School, but it is I who have been educated most by their family narratives that have provided profound educational resources. The Confucian values revealed in their lived experiences reinvigorate me in Confucian learning to reach out to Dewey's notion of education and experience. My inquiry into Chinese newcomer families' lived experience of cross-cultural schooling is a journey in search of home on landscapes in transition for my participants as newcomers. It is also a continued journey for me in my cross-cultural learning and inquiry for ways of bridging cultures on landscapes in transition.

I have continued this journey by working with Dr. Michael Connelly at OISE/University of Toronto in setting up a Toronto-Shanghai/Beijing Sister School Network for the purpose of facilitating reciprocal learning between Canadian and Chinese schools in collaboration with Toronto District School Board, East China Normal University, and China National Research Centre for Studies in Foreign Language Education (Connelly and Xu 2009). I have also developed the Pre-Service Teacher Education Reciprocal Learning Program between University of Windsor in Ontario Canada and Southwest University (SWU) in Chongqing China by collaborating with Drs. Shijian Chen and Yibing Liu at SWU (with Ling Li's initial assistance), in partnership with the Greater Essex Country District School Board with the essential support from Dr. Clara Howitt and her colleagues (Xu 2011a; Xu et al. 2015). I observe and am actively engaged in reciprocal learning with both pre-service and in-service teachers when I coordinate the yearly exchange visits of the Chinese and Canadian pre-service student teachers, and facilitate monthly Skype meetings between pairs of Windsor and Chongqing schools and related sister school interactions. In search of home on landscapes in transition, I keep my hope for reciprocal learning in teacher education and school education between the east and the west when working collaboratively with like-minded educators in Canadian and Chinese universities and schools through a seven-year partnership project co-directed with Dr. Michael Connelly in partnership with two Canadian universities, two Canadian school boards, four Chinese universities and over 30 associated Canadian and Chinese schools (Xu and Connelly 2013).

Home is where the best school is and hence the best education for our children. Home is where we can harmonize eastern learning with western knowledge in linguistic and cultural diversities. We search for home on landscapes in transition. Through reciprocal learning with mutual appreciation of knowledge and strengths from all cultures in a narrative unity, we can build a multidimensional bridge that leads to the home where diversity is celebrated in social harmony with our expanded and extended *we* in this interrelated and interdepended global world.

REFERENCES

Ames, R. T. (2004). Foreword. In J. Grange (Ed.), *John Dewey, confucius, and global philosophy*. Albany: State University of New York Press.
An, R. (2001). Traveling on parallel tracks: Chinese parents and English teachers. *Educational Research, 43*(3), 311–328.
Anisef, P., Kilbride, K. M., Ochocka, J., & Janzen, R. (2001). Study on parenting issues of newcomer families in Ontario. Joint Centre of Excellence for Research on Immigration and Settlement and Centre for Research and Education in Human Services. Toronto, Canada.
Aristotle, N. (1984). Topica. In R. McKeon (Ed.), *The basic works of Aristotle* (pp. 187–206). New York: Random House. Trans., W.A. Pickard-Cambridge.
Ayers, W. C. (2004). *Teaching the personal and the political: Essays on hope and justice*. New York: Teachers College Press.
Ayers, W. C. (2003). *On the side of the child: Summerhill revisited*. New York: Teachers College Press.
Ayers, W. C. (1998). Teaching as an ethical enterprise. *The Educational Forum, 63*(1), 52–57.
Ayers, W. C. (1993). *To teach: The journey of a teacher*. New York: Teachers College Press.
Baker, C. (2001). *Foundations of bilingual education and bilingualism* (3rd ed.). Multilingual Matters LTD. Bilingual Education and Bilingualism 27: Series Editors: Nancy Hornberger and Colin Baker. Buffalo, NY.
Beairsto, B., & Carrigan, T. (2004). Imperatives and possibilities. *Education Canada, 44*(2), 4–6 & 52.

Bender, B. (1995). *Landscape: Politics and perspectives*. Explorations in anthropology series. (Reprint; first published in 1993) Providence/Oxford: Berg Publishers.

Brown, R. (2006). *The TDSB grade 9 cohort study: A five-year analysis, 2000–2005*. Research Report, Toronto District School Board. Toronto, Canada: TDSB.

Bruce, M. (2010, December). China Debuts at Top of International Education Rankings. ABC News. Retrieved from http://abcnews.go.com/Politics/china-debuts-top-international-education-rankings/story?id=12336108, December 07, 2016.

Bruner, J. (1996). *The culture of education*. Cambridge: Harvard University Press.

Carey, E. (2002). Toronto: Canada's linguistic capital. *Toronto Star* (December 11).

Carter, K. (1993). The place of story in the study of teaching and teacher education. *Educational Researcher*, 22(1), 5–12.

Chao, R. C. (2013). Race/ethnicity and multicultural competence among school counselors' multicultural training, racial/ethnic identity, and color-blind attitudes. *Journal of Counseling & Development*, 91, 140–151.

Cheng, S., & Starks, B. (2002). Racial differences in the effects of significant others on students' educational expectations. *Sociology of Education*, 75(4), 306–327.

Chen, X., Cen, G., Li, D., & He, Y. (2005). Social functioning and adjustment in Chinese children: The imprint of historical time. *Child Development*, 76, 182–195. [PubMed: 15693766].

Chen, X., & Tse, H. (2010). Social and psychological adjustment of Chinese Canadian children. *International Journal of Behavioral Development*, 34(4), 330–338. doi: 10.1177/0165025409337546.

Chin, J. L. (2005). *Learning from my mother's voice: Family legend and the Chinese American experience*. New York: Teachers College Press.

Chong, S. (2005). The logic of Hong Kong teachers: An exploratory study of their teaching culturally diverse students. *Teaching Education*, 16(2), 117–129.

CIC Canada (2001). Facts and Figures 2001: Immigration Overview. Retrieved from http://www.cic.gc.ca/english/pub/facts2001/3tor-02.html, January 5, 2003.

CIC Canada (2004). Facts and Figures 2004: Immigration Overview, Permanent and Temporary Residents. Retrieved from http://www.cic.gc.ca/english/pub/facts2004, March 12, 2005.

CIC Canada (2005). CIC's Mandate, Mission and Vision. Retrieved from http://www.cic.gc.ca/english/department/mission.html, April 20, 2006.

CIC Canada (2015). Facts and Figures 2014: Immigration Overview. Retrieved from http://www.cic.gc.ca/english/resources/statistics/facts2014/index.asp, February 05, 2016.

Clandinin, D. J., & Connelly, F. M. (2000). *Narrative inquiry: Experience and story in qualitative research*. San Francisco: Jossey-Bass Publishers.

Clandinin, D. J., & Connelly, F. M. (1992). The teacher as curriculum-maker. In P. W. Jackson (Ed.), *Handbook of research on curriculum: A project of the American Educational Research Association* (pp. 363–401). Chapter 14. New York: Macmillan.

Coelho, E. (1998). *Teaching and learning in multicultural schools*. Bristol, United Kingdom: Multilingual Matters Ltd.

Collier, V. P. (1995). *Promoting academic success for ESL students*. Elizabeth, NJ: New Jersey Teachers of English for Other Languages-Bilingual Educators.

Conle, C. (1999). Why narrative? Which narrative? Struggling with time and place in life and research. *Curriculum Inquiry, 29*(1), 7–32.

Conle, C. (2000). Narrative inquiry: Research tool and medium for professional development. *European Journal of Teacher Education, 23*(1), 49–63.

Connelly, F. M., & Beattie, M. (1992). Keynote address: Narrative, storytelling and teacher education. In D. B. Maudsley (Ed.), Proceedings: The symposium on innovations in teacher education, May 15–17, 1991, (Vol. I, pp. 125–135). Toronto: Ministry of Education, Teacher Education Branch.

Connelly, M. F. (2001). Reverberations. *Journal of Critical Inquiry into Curriculum and Instruction, 3*(3), 58.

Connelly, F. M., & Clandinin, D. J. (1988). *Teachers as curriculum planners: Narratives of experience*. New York: Teachers College Press, Columbia.

Connelly, F. M., & Clandinin, D. J. (1990). Stories of experience and narrative inquiry. *Educational Researcher, 19*(5), 2–14.

Connelly, F. M., & Clandinin, D. J. (1992). Curriculum theory. In C. M. Alkin (Ed.), *Encyclopedia of educational research*, 6th ed. (pp. 287–292). N.Y.: Macmillan Publishing Co.

Connelly, F. M., & Clandinin, D. J. (1995). Narrative and education. *Teachers and Teaching: Theory and Practice, 1*(1), 73–85.

Connelly, F. M., He, M., Phillion, J., Chan, E., & Xu, S. J. (2004). Bay Street Community School: Where you belong. *Orbit, 34*(3), 39–42.

Connelly, F. M., & Xu, S. J. (2009). Cross-cultural school narratives of schooling: Shanghai-Toronto Sister School Network. A three-year standard research grant funded by Social Sciences and Humanities Research Council (SSHRC) of Canada.

Cook, G. (1996). Language play in English. In J. Maybin & N. Mercer (Eds.), *Using English: From conversation to anon*. London: Routledge with the Open University.

Cook, G. (2000). *Language play, language learning*. Oxford: Oxford University Press.

Costigan, C. L., Su, T. F., & Hua, J. M. (2010). Living up to expectations: The strengths and challenges experienced by Chinese Canadian students. *Canadian Journal of School Psychology, 25*, 223–245.

Coughlan, S. (2016). Pisa tests: UK lags behind in global school rankings. BBC News: Education & Family. Retrieved from http://www.bbc.com/news/education-38157811, December 06, 2016.

Creese, G., Dyck, I. L., & McLaren, A. T. (1999). Reconstituting the family: Negotiating immigration and settlement. RIIM (Research on Immigration and Integration in the Metropolis) Working Paper Series #99-10. Retried from http://Canada.metropolis.net, December 14, 2002.

Cummins, J. (1981a). *Bilingualism and minority language children.* Ontario: Ontario Institute for Studies in Education.

Cummins, J. (1981b). The role of primary language development in promoting educational success for language minority students. In California State Department of Education (Ed.), *Schooling and language minority students: A theoretical framework.* Los Angeles: California State Department of Education, Office of Bilingual Bicultural Education.

Cummins, J. (1983). *Heritage language education: A literature review.* Ontario: Ministry of Education.

Cummins, J. (1984a). *Bilingualism and special education: Issues in assessment and pedagogy.* Clevedon: Multicultural Matters.

Cummins, J. (1984b). Wanted: A theoretical framework for relating language proficiency to academic achievement among bilingual students. In C. Rivera (Ed.), *Language proficiency and academic achievement.* Clevedon: Multilingual Matters.

Cummins, J. (1986). Empowering minority students: A framework for intervention. *Harvard Education Review, 56*(1), 18–36.

Cummins, J. (1989). *Empowering minority students.* Sacramento, CA: California Association for Bilingual Education.

Cummins, J. (1993). The research base for heritage language promotion. In M. Danesi, K. McLeod, & S. Morris (Eds.), *Heritage languages and education: The Canadian experience.* Oakville: Mosaic Press.

Cummins, J. (1996). *Negotiating identities: Education for empowerment in a diverse society.* California: CABE (California Association for Bilingual Education.

Cummins, J. (2000). *Language, power and pedagogy: Bilingual children in the crossfire.* Clevedon: Multilingual Matters.

Cummins, J., & Corson, D. (Eds.) (1997). *Bilingual education* (Vol. 5). Dordrecht, The Netherlands: Kluwer Academic Publishers.

Cummins, J., & Danesi, M. (1990). *Heritage language: The development and denial of Canada's linguistic resources.* Toronto: Our Schools/Ourselves Education Foundation and Garamond Press.

Cummins, J., DeVillar, R. A., & Faltis, C. (Eds.) (1994). *Cultural diversity in schools: From rhetoric to practice.* Albany: State University of New York Press.

Deng, Z., & Gopinathan, S. (2016). PISA and high-performing education systems: explaining Singapore's education success. *Comparative Education, 52*(4), 449–472. doi: 10.1080/03050068.2016.1219535.

Dewey, J. (1887). Psychology. In *John Dewey: The early works, 1882–1898* (Vol. 2, pp. 125–126). Carbondale: Southern Illinois University Press.

Dewey, J. (1897). My pedagogic creed. *School Journal, 54*, January, 77–80.

Dewey, J. (1916/1961). *Democracy and education*. Old Tappan, N. J.: Macmillan.

Dewey, J. (1922/1964). The nature of aims. In R. D. Archambault (Ed.), *John Dewey on education: Selected writings*. With an introduction by Reginald D. Archambault. Chicago and London: The University of Chicago Press.

Dewey, J. (1938). *Experience & education*. New York: Kappa Delta Pi.

Dewey, J. (1932/1990). *The school and the society (1900, 1915, 1932); and, The child and the curriculum (1902): A centennial edition with a "lost essay"/ by John Dewey and a new introduction by Philip W. Jackson*. Chicago: University of Chicago Press.

Dillon, S. (2010, December). Top test scores from Shanghai stun educators. Retried from http://www.nytimes.com/2010/12/07/education/07education.html, December 11, 2016.

Dyson, L. L. (2001). Home-school communication and expectations of recent chinese immigrants. *Canadian Journal of Education, 26*(4), 455–476.

Elbaz-Luwisch, F. (1997). Narrative research: Political issues and implications. *Teaching and Teacher Education, 13*(1), 75–83.

Employment Equity Act (1995). Act current to March 3, 2006. Retrieved from http://laws.justice.gc.ca/en/E-5.401/238505.html, May 3, 2006.

Fallows, J. (2010, December) On Those "Stunning" Shanghai Test Scores. Retried from http://www.theatlantic.com/national/archive/2010/12/on-those-stunning-shanghai-test-scores/67654/, December 11, 2016.

Fei, X. (1947/1992). *From the soil: The foundations of Chinese society*. A translation of Fei Xiaotong's *Xiangtu Zhongguo* 乡土中国, *with an Introduction and Epilogue by Gary G. Hamilton and Wang Zheng. Berkeley and Los Angeles: University of California Press*.

Fraser, A. (2005). All the place is a stage – work as discourse: A narrative inquiry into workers' professional development. Unpublished doctoral dissertation, University of Toronto, Toronto, Canada.

Gagne, A. (2006). *Closing the gap: Exploring the relationships between immigrant parents and teachers*. Toronto: Ontario Institute for Studies in Education, University of Toronto.

Gagne, A. (2004). *Personal communication*. Toronto: Ontario Institute for Studies in Education, University of Toronto.

Gagne, A., Gambhir, M. R., Faez, F., Degamo, T., & Gershater, L. (Eds.) (2003). *Voices of English as a second language; students and their teachers: Compilation video*. Toronto, ON: ESL Infusion Initiative. Ontario Institute for Studies in Education, University of Toronto. Toronto District School Board. York Region District School Board.

Gibson, M. A. (1998). Promoting academic success among immigrant students: Is acculturation the issue? *Educational Policy, 12*, 615–633.

Gilligan, C. (1982). *In a different voice: Psychological theory and women's development.* Cambridge, MA: Harvard University Press.

Goldstein, T. (1999). Negotiating identities in Hong Kong, Canada: Opening small doors. *Bilingual Research Journal, 23*(2–3), 277–288.

Goodwin, A. L. (2002). Teacher preparation and the education of immigrant children. *Education and Urban Society, 34*(2), 156–172.

Government of Canada (1971). Multiculturalism: Policy and Legislative Framework. Canadian Heritage. Retrieved from http://www.canadianheritage.gc.ca/progs/multi/policy/framework_e.cfm, May 3, 2006.

Greene, M. (1978). *Landscapes of learning.* New York: Teachers College Press.

Greenfield, N. (1999). Asian and Chinese immigrants want a return to traditional methods in British Columbia. *The Times Educational Supplement*, No. 4312, February P.24.

Guo, Y. (2007). Multiple perspectives of Chinese immigrant parents and Canadian teachers on ESL learning in schools. *Diaspora, Indigenous, and Minority Education: An International Journal, 1*(1), 43–64.

Guo, Y. (2012). Diversity in public education: Acknowledging immigrant parent knowledge. *Canadian Journal of Education, 35*(2), 120–140.

Hall, D. L., & Ames, R. T. (1999). *The democracy of the Dead: Dewey, Confucius, and the hope for democracy in China.* USA: Carus Publishing Company.

Hamilton, G. G., & Wang, Z. (1992). Introduction and epilogue. A translation of Fei Xiaotong's (1947). *Xiangtu Zhongguo* 乡土中国 *(From the soil: The foundations of Chinese society).* Berkeley and Los Angeles: University of California Press.

Hardy, B. (1968). Towards a poetics of fiction: An approach through narrative. *Novel, 2*, 5–14.

Harrison, L. E., & Huntington, S. (2000). *Culture matters: How values shape human progress.* New York: Basic Books.

Hayhoe, R. (2006). *Portraits of influential Chinese educators.* Comparative Education Research Centre, The University of Hong Kong. Dordrecht, The Netherlands: Springer.

Hayhoe, R. (1997). Education as communication. In J. Montgomery (Ed.), *Values in education: social capital formation in Asia and the Pacific* (pp. 92–111). Hollis, New Hampshire: Hollis Publishing CO.

Hayhoe, R., & Pan, J. (Ed.) (2001). *Knowledge across cultures: A contribution to dialogue among civilizations.* Comparative Education Research Centre, The University of Kong Kong. Dordrecht, The Netherlands: Springer.

Hayhoe, R., & Li, J. (2017). Philosophy and comparative education: What can we learn from East Asia? In K. Munby, K. Bickmore, R. Hayhoe, C. Manion, & R. Read (Eds.), *Comparative and international education* (2nd ed, pp. 29–58). Toronto: Canadian Scholars' Press.

He, M. F. (2003). *A river forever flowing: Cross-cultural lives and identities in the multicultural landscape*. Greenwich, Connecticut, USA: Information Age Publishing.

He, M. F., & Phillion, J. (2002). Fluctuating landscapes, shifting thinking. *Curriculum Inquiry, 32*, 1.

Hing, B. O. (2001). Asians without blacks and Latinos in San Francisco: Missed lessons of the common good. *Amerasia Journal, 27*(2), 19–27.

Ipsos-Reid (2004). AP/Ipsos Polls: Reactions to immigration in leading nations. Retrieved from http://www.ipsos-na.com, October 16, 2004.

Jackson, P. W. (Ed.) (1992). *Handbook of research on curriculum: A project of the American Educational Research Association*. New York: Macmillan.

Jones, A. C. (2002). Where does the truth lie? *The Educational Forum, 66*, 110–115. Kappa Delta Pi.

Kibria, N. (2002). *Becoming Asian American: Second-generation Chinese and Korean American identities*. Baltimore: Johns Hopkins Press.

King, N. R. (1986). Recontextualizing the curriculum. *Theory Into Practice, 25*(1), 36–40.

Kim, S. Y., Wang, Y., Chen, Q., et al. (2015). *Journal of Youth Adolescence, 44*, 1263. doi:10.1007/s10964-014-0131-x.

Krashen, S. D. (1981). *Second language acquisition and second language learning*. Oxford: Pergamon.

Lai, Y., & Ishiyama, F. I. (2004). Involvement of immigrant Chinese Canadian mothers of children with disabilities. *Exceptional Children, 71*(1), 97–108.

Lee, O. (1997). Diversity and equity for Asian American students in Science Education. *Science Education, 81*(1), 107–122.

Lee, R. M., & Liu, H. T. (2001). Coping with intergenerational family conflict: Comparison of Asian American, Hispanic, and European American college students. *Journal of Counseling Psychology, 48*(4), 410–419.

Lee, S. J. (1996). *Unraveling the "model minority" stereotype: Listening to Asian American youth*. New York: Teaches College Press, Columbia University.

Lee, S. J. (2002). Learning "America": Hmong American high school students. *Education and Urban Society, 34*(2), 233–246.

Lee, S. J., & Hawkins, M. R. (2015). Policy, context and schooling: The education of English learners in new destinations. *Global Education Review, 2*(4), 40–59.

Leung, C. (2002). Reception classes for immigrant students in England. *TESOL Quarterly, 36*(1), 93–98.

Li, G. (2002). *East is East, West is West? Home literacy, culture, and schooling*. New York: Peter Lang.

Li, J. (2001). Expectations of Chinese immigrant parents for their children's education: The interplay of Chinese tradition and the Canadian context. *Canadian Journal of Education, 26*(4), 477–494.

Li, P. S. (1998). *Chinese in Canada* (2nd ed.) Toronto, ON: Oxford University Press.

Liu, E. (1999). *The accidental Asian: Notes of a native speaker.* New York: Vintage Books.

Louie, V. (2001). Parents' aspirations and investment: The role of social class in the educational experiences of 1.5 and second-generation Chinese Americans. *Harvard Educational Review, 71*(3), 438–474.

Louie, V. (2004). *Compelled to excel: Immigration, education, opportunity among Chinese Americans.* Stanford, CA: Stanford University Press.

Louie, V. (2005). Immigrant newcomer populations, ESEA, and the pipeline to college: Current considerations and future lines of inquiry. *Review of Research in Education, 29*, 69–105.

Macphee, J. (2003). New arrivals. *Child Education, 80*(9), 31–38.

Mapp, K. L. (1997). Making family-school connections work. *The Educational Digest, 63*, 36–39.

Martin, J. R. (1994). *Changing the educational landscape: Philosophy, women, and curriculum.* London: Routledge.

McKay, S. L., & Wong, S. C. (Eds.) (2000). *New immigrants in the United States: Readings for second language educators.* Cambridge, UK: Cambridge University Press.

McKay, L. S., & Wong, S. C. (1996). Multiple discourses, multiple identities: Investment and agency in second-language learning among Chinese adolescent immigrant students. *Harvard Educational Review, 66*(3), 577–608.

Minister of Public Works and Government Services Canada (2005a). *A Canada for all: Canada's action plan against racism.* Government of Canada: Minister of Public Works and Government Services Canada.

Minister of Public Works and Government Services Canada (2005b). *Annual Report on the operation of The Canadian Multicultural Act 2003–2004.* Government of Canada: Minister of Public Works and Government Services Canada.

Minister of State (Multiculturalism) (1988a). *Canadian Multiculturalism Act.* Retrieved from http://www.pch.gc.ca/progs/multi/policy/framework_e.cfm, August 4, 2005.

Minister of State (Multiculturalism) (1988b). *Canadian Multiculturalism Act.* Retrieved from https://www.pch.gc.ca/progs/multi/policy/act_e.cfm, August 4, 2005.

Mitchell, B. A. (2005). Canada's growing visible minority population: Generational challenges, opportunities and federal policy considerations. *Canada 2017: Serving Canada's Multicultural Population for the Future Policy Forum, Discussion Papers* (pp. 51–62). March 22–23, 2005. Government of Canada: Department of Canadian Heritage.

Mitchell, W. J. T. (Ed.) (1994). *Landscape and power.* Chicago: The University of Chicago Press.

Nieto, S. (1995). A history of the education of Puerto Rican students in U.S. Mainland schools. In J. A. Banks & C. A. McGee Banks (Eds.), *Handbook of research on multicultural education* (pp. 388–411). New York: Simon & Schuster Macmillan.

Nieto, S. (1999). *The light in their eyes: Creating multicultural learning communities.* New York: Teachers College Press, Columbia University.

Nieto, S. (2000). *Affirming diversity: The sociopolitical context of multicultural education* (3rd ed.). New York: Longman.

Noddings, N. (1992). *The challenge to care in schools: An alternative approach to education.* New York, NY: Teachers College Press.

OECD (2014). PISA 2012 Results in Focus: What 15-year-olds know and what they can do with what they know. Retrieved on December 7, 2016 from https://www.oecd.org/pisa/keyfindings/pisa-2012-results-overview.pdf

Oliver, S. J., & Klugman, E. (2003). Play and learning day by day—incorporating constructive play in the early childhood classroom. *Child Care Information Exchange, 149*(1/03), 62–65.

Ontario Government. (2005). *Many roots, many voices: Supporting English language learners in every classroom. A practical guide for Ontario Educators.* Toronto: Queen's Printer.

Ontario Government. (2008). *Supporting English language learners: A practical guide for Ontario educators Grades 1 to 8.* Toronto: Queen's Printer.

Park, C. C., Goodwin, A. L., & Lee, S. J. (Eds.) (2001). *Research on the education of Asian and Pacific Americans.* Greenwich, CN: Information Age.

Park, C. C., Goodwin, A. L., & Lee, S. J. (Eds.) (2003). *Asian American identities, families, and schooling.* Greenwich, CN: Information Age.

Park, H., & Bauer, S. (2002). Parenting practices, ethnicity, socioeconomic status and academic achievement in adolescents. *School Psychology International, 23*(4), 386–396.

Parker, W. C. (2003). *Teaching democracy: Unity and diversity in public life.* (A Volume in J. A. Banks (Ed.), Multicultural Education Series). New York: Teachers College Press, Columbia University.

Parry, L. J. (1998). Immigration and multiculturalism: Issues in Australian society and schools. *Social Education, 62*(7), 449–453.

Piper, H., & Garratt, D. (2004). Identity and citizenship: Some contradictions in practice. *British Journal of Educational Studies, 52*(3), 276–292.

Pham, S. (2010, December,). High Test Scores, but China Education Flawed. ABC News. Retried from http://abcnews.go.com/Politics/chinas-education-prepares-students-tests/story?id=12348599, December 07, 2016.

Phillips, D. C. (1994). Telling it straight: Issues in assessing narrative research. *Educational Psychologist, 29*(1), 13–21.

Phillips, D. C. (1997). Telling the truth about stories. *Teaching and Teacher Education, 13*(1), 101–109.

Phillion, J. (2002). *Narrative inquiry in a multicultural landscape: Multicultural teaching and learning.* Westport, Connecticut, USA: Ablex Publishing.

Phillion, J., He, M. F., & Connelly, F. M. (2005). *Narrative and experience in multicultural education.* Thousand Oaks, California: Sage Publications.

Rao, N., & Yuen, M. (2001). Accommodations for assimilation: Supporting newly arrived children from the Chinese mainland to Hong Kong. *Childhood Education, 77,* 5 part (annual theme issue), 313–318.

Resmovits, J. (2016). American teens' math scores fall on an international test. Los Angeles Times. Retried from http://www.latimes.com/local/education/la-me-pisa-2015-story.html, December 6, 2016.

Samuelsson, I. P., & Johansson, E. (2006). Play and learning—inseparable dimensions in preschool practice. *Early Child Development and Care, 176*(1), 47–65.

Schecter, S. R., & Cummins, J. (Eds.) (2003). *Multilingual education in practice: Using diversity as a resource.* Portsmouth, NH: Heinemann.

Schubert, W. H., & Ayers, W. C. (Eds.) (1992). *Teacher lore: Learning from our own experience.* New York: Longman.

Schwab, J. J. (1962). The teaching of science: The teaching of science as enquiry (The Inglis Lecture). In J. J. Schwab & P. F. Brandwein (Eds.), *Elements in a strategy for teaching science in the elementary school.* Cambridge, MA: Harvard University Press.

Schwab, J. J. (1971a). *Education and the structure of the disciplines.* Edited by I. Westbury and N. J. Wilkof. Chicago: The University of Chicago Press.

Schwab, J. J. (1971b). *The practical: A language for curriculum.* Edited by I. Westbury & N. J. Wilkof. Chicago: The University of Chicago Press.

Schwab, J. J. (1971c). *The practical: Arts of eclectic.* Edited by I. Westbury and N. J. Wilkof. Chicago: The University of Chicago Press.

Schwab, J. J. (1973). *The practical 3: Translation into curriculum.* Edited by I. Westbury and N. J. Wilkof. Chicago: The University of Chicago Press.

Schwab, J. J. (1983). The practical 4: Something for curriculum professors to do. *Curriculum Inquiry, 13*(3), 239–265.

Smith, P. K. (Ed.) (1984). *Play in animals and humans.* Oxford: Blackwell.

Solomon-Henry, G. (2005). African indigenous knowledges and education: Implicationsfor youth of African descent and Black focused schools in Toronto. Unpublished doctoral dissertation. Toronto: University of Toronto.

Soto, L. D. (1997). *Language, culture, and power: Bilingual families and the struggle for quality education.* Albany, NY: State University of New York Press.

Soto, L. D. (Ed.) (2002). *Making a difference in the lives of bilingual/bicultural children.* New York: Peter Lang.

Statistics Canada. (2001). Census of Canada. http://www12.statcan.ca/english/census01/home/index.cfm, retrieved May 4, 2006.

Statistics Canada. (2005). Study: Canada's visible minority population in 2017. Retrieved from http://www.statcan.gc.ca/daily-quotidien/050322/dq050322b-eng.htm. April 20, 2006.

Stevens, E. D. (2006). Of bricks and butterflies: Four teachers quest for professional growth. Unpublished doctoral dissertation. Toronto, Ontario: Institute for Studies in Education, University of Toronto.

Stevens, E. D., & Xu, S. J. (2005, April). Caring in schools: A cross-cultural exploration enabled by story and metaphor. Paper presented at American Education Research Association (AERA) Annual Conference, Montreal, Canada. (AERA Outstanding Research Paper Award).

Suárez-Orozco, M., & Páez, M. (Eds.) (2002). *Latinos: Remaking America*. Cambridge, MA: David Rockefeller Centre for Latin American Studies.

Suárez-Orozco, C., & Suárez-Orozco, M. (2003). The impact of H. R. 1 for English language learners and immigrant students. In *The challenge for education reform: Standards, accountability, resources, and policy* (Vol. 18, No. 2, pp. 41–52). The Aspen Institute Congressional Program.

Suárez-Orozco, C., & Suárez-Orozco, M. (2001). *Children of immigration*. Cambridge, MA: Harvard University Press.

Sutton-Smith, B. (1979). *Play and learning*. New York: Gardner.

Suzuki, B. H. (1989). Asian Americans as the 'Model Minority': Outdoing whites? Or media hype?. *Change: The Magazine of Higher Learning, 21*(6), 13–19.

Toronto District School Board. (2005). The 2013–2014 Environmental Scan of the Toronto District School Board Programs. Retrieved March 2, 2005, from http://www.tdsb.on.ca/

Toronto District School Board. (2013, May). 2011–12 Facts: Student and Parent Census. Issue #1.

Tu, W. (2002). 杜维明文集 *Tu Wei-Ming Wen Ji (Collections of Tu Wei-Ming's Works) (Vols 1–5)*. Edited by Guo Qi-Yong and Zheng Wen-Long. China: Wu Han Press.

Tu, W. (Ed.) (1994). *The living tree: The changing meaning of being Chinese today*. Stanford, California: Stanford University Press.

Tu, W. (1985). *Confucian thought: Selfhood as creative transformation*. Albany: State University of New York Press.

Valdés, G. (1996). *Con Respeto: Bridging the distances between culturally diverse families and schools: An ethnographic portrait*. New York: Teachers College Press, Columbia University.

Valenzuela, A. (1999). *Subtractive schooling: U.S.—Mexican youth and the politics of caring*. Albany: Sate University of New York Press.

Wong Fillmore, L. (1983). The language learner as an individual. In M. Clarke & J. Handscombe (Eds.), *Pacific perspectives on language learning and teaching*. Washington, D.C.: TESOL.

Wang, J.C-S. (2008). *John Dewey in China: To teach and to learn*. Albany: SUNY Press.

Westbury, I., & Wilkof, N. J. (1982). *Joseph Schwab. Science, curriculum, and liberal education: Selected essays*. Chicago: The University of Chicago Press.

Wong Fillmore, L. (1991a). When losing a second language means losing the first. *Early Childhood Research Quarterly, 6*(3), 323–347.

Wong Fillmore, L. (1991b). Second-language learning in children: A model of language learning in social context. In E. Blalystok (Ed.), *Language processing in bilingual children*. Cambridge: Cambridge University Press.

Wong Fillmore, L. (1992). Against our best interest: The attempt to sabotage bilingual education. In J. Crawford (Ed.), *Language loyalties: A sourcebook on the official English controversy*. Chicago: University of Chicago Press.

Wong Fillmore, L. (2000). Loss of family languages: Should educators be concerned?. *Theory into Practice, 39*(4), 203–210.

Wong, J. C.-S. (2007). *John Dewey in China: To teach and to learn. SUNY Series in Chinese Philosophy and Culture*. Albany, New York: Albany State University of New York Press.

Wong, S. C., & López, M. G. (2000). English language learners of Chinese background: A portrait of diversity. In S. L. McKay & S.-L. C. Wong (Eds.), *New immigrants in the United States: Readings for second language educators*. Cambridge, UK: Cambridge University Press.

World Bank. (2016, May). World Bank Study Shows Shanghai's #1 Global Ranking in Reading, Math, & Science Rests on Strong Education System with Great Teachers. Press Release. Retried from http://www.worldbank.org/en/news/press-release/2016/05/16/world-bank-study-shows-shanghais-1-global-ranking-in-reading-math-science-rests-on-strong-education-system-with-great-teachers, December 11, 2016.

Xu, J. (1999). *Reaching out to other people's children in an urban middle school: The families' views. The series on cultural interchange*. U.S.; New York: NCREST.

Xu, S. J. (2000). Perspectives of Chinese Visiting Scholars on English Teaching and Learning for Non-English Majors in China. Unpublished MRP (Master's Research Paper). York University, Toronto, Canada.

Xu, S. J. (2011a). *Broaden the horizons: Reciprocal learning program between University of Windsor and Southwest University China*. Canada: The University of Windsor Strategic Priority Fund Application Proposal. University of Windsor.

Xu, S. J. (2011b). Bridging the East and West dichotomy: Harmonizing Eastern learning with Western knowledge. In J. Ryan (Ed.), *Understanding China's education reform: Creating cross cultural knowledge, pedagogies and dialogue* (pp. 224–242). Ch 11. London, UK: Routledge.

Xu, S. J. (2015). Ethical boundaries and considerations in cross-cultural narrative inquiry. In S. Trahar & Y. W. Ming (Eds.), *Using narrative inquiry for educational research in the Asia Pacific* (pp. 136–151). Ch 10. New York: Routledge, Taylor and Francis Group.

Xu, S. J., & Stevens, D. (2004, May). Living in stories through images and metaphors: Recognizing unity in diversity. Paper presented at Narrative Matters 2004, Fredericton, New Brunswick, Canada

Xu, S. J., & Stevens, E. D. (2005). Living in stories through images and metaphors: Recognizing unity in diversity. *Mcgill Journal of Education, 40*(2), 303–319.

Xu, S. J., Connelly, F. M., He, M. F., & Phillion, J. (2007). Immigrant students' experience of schooling: A narrative inquiry theoretical framework. *Journal of Curriculum Studies, 39*(4), 399–422.

Xu, S. J., & Connelly, F. M. (2013). *Reciprocal learning in teacher education and school education between Canada and China*. Partnership Grant Proposal Package, Social Sciences and Humanities Research Council (SSHRC), Canada

Xu, S. J., Chen, S. J., & Huang, J. (2015). Pedagogies of working with diversity: West-East reciprocal learning in pre-Service teacher education. In L. Barak & C. Craig (Eds.), *International teacher education: Promising pedagogies*. U.K.: Emerald Publishing.

Yeh, T. L. (2002). Asian American college students who are educationally at risk. *New Directions for Student Services, 97*, 61–71.

Zhang, H. (2013). *John Dewey, Liang Shuming, and China's education reform: Cultivating individuality*. Lanham, MD: Lexington Books.

Zhou, M. (2003). Urban education: Challenges in educating culturally diverse children. *Teachers College Record, 105*(2), 208–225.

Zhou, M., & Kim, S. (2006). Community forces, social capital, and educational achievement: THe case of supplementary education in the Chinese and Korean immigrant communities. *Harvard Educational Review, 76*(1), 1–29.

Zhuang, J., & Nie, C. (2000). *Traditional Chinese painting: Silent poems in praise of nature and human life*. translated by Chen G. Beijing: China Intercontinental Press.

INDEX

A
Aboriginal, 190
Acculturation dissonance, 5
A Fluid and Open Inquiry, 7–11, 253
Allen, 10–11, 27, 29–32, 34, 37, 49–51, 58, 208, 233
American Chinese, 1, 234
Mr. Anderson, 10, 17, 34, 56–59, 90–96, 98, 128, 178
A practical guide for Ontario Educators, 191
Asian academic success, 192
Asian Heritage Month, 1
Asian model minorities, 4, 192, 228
Astronaut families, 192
At risk, 13, 127, 192, 200, 245–247

B
Bay Street Community School, 4, 5, 7–8, 10, 12, 20, 28, 33, 46, 48, 68, 73, 79–81, 83, 87, 89, 96, 111, 117, 124, 126–127, 142–146, 148–149, 151–152, 155–156, 160–161, 174–175, 183, 196, 200, 205, 207, 219, 224, 229, 232, 241

Beliefs, 5, 8, 17, 21, 84, 169, 192
Beliefs and values, 5, 21
Boat people, 16
Boundaries, 15, 20, 25, 125, 126, 187–189, 192, 197, 198, 211, 238, 242–244, 246–250, 252
Buddhist, 6, 47, 72, 207
Buddy Reading Program, 18, 34, 56–58, 87, 89–91, 128

C
Call seniors by their given name, 28
Canada Immigration and Citizenship, 2
Canada multiculturalism policy, 7, 9, 17, 190, 194, 195, 222, 226, 228, 230, 251
Canadian school system, 3, 9
Canadian, vii, 1–7, 9–11, 32–33, 39, 46, 74, 78–79, 84, 105, 115, 133, 143–154, 158–159, 162, 164, 168, 180–181, 184, 190–194, 201–204, 210, 222, 225, 227, 229–234, 236, 238–243, 248, 251

Cantonese, 16, 18, 23, 32, 36–37, 44, 46, 49, 55–57, 59, 63–64, 69, 71, 75, 93, 98–99, 109–110, 112, 117, 121–123, 197, 223–224, 230, 234, 248
Caregiver, 10, 22, 196, 215, 246
Carmen, 10, 16–20, 23–25, 28–29, 34–36, 49–50, 54–55, 57–60, 65, 69–72, 77, 83–84, 90–91, 96, 101, 123, 128, 205, 207, 243
Caucasian, 190
Census, 1, 3, 190
Centre for Research and Education in Human Services, 2
Childcare, 37, 51, 192, 196
Child discipline, 51, 192
Children's Aid, 54, 69–70, 122–123, 125, 137–139, 242–243
Chinese, vii, 1–10, 12–13, 15–18, 20–22, 23, 25–40, 42–47, 49–51, 53, 56–58, 61, 63–64, 66, 69–72, 74–78, 80, 82–98, 102, 105–106, 108–112, 114–115, 117–118, 121, 127–130, 132, 134, 136–141, 144–146, 148–149, 152–155, 157–160, 162–165, 168, 171, 174–178, 180–185, 188–215, 217, 219–220, 222–245, 247–251
Chinese family, 4, 12, 29, 51, 192, 195–197, 200, 208–209, 212, 222, 228, 243
Chinese handwriting, 23, 77
Chinese immigrants, 2–6, 9, 39, 180, 190, 222
Chinese newcomer families, 3–6, 13, 87, 191–193, 247, 249–250
Chinese New Year, 1, 29, 35, 47, 110, 134, 174
Chinese visiting professor, 7
Circle Time, 16, 18–19, 23, 34, 59, 128

Citizenship and Immigration Canada, 1, 16, 53, 152, 190
Classrooms, 10, 16, 28, 88
Commonplaces, 216–217, 221–222, 249
Communication Breakdown, 82
Communication of values, 6, 14, 249
Communitarianism, 214–217
Community, vii, 2, 4–6, 8–10, 13, 28, 45, 48, 72, 83–84, 89, 114, 123, 126, 129, 146, 149, 164, 171, 183, 190–191, 197, 199–200, 202, 209, 214–215, 217–218, 220–221, 225, 241, 243, 245–246, 252
Confucian, 6, 39–40, 42, 51–52, 188–189, 192–193, 196–199, 202–210, 214–218, 224–225, 236–237, 240
Contemporary anti-revolutionary, 40
Continuity, 9, 25, 188–189, 197–198, 214, 218, 220–221, 232, 245, 252
Contributions, 193
Core Family Stories, 11–12, 14, 26
Core values, 6
Cross-cultural, vii, 3, 5–6, 8–9, 20, 22, 26, 28, 51, 88–89, 126, 149, 189, 193, 197, 200, 209, 213, 219, 221, 227, 232, 234, 236, 249–250, 252
Cross-Cultural Schooling Experience, 3
Cultural, vii, 4, 6, 8–9, 20–21, 25, 27, 44, 46, 58, 86, 113, 126, 128, 181, 185, 188–189, 191–197, 199, 201–204, 212–214, 216, 218–219, 224–225, 232–238, 240, 247–252
Cultural boundaries, 250
Cultural group, 4, 8, 219, 232, 235, 248, 251–252

Cultural narrative, vii, 25, 192, 196, 203, 213, 224–225, 232, 236, 238, 240
Cultural revolution, 39–40, 170, 173, 199, 201, 203, 205–206
Cultural tensions, 6, 193, 195
Culture broker, 13, 197, 241
Culture, vii, 5, 26, 28–29, 51, 94, 98, 181, 188–189, 193–195, 197–198, 216, 228, 235–236, 241, 246–247, 249–252
Curriculum, 6, 9, 20, 79, 81, 83, 88, 96, 101, 111, 127, 149n1, 151, 152, 160, 191, 195, 196, 206, 216, 220–221, 222, 225, 228–230, 232, 233, 236, 241, 248, 249
Customary, 28, 39, 207

D

Danny, 18, 22–24, 59
Descendants of the Dragon, 1, 5
Dewey, 8, 189, 213–216, 220–221
Discontinuities, 9, 25
Discrimination, 114, 175
Dissatisfaction, 33
Dissonance, 29, 90, 180
Diverse, 2, 4, 6, 9, 13, 15, 20–21, 25, 86, 195, 217–218, 232–234, 241, 247–248, 251–252
Double agendas, 25–26
Dreams and hopes, 12
Dropped out of high school, 12

E

East and West dichotomy, 5, 27, 218
East Asian students, 3, 212
Economic, vii, 6, 234, 249, 251
Educational, vi, vii, 4–6, 8–9, 14–15, 17, 21–22, 25, 39, 62, 73, 126, 149, 161, 184–185, 189–192, 195, 201–203, 210, 213–217, 220, 222, 225–226, 228–230, 234–237, 243, 245–250, 252
Educational experience, 39, 161, 217, 220
Educational needs, 4, 6, 195, 250
Egocentric, 198, 210
Elementary education, 33, 160, 231
Eleven influential Chinese educators, 194, 238
English, viii, 2–4, 9, 18, 27, 34–36, 44–46, 48–49, 55–56, 60, 63–64, 70–78, 80–81, 84–85, 88, 90, 92–96, 100–101, 103, 107–108, 112, 115, 126–127, 129–130, 132, 138, 140, 147, 151, 153–161, 163, 165, 167–168, 171–172, 175–176, 178, 180–183, 191, 199, 202, 204, 222–230, 235, 238, 240, 242, 248
ESL, 9, 28, 35–36, 48, 51, 54, 72–73, 76, 81, 84, 101, 123–124, 127, 129, 145, 160, 162, 165–166, 176, 183, 208, 225–227, 229
Ethnic, 191
Excellent in learning, 153, 170
Experiences, 8, 25, 56, 189, 228
Experiential phenomena, 188

F

Families of boys, 12
Family, 2–3, 5–6, 8–9, 11–14, 22–24, 26–29, 38–54, 56, 60–62, 64–67, 69, 72, 75–77, 81, 83, 86, 93, 100–101, 109, 113, 115–116, 118, 123, 125–126, 133–134, 137–141, 144, 148–149, 152–153, 158, 161–162, 165, 184–185, 188–189, 191–202, 204–212, 214–215, 219, 221, 228–230, 233, 235–236, 244–246, 248, 250, 252

The Family of Confucian scholars, 198
Family of four generations, 199, 208
The Family of Taoist scholars, 198
Family responsibilities, 13
"Family Reunion," 16
Fell in between, 12
Field notes, 9, 16, 149, 241
Field trips, 9–10, 13, 28, 59, 88, 94, 97, 145, 157, 178
Fieldwork, 3, 5, 9, 11, 13, 28, 83, 85, 96, 201, 208, 219, 223, 243–244
First language, 2–4, 191, 226, 228–229
Fluidity of the inquiry, 10
Focus, vii, 4–5, 12, 74, 108, 159, 164, 168, 193, 209, 214, 221, 224, 231, 239, 243, 249
For the sake of their children, 2, 7, 86
Fragmented, 12, 23–25, 51, 100, 126, 149, 227, 247
Freeman, 10, 13, 16–19, 24, 27–28, 36, 38, 43–47, 50, 54, 58–60, 69–70, 80, 82–84, 90, 92, 96, 123, 129, 193, 197, 202, 205–206, 208, 223, 230, 251
Friend to the families, 13
Frustration, 17, 25, 103, 108, 115, 125
Fujian, 12, 16, 34, 87, 90, 93, 98, 104, 127–128, 153, 160, 176, 183, 222–223, 234
Fujian dialects, 16, 93, 223
Fund-raising, 59, 129–130

G

Generational, 6, 51, 184, 193, 195, 198
Grandchildren, 24, 28, 37–39, 43, 50, 193, 196–199
Grandpa Jiang, 28, 38–42, 51, 86, 193, 197–198, 205–206
Grandparents, 9, 10, 12, 13, 16–18, 20, 25, 27–52, 58, 66, 69, 70, 89, 93, 104, 109, 129, 133, 134, 153, 174, 184, 189, 192–194, 196–203, 218, 223, 231, 232
Greater Toronto area, 2
Growing up to be a good man even if they may not succeed in school, 194
Guangdong, 12, 16, 24, 27–28, 32, 34, 37, 44, 60, 87–88, 109, 153, 222–223, 227, 234
Guangzhou, 28, 33, 60–61, 110, 196
Gym, 28, 82, 148

H

Happiness, 7, 38, 169, 199
Harmony, 21, 38, 42–43, 51–52, 189, 197–198, 204, 216, 218, 248
Have to be pushed, 33
Hidden needs, 193
Home(s), 2–3, 10, 27–52, 62–64, 142–143, 147, 152, 198, 204, 208, 209, 219–252
Homework, 7, 32, 35, 65, 69–70, 73, 75, 77–78, 80–82, 85, 103, 105, 112, 120, 162, 167–168, 170, 178–179, 184, 197, 202–204, 224–226, 231–232, 238
Homogeneous, 13
Hui Lan, 10, 12, 36, 38, 50, 52–55, 59–75, 77–86, 92, 114, 138, 152, 164, 192–193, 199, 201–202, 205–207, 212, 223–225, 230–231, 233, 239, 241, 251
Humanity, 42, 86, 198, 204, 208, 209, 237

I

Identify, 6, 11, 86, 250
Immigrants, 1–6, 9, 12, 39, 53, 152, 172, 180–181, 190–193, 209, 222, 234–235
Individuals, 4, 189, 211, 215
Inquiry attitude, 17
Insights, 6, 195, 198, 213–214, 219, 247, 250–251
Interpreter, 13, 69, 100, 123
Issues and challenges, 15

J

Jane, 28, 30–31, 39
Jeff's Grandpa, 19
Jia Ming, 10, 12, 95–96, 126, 129–130, 151–185, 192–193, 200–203, 206, 208–209, 222–225, 227–229, 231, 233, 239, 248, 251
Joint Centre of Excellence for Research on Immigration and Settlement, 2
Julian, 7, 10–11, 18, 23, 27–30, 32–33, 36–37, 45, 49–51, 58–59, 79, 105, 196, 202, 232
Julian's grandma, 7, 10–11, 18, 23, 27–39, 43–51, 57–59, 73, 79, 92, 129, 193, 196–199, 202, 206, 208, 223, 232, 236
Julian's little brother, 11, 27, 208, 233

K

Key form of experience, 26
Key way of writing and thinking, 26

L

Landscapes in transition, 3–6, 8–9, 12, 22, 25, 51, 187–189, 191, 193, 196–197, 204, 213, 219–220, 222, 232, 241, 243, 247, 249, 251–252
Language, 2, 3, 4, 9, 16, 28, 29, 33, 44, 46, 48–49, 72, 90, 92–93, 132, 165–166, 224–230, 234, 247
LEAP program, 54, 81, 89, 96, 101, 151–152, 163, 174, 179, 223, 227, 230, 233, 243
Lens of Generational Narratives, 195–196
Library, 28, 65, 73, 78–79, 83, 88, 91, 96–97, 144, 152, 161, 174, 178, 181–182
Life, 2, 5–14, 16–17, 20–26, 28, 31, 38, 41–43, 48–51, 53–54, 61–62, 64–65, 75, 88–89, 93–94, 100, 109, 111, 115, 121–122, 125–126, 128, 130, 133, 137–138, 147, 149, 157–158, 161, 169, 173–174, 177–179, 181, 184, 187, 196–203, 205, 207–209, 213, 215, 217, 220, 222, 231, 233, 237, 239, 242–243, 245, 247–248, 252
Linguistically and culturally diverse, 3, 5, 10, 13–14
Literature, viii, 216, 234
Lived experience, 5, 9, 15, 20–22, 25–26, 53, 114, 187, 193, 196, 219–221, 225, 230, 234–235, 245, 247, 249, 251
Longitudinal, 3–4

M

Main Office, 28, 88, 95, 100, 102, 108, 134–145
Mainstream, 4–6, 181, 191–195, 197, 199, 201, 235, 247, 251–252

274 INDEX

Make meaning, 6, 20–21, 236
Mandarin, 9, 16, 18, 23, 29, 32, 36, 38, 44–46, 55, 64, 71, 92, 96, 112, 117, 152, 165, 222–224, 229–230
Marginalization, 194, 235, 249
Marginalize groups, 4
Mencius, 152, 196, 198, 199
Metropolitan, 2
Michael Connelly, 3–4, 7–9, 15, 17, 20, 22, 25–26, 187, 220–222, 248
Michael's mother, 18
The Midst of Stories, 15, 21
Minority groups, 190, 194, 200, 250
Misbehaving, 13, 70, 82, 88–89, 130, 240
Misbehavior, 16, 58, 68–69, 100, 128, 136, 233, 239, 248
Mom Cares About Me Most, 120
Mother tongue, 1–2
Mr. Wiseman, 79, 152
Ms. Campbell, 96, 99, 152, 175–176, 178
Ms. Corter, 89, 96–102, 104, 109, 117, 131–137, 140, 145–147, 176, 201
Ms. Tan, 96, 152, 165
Multicultural, 4, 6, 14, 88, 180, 189, 191, 193–195, 197, 230, 249, 252
Multiculturalism, 190, 194, 226
Multidimensional Bridge across Cultures, 249–252
Multi-point perspective, 188
Mutual communication, 7

N

Narrative, vii, 3, 5–6, 8–9, 11, 14–15, 21–22, 24–26, 39, 51–53, 87, 105, 126, 187, 189–190, 192–193, 195, 197, 204, 214, 220–221, 225, 227–228, 234–235, 241, 249

Narrative culture of the text, 26
Narrative inquiry, 3, 8, 15, 25–26, 189, 220
Narrative methodology, 6
Narrative thinking, 9, 14, 26
Narrativization, 22, 24, 109, 114, 241
Narrativized, 22, 109, 113–114
Nation family, 198
Negotiation, 169, 171, 192
Newcomer, 2–6, 10, 12–13, 17, 34, 54, 56, 58, 87–92, 94, 96, 98–99, 101–102, 125–128, 131, 147, 149, 151, 157, 162, 172, 174–176, 183, 185, 189, 191–196, 200–203, 209–214, 216–217, 219, 222, 224–226, 228–230, 232–235, 239, 241, 243–247, 249–252
Non-Chinese families, 10
Non-English languages, 3
Notion of being, 209, 210, 215, 218n4
Notion of home, 6, 193, 196, 204
Notion of landscape, 187, 195
Notion of learning, 6, 20, 193, 196, 204, 220

O

On Landscapes, 1, 3, 187
Othered, 6
Others, 22, 30, 189–190, 193, 203, 205–209

P

Parental Involvement, 163, 184
Parent Centre, 7, 9–11, 13, 16–17, 19–20, 22–25, 27–35, 37–39, 42, 44, 46, 48–50, 54–59, 66–71, 79–80, 83–84, 87–91, 96–97, 101, 104–107, 109, 115, 128, 138, 161, 196, 201, 205–207, 223, 232, 241, 243

Parenting issues, 2, 192
Parents not helping, 16–17, 22
Peer Influence, 12, 160
People's Republic of China, 2, 39, 190
Perceive reality, 188
Phenomenon, 15, 25–26, 208–210, 213, 235
Philosophies of education, vii
Place, 8–9, 15, 19, 23, 28, 31, 40, 50, 64–65, 68, 95, 125, 129, 187, 212, 215, 221
Prelude, 11, 88
Pretended, 30, 165
Proudly, 32
Punished, 30, 105

R
Reciprocal learning, vi–viii, 3, 7, 184–195, 213–214, 216, 252
Reciprocity, 193, 209, 217
Re-education, 40, 152
Reflection, 11, 51, 157, 219
Reluctant, 30, 72–73, 85, 165
Research sites, 3
Resources, 6, 126, 195, 210, 235, 243, 245, 249
Respect the Elderly and Care for the Young, 174
Role modeling, 194, 199–202

S
Sacrifice, 2, 3, 37, 49–52, 192, 197–198, 209
Sacrifice everything to come here, 2
Sally's grandma, 27, 59
School Council Meetings, 9–10, 13, 28, 69, 79–80, 88, 99, 128, 152, 160, 243, 245
School events, 9–10, 13, 28, 79, 88, 111, 152, 160, 243

Schooling experience, 17, 189, 213, 219, 227, 232, 234, 249–250
Schools, viii, 2–7, 9, 11, 15, 23, 26, 32–33, 39, 54, 79–80, 87, 89, 101–102, 105, 111, 113, 121–126, 146, 148–149, 153, 158–160, 162, 168, 184, 191, 194, 197, 202–203, 205, 207, 213, 227, 230–231, 234–235, 239, 241–244, 247–249
Schwab, 9, 216–217, 220–221, 249
Sense of Home, 27
Self, 52, 78, 172, 180, 188, 198, 209, 210–212, 215–217
Self-cultivation, 198, 210, 213, 217
Shared obligations, 250
Shijie, 198
Shirley Zhang, 151
Situations, 220
Skilled Workers, 16
Social, 6, 8, 9, 13, 21, 25–26, 42, 51, 78, 108, 117–118, 124–126, 149, 159, 161, 171–172, 185, 187–190, 192, 198, 200–203, 208–211, 213, 215–217, 220, 234–235, 237, 241–247, 249–251
Social dimension, 8, 25
Society, viii, 4–7, 38, 42–43, 51–52, 130, 177, 190, 192–195, 197–198, 201, 203–204, 206, 210–211, 215, 237, 241, 244–245, 247, 252
Sophisticated, 17
South Asian students, 3
Sponsor, 30, 49, 134
Spoon-feeding, 7, 32
Stephen's grandpa, 27

Stories, 5, 11–12, 14–17, 20–29, 31, 39, 41–43, 51–52, 56–58, 60, 62–63, 65, 67, 70, 86–87, 89–92, 100, 104, 109–110, 113–114, 120, 128, 142, 149, 152–153, 158, 165, 169, 176, 187–189, 192–194, 197–199, 205, 208–209, 212–213, 223–225, 227–228, 231, 233–235, 239, 245, 247
Struggles, 5, 149, 191, 221, 235
Success of their childrens education, 12
Summary, 11, 189, 232, 252
Sympathetic, 32

T
Taoist, 6
TDSB, 3
Teacher, vi, viii, 3, 6, 9–11, 13, 17, 27–28, 32, 34, 36, 44, 51, 56, 58, 60, 69–71, 77–82, 84, 88–89, 92, 95–97, 99–100, 102–103, 105, 107, 109–111, 113, 115–117, 121–122, 128, 132–138, 140, 142, 144–145, 149, 152–154, 156–157, 159–160, 162–168, 170, 176, 178–179, 183, 195–196, 201–203, 206–207, 213, 216, 221, 224–227, 229–230, 236–246, 248–249
Temporal dimension, 8
Thinking Narratively, 9, 21–22
Think of others, 208
Three-dimensional narrative inquiry space, 8, 11, 149, 193, 249
To be human, 194, 197, 199, 204, 205, 209, 215, 218n3, 233
"To Believe is to See," 15, 17
Tommy's grandma, 27, 37–38

Toronto, vi, 1–3, 5, 7–8, 11, 20, 28–29, 31, 34–37, 46, 50–51, 53–54, 62–63, 67–68, 72, 85, 93, 105–106, 108, 114–115, 127, 129–130, 133, 136, 142–148, 154–159, 161–168, 170–174, 178–179, 182–184, 190, 196, 200–201, 223–225, 228–230, 243
"To See is to Believe," 15, 17
Traditions, 25, 173, 197, 217–218
Transition, 1, 3, 87–88, 111, 127, 151, 155, 187
Truth in narrative, 15, 17
Typical Chinese mother and wife, 12

U
Unfolding narratives, 14
Unities, 9, 25
University, 53, 82, 85, 113, 121, 130, 142, 143–145, 158, 161, 175–177, 183, 184, 199, 201, 203, 204, 225, 230, 239
Untold, 22–25, 29
Untold Stories, 23

V
Values, 4, 6–8, 12, 17, 22, 25, 39, 47, 51–52, 61, 65, 86, 133, 161, 168, 173, 181, 185, 190, 194–197, 199, 202–204, 206, 208–210, 218, 222, 225, 233, 237, 249–252
Values of democracy, 250
Video games, 12, 65, 74, 76, 89, 103, 106, 108, 114, 116, 119, 121, 125, 129, 134–135, 137–141, 147, 157, 164, 225–226, 233, 239

Visible majority, 2
Visible minorities, 6, 190, 194, 235, 251–252
Visitor's visa, 29, 49

W

Wage earner, 192
We-consciousness, 217, 252
Well educated, 17, 21
Western, 8, 17, 27, 51, 156, 199, 201, 204, 209–211, 213–218, 237, 245
The West, vii, 6, 17, 26, 127, 159, 189, 199, 204, 209–211, 213–217, 244–245
What I think or believe what I hear, 22
What I think or believe what I see, 22
Work overtime, 31

Y

Yang Yang, 12–13, 100–101, 104, 127–149, 177, 192, 194, 200–202, 204, 212, 224–229, 233–235, 238–239, 246, 248, 250
Year of the Monkey, 37
Yong Chang, 54, 56, 60, 63–67, 72–73, 75–77, 79–84, 114, 152, 164, 175, 178, 207, 222, 225, 230, 233, 238
Yong Sheng, 18–19, 23–24, 28, 36, 53–60, 62–63, 66–68, 72–74, 77–79, 83–85, 91, 207, 224, 230–231

Z

Zhidao, 198
Zhi Gao, 10, 12–13, 87–89, 92–126, 128, 130–133, 136, 146, 149, 177, 192–194, 200–202, 204, 210, 225–229, 233–235, 238–239, 242–246, 248, 250

GPSR Compliance

The European Union's (EU) General Product Safety Regulation (GPSR) is a set of rules that requires consumer products to be safe and our obligations to ensure this.

If you have any concerns about our products, you can contact us on

ProductSafety@springernature.com

In case Publisher is established outside the EU, the EU authorized representative is:

Springer Nature Customer Service Center GmbH
Europaplatz 3
69115 Heidelberg, Germany

www.ingramcontent.com/pod-product-compliance
Lightning Source LLC
Chambersburg PA
CBHW071702100426
42873CB00017B/386